America and the Cold War, 1941–1991

America and the Cold War, 1941–1991

A REALIST INTERPRETATION

Volume 1

Norman A. Graebner, Richard Dean Burns, and Joseph M. Siracusa

Praeger Security International

 PRAEGER

AN IMPRINT OF ABC-CLIO, LLC
Santa Barbara, California • Denver, Colorado • Oxford, England

Library of Congress Cataloging-in-Publication Data

Graebner, Norman A.
  America and the Cold War, 1941-1991 : a realist interpretation / Norman A. Graebner, Richard Dean Burns, Joseph M. Siracusa.
    p. cm.
  Includes bibliographical references and index.
  ISBN 978–0–313–38525–4 (hard copy : alk. paper) — ISBN 978–0–313–38526–1 (ebook)
1. United States—Foreign relations—1945–1989. 2. United States—Politics and government—1945–1989. 3. United States—Foreign relations—Soviet Union. 4. Soviet Union—Foreign relations—United States. 5. Cold War. I. Burns, Richard Dean. II. Siracusa, Joseph M. III. Title.
E744.G683   2010
327.73009′04—dc22   2010000523

ISBN: 978–0–313–38525–4
EISBN: 978–0–313–38526–1

14 13 12 11 10   1 2 3 4 5

This book is also available on the World Wide Web as an eBook.
Visit www.abc-clio.com for details.

Praeger
An Imprint of ABC-CLIO, LLC

ABC-CLIO, LLC
130 Cremona Drive, P.O. Box 1911
Santa Barbara, California 93116-1911

This book is printed on acid-free paper ∞

Manufactured in the United States of America

Contents

Volume 1

Preface   vii

Introduction   1

Chapter 1   The Grand Alliance   17

Chapter 2   The Road to Yalta   37

Chapter 3   A Troubled World at Peace: 1945   65

Chapter 4   End of the Grand Alliance   97

Chapter 5   The Stabilization of Europe   115

Chapter 6   The Cold War in East Asia   153

Chapter 7   The National Security State   181

Chapter 8   High Tide: The Eisenhower Years   211

Chapter 9   The Kennedy Years   251

Volume 2

Chapter 10 The Cold War at Mid-1960s: The Johnson Years   283

Chapter 11 Watershed: The War in Vietnam   313

Chapter 12 The Search for Détente: Nixon, Kissinger,   343
            and Ford

Chapter 13 The Carter Years   393

Chapter 14 Rise and Fall of the Second Cold War: 441
            Reagan and Gorbachev

Chapter 15 The Final Days of the Cold War   487

Chapter 16 Reflections   513

Notes   527

Selected Bibliography   625

Index   645

Preface

Early academic historians of America's Cold War focused on the exercise of power; that is, they questioned Washington's goals and the means available to achieve these ends. These historians of power assessed American policies in realist terms, namely, their relationship to national interests and the limits of the nation's power. Much of the post-1960s literature, however, ignored traditional diplomatic and political history and turned instead to a variety of themes that diffused the element of power and led to Cold War histories that generally ignored the realist tradition in American foreign policy. In drafting the core of this critical analysis of America's Cold War experiences, Norman A. Graebner, the doyen of the realist school of diplomatic history, has applied the basic precepts of the realist tradition. Not only have he and his coauthors employed realist principles to evaluate policies and actions in America's Cold War, they have done so largely by emphasizing contemporary sources. As files released from the archives of the superpowers and their allies since the end of the Cold War have consistently revealed, these judgments usually anticipated archival documentation. This was not surprising.

Our essential concern, as the lead author Professor Graebner has noted in his memoirs, "was not the motives behind national decisions —which [can be] exceeding elusive." For us "major decisions seldom arose in a policy vacuum, reflecting largely domestic economic concerns, but were the products of external pressures and events that often permitted the country only limited responses. Most resulting policies were made in the upper reaches of government and then sold to Congress and the public."[1] Consequently, our study emphasizes, in the considered judgment of three generations of diplomatic historians, Washington's excessive anti-Communism, the resulting major policies (where there were coherent policies), the public rationalizations in support of the policies, and the most notable events of the Cold War. In another sense, this study is also a historical tribute to the journalists, analysts, and other writers—critical-thinking Americans and West Europeans—who fully appreciated that contemporary polices often greatly exceeded Washington's ability to achieve them and who fully recognized that the policies would not resolve the very problems they were meant to address.

For some present readers, the Cold War rivalry between the United States and the Soviet Union is already a fading memory. For most, it is not a memory at all. Today's college students were mere infants when the infamous Berlin Wall fell in 1989. If diplomatic historians enjoy digesting archival sources that explain long-past events, they also have an obligation, we maintain, to provide the principles by which citizens and leaders may assess and shape the public discourse about contemporary foreign policies.[2] It is absolutely crucial, then, that students of modern politics and history, no less than the political successors of Ronald Reagan and Mikhail Gorbachev, develop these conclusions with far more care than has been characteristic in the pre-nuclear past.[3]

We have sought in the following pages to write a sweeping interpretive history of America's Cold War, chronicling the events of U.S.-Soviet relations from World War II to the collapse of Moscow-dominated Communism, while employing realist principles that may prompt current and future denizens of the White House and the Kremlin —and the American public—to develop and assess foreign policies with far more care than has been characteristic recently.[3] The First Red Scare, 1919–1920, may have crystallized the anti-Communist views of America's elite, but the seedtime of the Cold War can be found in the political differences that emerged during World War II. The interplay found Washington's policies consistently emphasizing a return to post-Versailles *status quo*, while Moscow insisted that the postwar realignment eliminate hostile forces ringing its borders and enhance the Soviet Union's security. The Truman administration's continued insistence on self-determination for Central and Eastern Europe, which Moscow perceived as the likelihood of returning governments hostile to the Soviet Union along its much contested frontier, ended the Grand Alliance and launched the full-blown Cold War. By the mid-1960s, the original political confrontations, centering on democratic governments for Central and Eastern Europe, were superseded by the escalating nuclear arms race. For America's elite during this and following decades, according to two recent students of the subject, "the general portrayal of the Soviet menace" and Washington's "willingness to meet that menace became, in and of itself, the defining objective of American policy."[4] Throughout this formulation of policy, they continued, "the connection between means and ends remained undefined." We concur.

A work of this size and magnitude has incurred incalculable debts, intellectual and otherwise. Our intellectual debts are at once overwhelming and obvious and are recognized in the text, endnotes, and selected bibliography. We should also like to acknowledge the role played by our editor Steve Catalano, at ABC-CLIO, for his part in bringing this manuscript to light, as well the valuable assistance of our research associate, Candice Maddison, in formatting the initial text and notes. Needless to say, the authors alone are responsible for any errors.

Norman A. Graebner
Charlottesville

Richard Dean Burns
Claremont

Joseph M. Siracusa
Melbourne

Introduction

For some Americans the euphoria of victory and peace in 1945 evaporated quickly. That the Soviet Union's total victory over Nazi Germany had upset the historic European balance of power mattered little to Americans who had lauded the U.S.S.R. for its costly and necessary contributions to the Allied successes. But for a small minority of U.S. officials and writers, well conditioned to distrust the Kremlin, the continued Soviet occupation of Eastern Europe merely enhanced that country's strategic position in the Balkans and rendered bordering regions vulnerable to further Soviet expansion.[1] It required only the Kremlin's postwar demands on Iran and Turkey to unleash visions of Soviet military expansion reminiscent of the Italian, German, and Japanese aggressions that, so recently, had brought war to the world. Joseph and Stewart Alsop, writing in the May 20, 1946, issue of *Life*, defined the emerging Soviet threat in Hitlerian terms:

Already Poland, the Baltic States, Rumania, Bulgaria, Yugoslavia and Albania are behind the Iron Curtain. Huge armies hold Hungary and half of Germany and Austria. Czechoslovakia and Greece are encircled. . . . In the Middle East, the Soviets are driving southward. Iran is in danger of being reduced to puppethood; Turkey and Iraq are threatened. Finally, in the Far East, the Kuriles has been stripped and left in condition to be transformed at will and half of Korea are occupied and Manchuria into another Azerbaijan. The process still goes on. One . . . must also wonder whether they will ultimately be satisfied with less than dominion over Europe and Asia.[2]

Responding to Soviet pressures on Turkey for a new Straits settlement in August 1946, Acting Secretary of State Dean Acheson and the Chiefs of Staff, with advice from State Department experts, prepared a memorandum on Turkey for the president. The memorandum, signed by

Acheson, Navy Secretary James Forrestal, and Secretary of War Robert Patterson, warned: "If the Soviet Union succeeds in its objective of obtaining control over Turkey, it will be extremely difficult, if not impossible, to prevent the Soviet Union from obtaining control over Greece and over the whole Near and Middle East . . . (including) the territory lying between the Mediterranean and India. When the Soviet Union has once obtained full mastery of this territory . . . it will be in a much stronger position to obtain its objectives in India and China."[3]

Such rhetorical portrayals of Soviet territorial ambitions far exceeded Soviet military capabilities and intentions. Stalin was no Napoleon or Hitler. The Kremlin had already demonstrated its extreme reluctance to confront the West militarily along its Iranian and Turkish borders where its strategic advantage was profound. Confronted by the predictable resistance of the non-Soviet world, Kremlin leaders understood that any military venture would end in disaster. Indeed, U.S. military officials concluded as early as 1946 that the Soviet Union had no intention of embarking on a career of armed aggression. That conviction, however, scarcely constrained the country's burgeoning insecurities.

* * *

All of this played out against the background of previous unpleasant experiences that ultimately had some influence on both Soviet and American decisions. First-generation Bolsheviks retained the memory of Allied interventions in Northern Russia, the Crimea, and Siberia that persisted after World War I. Although the British negotiated a trade agreement with the Soviets in 1921, which extended de facto recognition of the government, the United States did not formally recognize the Soviet Union until November 1933. Perhaps the only bright spot in Soviet-American relations occurred in 1921 when Herbert Hoover established a relief program that fed thousands of starving Russians. In the post–World War II years, however, Soviet officials would often focus back to their grievances resulting from Allied interventions and interwar diplomatic isolation.

In America, the appearance of the Lenin government prompted a domestic reaction that culminated in the nation's first "Red Scare" of 1919–1920 and briefly threatened the nation's cherished civil liberties. This prompted newspaper columnist Walter Lippmann to write, "the people are shivering in their boots over Bolshevism. They are far more afraid of Lenin than they ever were of the [German] Kaiser. We seem to be the most frightened lot of victors that the world ever saw." Many American had come to view all radicals—including socialists, anarchists, and union activists—as inspired, if not led, by foreign Communists who would subvert American values and society. Red baiting became part of the American political scene. During the election of 1944, for example, Thomas Dewey insisted that the Democratic Party was "subject to capture, and the forces of Communism are, in fact, now capturing it." In July 1945, *Life* magazine asserted that "the fellow-traveler [of Communism] is everywhere: in Hollywood, on college faculties, in government bureaus, . . . even on the editorial staffs of eminently capitalist journals."[4] Five years later there was a near hysterical outpouring of anti-Communist emotions symbolized by the "Era of McCarthyism" from 1950 to 1954—or the second Red Scare—that greatly affected not only American society, but the nation's foreign policies.

At issue in the growing fear and distrust of the U.S.S.R. was not only the American dislike of Communism. It was evident that overwhelmingly U.S. citizens opposed Communism as inimical to Western principles of liberal democracy. But for most the ideological foundations of the Soviet state were not an American concern. What seized the country's emerging anti-Communist elite was the fear that the real Soviet danger, one that rendered military aggression irrelevant, lay in the limitless promise of Soviet ideological expansion. Soviet rhetoric had long predicted Communism's ultimate conquest of the world. For those Americans who took the Soviet rhetoric seriously, the U.S.S.R., as the self-assigned leader of world Communism, possessed the power and will to incite or support Communist-led revolutions everywhere, imposing on them its influence, if not its direct control. Ideological expansionism, assuring future Soviet triumphs without war, transcended the limited possibilities and high costs of military adventurism by enabling the U.S.S.R. to extend its presence over vast distances without projecting military force. It mattered little whether Soviet troops or even Soviet officials were present at all. The alleged capacity to expand far beyond the reach of its armies seemed to transform the U.S.S.R. into an international phenomenon of unprecedented expansive power. The immediate danger to Western security lay in the chaotic economic, social, and political conditions that prevailed throughout much of postwar Eurasia, offering unlimited opportunities for Soviet ideological exploitation. The doubtful validity of liberal ideas and capitalist institutions in a revolutionary environment suggested that much of the world's resources might still escape the West and fall into the clutches of the Kremlin.

As early as 1946 anti-Communist writers and spokesmen detected few limits to the Kremlin's external needs and ambitions. George F. Kennan's famed Long Telegram of February 1946 attributed the Kremlin's insatiable designs on the United States to a paranoia that demanded the destruction of all competing power. "We have here," he warned, "a force committed fanatically to the belief that with the United States there can be no permanent *modus vivendi*, that it is desirable and necessary that the internal harmony of our society be disrupted, our traditional way of life destroyed, the international authority of our state broken, if Soviet power is to be secure."[5] Kennan's analysis created a sensation in official Washington, especially among those who shared the mounting fears of Soviet expansionism. Taking his cue from the Long Telegram, State Department official H. Freeman Matthews observed in April that for the Kremlin, "the Soviet and non-soviet systems (could not) exist in the world side by side." Writing for *Life* magazine, foreign policy expert John Foster Dulles warned the country, in June, that the Soviets intended "to have governments everywhere which accept the doctrine of the Soviet Community Party." The achievement of that goal, he acknowledged, would give the Soviet Union world hegemony. Also that year former Ambassador William C. Bullitt averred, "As conquest of this earth for Communism is the objective of the Soviet government, no nation lies outside the scope of its ambitions."[6] The report of Clark Clifford and George Elsey on the Soviet danger, presented to the president in September 1946, reflected the broad convictions of Washington insiders. "The key to understanding of current Soviet policy," the report concluded, " . . . is the realization that Soviet leaders adhere to the Marxian theory of ultimate destruction of capitalist states by communist states."[7]

Anti-Communism's central assumption was the threatening power of Soviet ideological expansionism. But ideology was no expansive force. Nationalism and the pursuit of self-determination comprised a universal defense against Soviet ideological expansionism. Without access to external military support that mattered, Communist struggles for power, invariably indigenous, always succeeded or failed on their own. No Communist regime would war on sentiments of patriotism and national allegiance, or compromise its country's sovereignty, to serve the interests of the Kremlin. Therefore, any alleged Communist threat to global security would fall below the threshold of an American military response. If the U.S.S.R. would not expand militarily and could not expand ideologically, how was it to conquer anything? Possessing no expansive power other than military force, the Kremlin, relying on generally risk-free policies, gained nothing territorially, or even politically, throughout the decades of Cold War.

Any purposeful crusade against alleged Communist dangers would require the destruction of governments and embrace global objectives beyond the capacity, effectiveness, or relevance of U.S. military power. Finally, anti-Communism's boundless rhetorical fears, demands, and aspirations left little room for the day-to-day decisions required for successful coexistence—the inescapable condition required by the interests of humanity. Constrained by such limitations, Washington never pursued a genuine anti-Communist program. It never made a serious attempt to free Eastern Europe, China, the Soviet Union, or any other region of the globe, from Communist control. Indeed, what perpetuated the decades of laudable superpower coexistence was the decision of successive administrations to abjure the dictates of ideology and pursue the limited goals of containment, with their acceptance and defense of the *status quo*, where it mattered, as well as their studied avoidance of direct and unnecessary conflict with the Soviet Union.

* * *

The Truman administration's widely repeated rationale for the defense of Greece and Turkey established avoidance of the Munich syndrome as the guiding principle in meeting the Soviet challenge. Greece and Turkey had become the symbols of the *status quo*; their fall, like that of Austria, the Sudetenland, and Czechoslovakia after 1938, would, the president in his message to Congress on March 12, 1947, advised, "undermine the foundations of international peace and hence the security of the United States."[8] Others quickly embellished the requirement that the country take a stand on Greece and Turkey.

But nowhere did the Munich rhetoric of 1947 correspond to the realities of 1938. What the West faced at Munich was open German aggression on a massive scale. German forces already occupied Austria. Huge Nazi armies stood poised to mass along Germany's borders with Czechoslovakia and Poland, preparatory to invasion and war. But in 1947 no Soviet forces awaited orders to advance against a neighboring state. Indeed, the rhetorical references to Munich, designed to rationalize the defense of Greece and Turkey, never contemplated Soviet military aggression; nor did they advocate any crash program to prepare the West for war. They described threats reaching across Europe, the Middle East, South Asia, and Africa, encompassing territories hundreds, even thousands, of miles from Soviet territory, with no reference to the means whereby the Soviets intended to expand anywhere. Furthermore, those who described the Kremlin's territorial objectives never seemed to agree on what they were or why the Soviets deemed them vital. What mattered to them were the Soviet Union's apparently limitless, putative power and determination to expand, and the dangers that it conveyed. The Munich analogy, along with its counterpart, the domino theory, provided a necessary rhetorical extension to the doctrine of anti-Communism. The verbal images of the Kremlin's unprecedented capacity to expand indefinitely through the exploitation of successive gains, always unhampered by historic restraints, found their necessary rationale in the power of Soviet ideology to conquer and absorb.

American portrayals of Soviet territorial ambitions beyond Greece and Turkey far exceeded what the Kremlin could have achieved peacefully or afforded at the price of war. Moreover, the rhetorical depictions of the Soviet Union's expansive power neither considered its devastating losses suffered during the recent war nor took measure of the West's economic, political, and diplomatic predominance. During the two years that followed congressional approval of the Truman Doctrine, the Western powers achieved an unbroken succession of diplomatic triumphs that demonstrated its total superiority. The sometimes astonishing successes began in 1948 with the elimination of Communists from the French government. Although the French Communists never revealed any affinity for Soviet causes, U.S. officials feared that a French Communist victory at the polls would carry that country into the Soviet orbit and endanger Western interests in Europe, Africa, and the eastern Mediterranean. Similarly Washington's varied economic pressures and electioneering efforts in Italy paid off in the April 1948 election that brought a new government, free of Communists and Socialists, into power. In June, Marshal Tito, Yugoslavia's staunch Communist leader, broke with the Kremlin to demonstrate that Communism could not erode the power of nationalism, and that Kremlin control extended only as far as the reach of Soviet armies.

During subsequent months, America's varied policies aimed at the containment of Soviet power emerged victorious. In Greece the U.S.-supported government finally eliminated the Communist-led insurgency in August 1949, driving the surviving guerrillas into Albania. President Truman proclaimed victory on November 28.[9] Meanwhile, U.S. officers organized and modernized the Turkish army, vastly improved the country's military capabilities with shipments of equipment and aircraft, and constructed new roads and airstrips. Even greater triumphs came with the passage of the Marshall Plan in 1948 to set Western Europe on a course of unparalleled economic growth. During May 1949 Stalin lifted the Berlin blockade, instituted a year earlier to prevent the unification of Germany's three western zones. A month later the Paris Foreign Ministers Conference announced the formation of the Federal Republic of Germany, an achievement long opposed by the Kremlin.[10] Finally, in April 1949, 12 Western countries formed the North Atlantic alliance to underwrite the stability and security of Western Europe.[11]

Washington, amply supported by the European powers, gained the full spectrum of its immediate objectives consistently, even overwhelmingly, because Europe's postwar challenges gave the economic supremacy of the United States a special relevance. With Europe in ruins and the Soviet Union reeling from near disaster, America's economic superiority was absolute. The war had rained destruction on every major power of Europe and Asia, destroying countless cities, factories, and rail lines. By contrast, the United States, with its many accumulating elements of power, had escaped unscathed. Its undamaged industrial capacity now matched that of the rest of the industrialized world. Its technological superiority was so obvious that the world assumed its existence and set out to acquire or copy American products. During the immediate postwar years the United States reached the highest point of world power achieved by any nation in modern times.[12] Abroad, the United States gained its marvelous triumphs where it mattered, the virtual re-globalization of the world: the economic rehabilitation of Western Europe and Japan, the promotion of international trade and investment, and the maintenance of a defense structure that underwrote the containment effort and played an essential role in Europe's postwar political development and burgeoning confidence. These contributions to the world's unprecedented security and prosperity comprised the essence of the nation's postwar international achievement. By 1949, the U.S.S.R. faced the greatest manifestation of opposing power in the peacetime history of the world. The persistent Soviet retreats were evidence enough that Europe's balance of forces had turned against it.[13]

* * *

Western superiority on the international scene, however, offered reassurance only to those who measured the Soviet danger by Soviet behavior and comparative levels of economic and military power. For American anti-Communists, whose central concern was Soviet ideological expansionism, the Soviet threat to Western security was only emerging. By 1948 the official American worldview could detect no visible limits to Soviet expansionism—which now embraced the entire globe.

The National Security Council's study, NSC 7, dated March 30, 1948, defined the Kremlin's challenge in precisely such terms. "The ultimate objective of Soviet-directed world communism," the document averred, "is the domination of the world. To this end, Soviet-directed world Communism employs against its victims in opportunistic coordination the complementary instruments of Soviet aggressive pressure from without and militant revolutionary subversion from within." With its control of international Communism, NSC 7 continued, the U.S.S.R. had engaged the United States in a struggle for power "in which our national security is at stake and from which we cannot withdraw short of national suicide."[14] The more pervading NSC 20/4, approved by the president on November 24, 1948, defined the danger in similar terms. "Communist ideology and Soviet behavior," the document began, "clearly demonstrate that the ultimate objective of the leaders of the U.S.S.R. is the domination of the world."[15]

Designed specifically to kindle the nation's insecurities, NSC 68, of April 1950, comprised the final and most elaborate attempt of the Truman Cold War elite to arrive at a definition of national defense policy. This document, like its predecessors, described the danger of Soviet expansion in global, limitless terms. It concluded that the U.S.S.R., "unlike previous aspirants to hegemony, is animated by a new fanatic faith, antithetical to our own, and seeks to impose its absolute authority over the rest of the world." For the Soviets, conflict had become endemic, waged through violent and nonviolent means in accordance with the dictates of expediency. "The issues that face us," NSC 68 continued, "are momentous, involving the fulfillment or destruction not only of the Republic but of civilization itself." Defeat at the hands of the Soviets would be total.[16] With such a determined enemy, diplomacy was scarcely promising.

Still neither NSC 68 nor any of its predecessors offered a response commensurate with its rhetoric of fear. None of them anticipated the necessity of force to counteract the dangers. NSC 20/4 averred that the United States could achieve the goal of promoting the gradual retraction of Soviet power and influence, until they ceased to be threatening, simply by placing massive political and economic strain on the Soviet imperial structure.[17] Such ill-defined means for victory defied effective policy implementation. Similarly, NSC 68 assumed that the United States, with "calculated and gradual coercion," could unleash the forces of destruction within the Soviet empire itself. In its need to limit Soviet ambitions, the United States could anticipate support within the U.S.S.R. "If we can make the Russian people our allies in this enterprise," NSC 68 predicted, "we will obviously have made our task easier and victory more certain." In the process of inducing change, the United States would avoid, as far as possible, any direct challenge to Soviet prestige and "keep open the possibility for the U.S.S.R. to retreat before pressure with a minimum loss of face."[18] However grave the dangers portrayed by this most terrifying of documents, their elimination required neither risk nor war.

Ultimately the rhetorical suppositions of a global Soviet challenge would find their chief affirmation, not in Europe where the Soviets made no advances, but in East Asia. Whereas in Eastern Europe the West faced an unmovable Soviet occupation, in East Asia the U.S.S.R. had neither conquering nor occupying armies. There any proclaimed Soviet expansion could result only from the Kremlin's power to command and exploit local Communist-led revolutions. In attributing to the Soviet Union the capacity to pursue a career of global conquest across Asia and elsewhere without the presence of armed forces, U.S. officials, by mid-century, could, at last, demonstrate the Soviet Union's limitless power to expand through ideological affinities alone. Washington's responses, however, never conformed to the dangers so perceived. Every Communist movement in postwar Asia was indigenous and defiant of Soviet control. Never would the United States confront the Kremlin directly or militarily over any alleged Soviet-backed Communist aggression outside Europe.

* * *

What underwrote U.S. fears of Soviet expansion across East Asia was the overwhelming conviction, anchored to a troubling rhetoric, that the powerful Communist movements in China and Indochina were totally under Moscow's command. John Moors Cabot, U.S. consul general in Shanghai, warned as early as February 1948 that if the Communists succeeded in gaining control of China they would "install in China a tyranny as subservient to Russia and a terror as brutal as Tito's."[19] Despite the absence of Soviet forces in East Asia, a State Department memorandum of October 1948, prepared by the department's China experts, concluded that Soviet policy was designed to install Soviet control and predominance in China as firmly "as in the satellite countries behind the Iron Curtain."[20] Secretary Dean Acheson, in the China White Paper's letter of transmittal, again presumed that China had fallen victim to Kremlin control. "The Communist leaders," he concluded, "have foresworn their Chinese heritage and have publicly announced their subservience to a foreign power, Russia."[21]

Mao Zedong's final triumph in China, late in 1949, demonstrating graphically the alleged expansive might of Soviet ideology, appeared to place what remained of East and Southeast Asia in danger of Soviet conquest. Ambassador Edwin F. Stanton, writing from Bangkok, warned Washington that Soviet pressures, unless countered effectively, would cause *"the whole of Southeast Asia [to] fall a victim to the Communist advance, thus coming under Russian domination without any military effort on the part of Russia."*[22] This presumption of the Kremlin's capacity to conquer without military force quickly exposed Washington's deepest fears. The noted National Security Council Document NSC 48/1 of December 23, 1949, described fully the terrible consequence of events in China: "The extension of Communist authority in China represents a grievous political defeat for us; if southeast Asia also is swept by communism we shall have suffered a major political rout the repercussions of which will be felt throughout the rest of the world, especially in the Middle-East and in a then critically exposed Australia." If the Kremlin could establish no forcible control over neighboring Communist-led Yugoslavia, it was not clear how it could do so over a Communist government in a huge, distant, self-centered, sovereign, historically antagonistic, and highly nationalistic country such as China, especially without a huge bureaucracy backed by an overpowering army. The Chinese Communist Party was indigenous, both organizationally and ideologically; it owed little or nothing to the Soviets for its success.[23] Thus China, unoccupied by Soviet forces, pursued its external relations in accordance with its own interests.

Long convinced that the Kremlin would exploit any opportunity to advance its influence across Asia, U.S. officials attributed the North Korean invasion of South Korea in late June 1950 to Soviet expansionism. The president declared that the attack on Korea "makes it plain beyond all doubt that Communism has passed beyond the use of subversion to conquer independent nations and will now use armed invasion and war."[24] The generally unquestioned presumption that the Kremlin had designs on broad areas of the Pacific recalled the Munich paradigm. For Truman the North Korean attack, unless challenged, meant a third world war. "My thoughts," he wrote, "kept coming back to the 1930s–to Manchuria-Ethiopia-the Rhineland-Austria and finally to Munich. If the Republic of Korea was allowed to go under, some other country would be next, and then another, just like in the 1930s."[25] No less for presidential candidate Dwight D. Eisenhower, the United States responded to the North Korean invasion to prevent World War III. He declared on October 24, 1952: "World War II should have taught us all one lesson: To vacillate, to hesitate, to appease—even by merely betraying unsteady purpose—is to feed a dictator's appetite for conquest and to invite war itself."[26] For Truman and Eisenhower alike, the Kremlin, unless confronted with counterforce, would topple dominoes into another world war.

Still, the American military buildup never contemplated war against the U.S.S.R., even when official U.S. rhetoric attributed the Chinese entry of November 1950 to Soviet influence and ambition. Acheson warned the country in a nationwide radio address on November 29, "Those who control the Soviet Union and the international Communist movement have made clear their fundamental design. It is to hold and solidify their power over the people and territories within their reach." Truman declared on the following day, "We hope that the Chinese people will not continue to be forced or deceived into serving the ends of Russian colonial policy in Asia."[27] Even the normally sober *New York Times* proclaimed on December 8, "The Chinese Communist dictatorship will eventually go down in history as the men who sold out their country to the foreigners, in this case the Russians, rather than as those who rescued China from foreign 'imperialism'."[28]

Thereafter Washington continued to dwell on the alleged Chinese subservience to Kremlin direction. The president reminded the American people in his State of the Union message of January 1951: "Our men are fighting . . . because they know, as we do, that the aggression in Korea is part of the attempt of the Russian communist dictatorship to take over the world, step by step."[29] It was left for John Foster Dulles to carry the full might of Soviet influence in the Far East to its ultimate conceptualization. "By the test of conception, birth, nurture, and obedience," he informed a New York audience in May, "the Mao Tse-tung regime is a creature of the Moscow Politburo, and it is on behalf of Moscow, not of China, that it is destroying the friendship of the Chinese people towards the United States."[30] Not even such graphic suppositions of Soviet control over vast regions of Asia, thereby threatening the world's balance of power, produced any direct confrontation with the Kremlin.

* * *

Again it was the doubtful application of the Munich syndrome to the struggle for Vietnam that rendered Saigon's victory essential for Western security in East Asia and the Pacific. The domino theory, applied to the Vietnam War, comprised a dramatic warning that a peripheral contest could, if not resolved, become one of pivotal importance.

Eisenhower offered such terrifying imagery to a press conference in April 1954 by warning that if one knocked over the first domino in a row of dominoes, the last would fall very quickly and create a disintegration of profound significance. The loss of Indochina, he warned, would lead to the possible loss "of Burma, of Thailand, of the Peninsula, and Indonesia." From that geographic advantage the Communists could "turn the island defense chain of Japan, Formosa, of the Philippines and ... threaten Australia and New Zealand."[31] Similarly General Douglas MacArthur warned the country against any appeasement of aggression in Vietnam. "The Communist threat," he said, "is a global one. Its successful advance in one sector threatens the destruction of every other sector. You cannot appease or otherwise surrender to communism in Asia without simultaneously undermining our efforts to halt its advance in Europe."[32] Adopting such imagery, John F. Kennedy instructed the Senate, in June 1956, that Vietnam comprised "the cornerstone of the Free World in Southeast Asia, the keystone to the arch, the finger in the dike." If the red tide swept across Vietnam, he warned, it would engulf "Burma, Thailand, India, Japan, the Philippines, and obviously Laos and Cambodia."[33] In his Gettysburg College address of April 1959, Eisenhower warned those who doubted the wisdom of the ever-broadening U.S. commitment to the Saigon regime. "Strategically," he said, "South Vietnam's capture by the Communists ... would set in motion a crumbling process that could, as it progressed, have grave consequences for us and for freedom."[34]

Even as President Lyndon B. Johnson contemplated the Americanization of the war during the early months of 1965, the imagery of falling dominoes assured the necessary congressional and public support for the mounting death and destruction. Always that imagery centered on the Munich tragedy and the need to prevent further aggression and another world war by turning back the Communist enemy. Addressing the American Society of International Law in April 1965, Secretary of State Dean Rusk asserted that "surely we have learned over the past three decades that the acceptance of aggression leads only to a sure catastrophe. Surely we have learned that the aggressor must face the consequences of his action and be saved from the frightful miscalculation that brings all to ruin."[35] Washington's Senator Henry Jackson reminded Americans, "our sacrifices in this dirty war in little Vietnam will make a dirtier and bigger war less likely." Thomas J. Dodd of Connecticut warned the Senate: "The situation in Vietnam today bears many resemblances to the situation just before Munich. ... We are again confronted by an incorrigible aggressor, fanatically committed to the destruction of the free world, whose agreements are as worthless as Hitler's. If we fail to draw the line in Vietnam, in short, we may find ourselves compelled to draw a defense line as far back as Seattle and Alaska."[36] For the Joint Chiefs of Staff the war against South Vietnam was "part of a major campaign to extend Communist control beyond the periphery of the Sino-Soviet bloc. . . . It is, in fact, a planned phase in the Communist timetable for world domination."[37]

Unfortunately the Munich syndrome, with its exaggerated, pathological images of Communist expansion far beyond Vietnam, uninhibited by the costs, risks, and limitations of military conflict, determined the manner that official anti-Communist rhetoric perceived the Soviet danger. Never did the predictions of Soviet expansion prove valid because the Soviets had no intention of fighting in Southeast Asia. The domino theory, moreover, never recognized the power of nationalism or the individuality of nations that rendered all Southeast Asian countries resistant to external encroachments. Thus no Washington official could define the enemy that, having acquired Saigon, would thereafter spread Communist aggression across East Asia and the Pacific. If Moscow and Beijing were the enemy, fighting Hanoi was irrelevant. If Hanoi's defeat assured the peace and stability of Asia, as U.S. policy presumed, what was the meaning of falling dominoes? Hanoi, driven by its conception of self-determination, possessed the power to unite Vietnam; it possessed neither the power nor the intention to expand across Asia and the Pacific. It was not strange that criticism of the American Vietnam involvement kept pace with official efforts to escalate the costs and the importance of the struggle. The unleashing of huge quantities of destruction against a jungle population on the Asian mainland challenged both the credulity and the moral sensibilities of millions of Americans for whom the Soviet Union comprised no threat to Southeast Asia—or any other Third World region. Yet the concept of falling dominoes underwrote the later fears of Communist expansionism in such countries as Angola, Afghanistan, Nicaragua, El Salvador, and Grenada.

* * *

In any case, and within the space of 31 years, 1914–1945, the world experienced two global wars of tremendous violence, "total wars"— the first marked by the march toward a mainly European tragedy in the trenches of 1914–1918, the second reaching a death toll of probably 60 million, a figure that included the 6 million murdered because they were Jewish. During these years America witnessed two revolutions—Russian and Chinese—of extreme intensity and cruelty. It also saw the collapse of five empires—the Ottoman, the Austro-Hungarian, German, Italian, and Japanese—as well as the decline of the British and French imperial systems. Thus during the span of one generation, American politicians, policy-makers, and diplomats of the emerging Cold War had experienced the disillusionment of the Versailles system; struggled through the Great Depression with one-quarter of the nation unemployed; witnessed the rise of Communism (with its forced collectivization and purges), fascism, and Nazism; recoiled from the West's abandonment of Czechoslovakia to Hitler in 1938, under the aegis of appeasement; and were dragged into a second world war in their lifetime. Moreover modern warfare, with its awful weapons of death and destruction and the equally awful contemplation they could be delivered anywhere with impunity, caused the majority of Americans to rethink past policies and their role in the world, as the historic balance of power had been fundamentally altered.

Washington's basic problem was to make sense of the U.S.S.R. Americans were as perplexed about the motives and intentions of the Soviet Union in 1941 as they were in 1917. What had occurred to cause a nation still enjoying the taste of victory to turn on its recent ally in the Grand Alliance? How does a nation deal with a regime that it seemingly regards as the root and branch of all evil? In the end, American attitudes toward the Bolsheviks revolved around a single question: Was the Soviet Union a messianic ideology in the service of a traditional Great Power, or was it a traditional Great Power in the service of a messianic ideology? Uncertain initially, and with the bitter taste of the Nazi experience still in its mouth, Washington, with the prompting of the British, chose to believe the worst. Post–Cold War revelations from Soviet archives proved Washington and (London) right on one score: Stalin could be a monster, with the soul of a killer.[38] Still, as a Cold War opponent, the same archives proved he was at once an opportunist and a realist, taking what he could while understanding the limits of his own power.

Seeking to understand Soviet motives and intentions, this study begins with the seedtime of America's Cold War that originates with United States entry into the Second World War. The political interplay during these four years found American officials, who understood that Nazi Germany could not be defeated without a huge assist from the Red armies, consistently urging a return to the prewar European *status quo* with democratic governments chosen by free elections. Meanwhile, the Kremlin continually pressed for a postwar realignment in Central and Eastern Europe that would install "friendly" governments along its borders and enhance the Soviet Union's security. When its proposals were rebuffed, Washington instituted a strategy, of postponing decisions until Hitler was vanquished, that at various conferences papered over the essential points of contention with Moscow. The Truman administration's response to the unresolved issues was a continued insistence on self-determination for Central and Eastern Europe, which Moscow perceived as the likelihood of returning governments hostile to the Soviet Union along its much contested frontier. The Grand Alliance ended and thereafter followed the full-blown Cold War.

CHAPTER 1

The Grand Alliance

When the Japanese attack on Pearl Harbor, December 7, 1941, brought the United States into the Second World War, one of the greatest military confrontations of all time was raging along an eight hundred mile front stretching across the Soviet Union from the Baltic to the Black Sea. That gigantic Soviet-German clash on the Eastern Front endangered what remained of Europe's internal balance that had long underwritten America's historic security in the Atlantic world. The old European equilibrium could not survive a total victory of either Germany or the U.S.S.R. over the other, for the potential strength of these two giants vastly exceeded that of France and Britain. The Western democracies had disposed of German and Russian expansive power during the Great War of 1914; they would not do so again. As late as 1945 the U.S.S.R. carried the full burden of the war against Germany in the East, a war four times as massive as the war in the West. The Western Allies could not emerge from the war victorious without leaving their ally, the Soviet Union, the predominant power on the European continent.[1]

Yet this inescapable assault of the Allied war effort on the historic European balance of power was scarcely a matter of concern to Washington. Throughout the war, U.S. leaders anticipated no less than the restoration of the 1919 Versailles order, with territorial arrangements and legal principles that defined the ideal world of the Western democracies. In August 1941, President Franklin D. Roosevelt and British Prime Minster Winston S. Churchill met at Placentia Bay off Argentia, Newfoundland, and there drafted the famed Atlantic Charter, with principles on which they based "their hope for a better future for the world." In the first three articles of the Charter, the two leaders declared that their governments sought "no aggrandizement, territorial or other," that they opposed territorial changes contrary to the free wishes of the people concerned, and that they respected the right of all peoples to self-government.

The Charter recommended no program, but, in offering the restoration of the Versailles order, it promised independence for all European peoples living under externally imposed governments. Much of the Western World at war with Germany adopted the Atlantic Charter as the standard to which they would hold those responsible for the postwar reconstruction of Europe.[2] In December 1941, Secretary of State Cordell Hull, to protect the principles of the Atlantic Charter against any secret wartime agreements, announced the American policy of postponing all territorial and political decisions for Europe until the end of the war.[3] The Kremlin, however, was not reticent about pressing its demands for postwar changes.

Washington and London accepted the challenge to uproot the war-making power of Germany and Italy as the necessary prelude to an acceptable peace. Their strategies for victory reflected the wartime conviction that the world comprised two categories of nations, expansionist and peace-loving. The aggressiveness that appeared to characterize Axis

Figure 1.1
President Roosevelt and Prime Minister Winston Churchill at the Atlantic Conference, 1941 (Courtesy: National Archives)

behavior was, to Washington especially, an inherent national quality. Clearly, Hull informed the nation in July 1942, the United States had no choice but "to destroy the worldwide forces of ruthless conquest and brutal enslavement." To assure the elimination of Nazi and Fascist expansionism, Roosevelt announced, at the Casablanca Conference of January 1943, the allied wartime objective of unconditional surrender. "It is clear to us," he informed Congress," that if Germany and Italy and Japan—or any of them—remain armed at the end of this war . . . , they will again, and inevitably, embark upon an ambitious career of world conquest."

Roosevelt recalled vividly the German "stab in the back" theory of an undefeated German army in 1918, and its role in the rebirth of German militarism. It was essential that the Axis powers not only experience defeat, but also acknowledge it. Churchill accepted the policy of unconditional surrender, although Roosevelt's announcement caught him off guard.[4] Unconditional surrender presumed that the United States and its allies, at the war's end, would possess the coordination, wisdom, and control of all essential elements in the peace process to create, in the absence of the Axis aggressors, the perfect postwar settlement. Unconditional surrender, Roosevelt proclaimed at Casablanca, "means a reasonable assurance of world peace, for generations."[5] Unfortunately, unconditional surrender, by denying enemy states the right to any control over their postwar economic, political, or territorial destiny, assumed the danger of converting the war into a zero-sum contest of limitless death and destruction. Without the assurance of some acceptable offer of accommodation, nations might resist capitulation even at the price of total disaster.

America's wartime hopes for achieving both the destruction of Axis power and the reconstitution of the Versailles order rested on the performance of the Grand Alliance. Unfortunately, the alliance, despite its promise of ultimate victory, was never cohesive. Hitler's decisions had brought Great Britain, the U.S.S.R., and the United States into the war at different times and under different circumstances.[6] Entering the struggle individually and without agreed-upon objectives other than the defeat of the Axis, each could never escape the thinly disguised suspicion, at times approaching animosity, that their allies were using them to achieve purposes totally divorced from the common goal of defeating the enemy. The varied wartime opportunities for the enlargement of power and influence that each ally experienced merely magnified the tensions as the war progressed. The Soviet advantages for self-aggrandizement were unique largely because Germany and the

U.S.S.R. had entered the war as the real poles of the European equilibrium, creating in their mammoth confrontation across Eastern Europe
the assurance that one would emerge from the war predominant in
European affairs. That victor could only be the Soviet Union.

Had the Kremlin shared the Anglo-American vision of postwar
European reconstruction, Soviet mastery, conterminous with the
reach of the Soviet armies, would have mattered little. But Stalin never
denied his intention of acquiring tangible emoluments of victory
through the expansion of the Soviet sphere of influence into Eastern
Europe—at the expense of principles proclaimed in the Atlantic
Charter. Soviet territorial ambitions were implicit in the entire range
of Soviet diplomacy from the negotiation of the Nazi-Soviet Pact of
August 1939 until Hitler's invasion of the Soviet Union in June 1941.

Invited by the Nazi-Soviet pact of August 1939, Stalin quickly absorbed
eastern Poland; the Baltic states of Estonia, Latvia, and Lithuania;
Finland's Karelian Peninsula; and Bessarabia and Northern Bukovina,
two regions formerly belonging to Rumania. Even as the war engulfed
the U.S.S.R., Soviet diplomats sought British and American recognition of these annexations. Churchill responded to the Nazi invasion
of the U.S.S.R. with an immediate promise of support. Harry Hopkins,
visiting London in late July 1941, reported that Stalin "had not been
tremendously impressed by Britain's offer of aid, but had been concerned, from the very beginning, with the political aspects of the
enforced alliance." With its very existence in peril, Hopkins recalled,
"the Soviet Government appeared to be more anxious to discuss future
frontiers and spheres of influence than to negotiate for military
supplies."[7]

Determined to retain occupied territories at the war's end, the
Soviets viewed the Atlantic Charter with deep distrust. Roosevelt and
Churchill, in framing the Charter without reference to the Kremlin,
believed either that Moscow would accept it willingly or that the
Soviet reaction did not matter. Both presumptions were grievously
wrong. Soviet leaders complained vehemently that the two Western
powers, the United States not even belligerent, were attempting to
exclude them from the postwar settlement. Nevertheless, the Soviets
set aside their suspicions long enough to join nine other nations in
London, on September 24, 1941, to declare their adherence to the
principles of the Charter. Soviet ambassador Ivan Maisky declared that
"the Soviet Union has applied, and will apply, in its foreign policy the
high principle of respect for the rights of people." The Soviet application of that principle, he added for those who cared to listen, would

"necessarily adapt itself to the circumstances and historic peculiarities of particular countries." The Soviets signed the UN Declaration of January 1, 1942, which restated the principles of the Atlantic Charter.[8]

During subsequent months State Department planners examined the German and Eastern European disputes that had undermined Europe's stability of the late 1930s, with the intention of eliminating them from the postwar world. Their immense efforts presumed that the United States would dictate the Eastern European settlement.[9] Yet the expectation that Soviet leaders would give up their territorial ambitions in conformity with the American principle of self-determination, which the Western allies could not enforce, simply denied the reality of Russia's emerging power and its historic designs on Eastern Europe.

* * *

Shortly before Pearl Harbor, Secretary of State Hull formulated a U.S. response to the Soviet Union's territorial ambitions in Eastern Europe. On December 4, the British Foreign Office informed Washington that Foreign Secretary Anthony Eden would shortly visit Moscow to allay Soviet doubts regarding Western intentions toward Eastern Europe. Hull warned the London government against any secret arrangements regarding that region's future. U.S. policies, he added, "have been delineated in the Atlantic Charter which represented the attitude of the United States, Britain, and the Soviet Union." To meet the Soviet challenge, Hull offered the program of postponing all political and territorial decisions until the conclusion of the war. That program faced an immediate challenge.

In late December, Stalin confronted Eden, then in Moscow, with a far-reaching plan for the reconstruction of Eastern Europe. The Soviet sphere of influence would include all territory under Soviet control in June 1941, when the Germans launched their attack on the U.S.S.R. He included the Curzon line in Poland, but declared that the immediate Soviet concern was "the position of Finland and the Baltic states and Rumania ... It is very important," he asserted, "for us to know whether we shall have to fight at the peace conference to get our western frontiers." When Eden observed that the Atlantic Charter pledged Britain "to take into account the wishes of the inhabitants," Stalin replied: "I thought that the Atlantic Charter was directed against those people who were trying to establish world dominion. It now looks as if the Atlantic Charter was directed against the U.S.S.R." Eden escaped the dilemma momentarily by explaining that, in view of prior negotiations with the United States, "it was quite impossible for His Majesty's Government to commit themselves at this stage to any postwar frontiers in Europe."[10]

British Prime Minister Winston Churchill agreed to this policy of procrastination. "There can be no question whatever of our making such an agreement," he wrote en route to Washington, "... without prior agreement with the United States. The time has not yet come to settle frontier questions, which can only be resolved at the Peace Conference when we have won the war."[11] To approach Roosevelt with such proposals, he surmised correctly, would court a blank refusal. Churchill advised Eden from Washington on January 8, 1942, that the "transfer of the peoples of the Baltic states to Soviet Russia against their will would be contrary to all the principles for which we are fighting this war and would dishonor our cause."[12] This was the last time that British leaders would assume such an uncompromising posture on the territorial issue.

By February, the British were ready to propose a more expedient approach to the question of Soviet territorial ambitions. Eden reminded Washington that at issue in Stalin's demands was the necessity of working with the Kremlin, both during and after the war. He warned that it would be unsafe "to gamble on Russia emerging so exhausted from the war that she will be forced to collaborate with us without our having to make any concessions to her." Eden then attacked the concept of postponement as dangerous and unrealistic. Prudence, he wrote, required the Western powers to base their plans on the assumption that postwar Soviet cooperation would require allied policies advantageous to the U.S.S.R. "The application of this policy will be a laborious and lengthy process," he added. "If we are to adopt it we must start now and not wait until the war is over." Meanwhile, the British Foreign Office revealed increasing concern over the Soviet insistence on a favorable British reply. On February 18, Sir Stafford Cripps, former British ambassador to Moscow, advocated British acquiescence to Soviet demands. By March Churchill had reached the point of capitulation. For him it served no purpose to maintain a position based on principle that could not be maintained with any available policy. To Roosevelt he wrote:

The increasing gravity of the war has led me to feel that the principles of the Atlantic Charter ought not to be construed so as to deny Russia the frontiers she occupied when Germany attacked her. This was the basis on which Russia acceded to the Charter. ... I hope therefore that you will be able to give us a free hand to sign the treaty which Stalin desires as soon as possible. Everything portends an immense renewal of the German invasion of Russia in the spring. And there is very little we can do to help the only country that is heavily engaged with the German armies.[13]

That month the British decided to conclude a treaty with Russia that would incorporate the political guarantees demanded by Stalin. Eden explained that Britain could not "neglect any opportunity offered to establish close and friendly relations with Stalin." If the Soviet leader adopted an anti-British policy because of England's obstinacy on the frontier issue, he warned, the results for Britain would be disastrous. Washington responded to this approaching crisis in allied diplomacy with a promise to accede to another of Stalin's demands: the immediate establishment of a second front in Europe. Stalin acknowledged in moments of candor that the establishment of a second front lay well beyond immediate Western capabilities, but the persistent repetition of the request served as a reminder that the U.S.S.R. was carrying the brunt of the European war. To quiet Stalin and simultaneously extract Britain from its diplomatic dilemma, Roosevelt, in April, addressed a note to the Soviet leader, assuring him of the U.S. intention to establish a second front in the near future. Stalin responded by dispatching Molotov to Washington.

While Roosevelt broached the subject of a second front, Hull continued to confine U.S. policy to the narrow compass of the Atlantic Charter. Early in February, he reminded the president that any concession to the Soviet demands would destroy the Charter's integrity. "Our attitude," ran the theme of his memorandum, "had been predicated on our general policy not to recognize any territorial changes that had been made in European frontiers since the outbreak of the war and not to enter into any territorial commitments that might hamper the proceedings of the postwar peace conference."[14] When Hull, after a period of illness, returned to his desk in May, Ambassador John Winant informed him that Molotov's conversations with Eden in London, aimed at producing a wartime pact, were progressing well and that the Soviet minister was holding to Stalin's request for the Baltic States and the new Finnish line. Hull warned Roosevelt that any treaty which included such a territorial settlement would undermine the cause of the nations fighting Germany, and that "if the treaty in its proposed form were signed, we might not be able to remain silent since silence might give tacit consent. On the contrary we might have to issue a separate statement clearly stating that we did not subscribe to its principles and clauses."[15]

In London, on the evening of May 24, Winant conferred with Molotov and Maisky, explaining to them that the U.S. government desired to cooperate with the Soviet Union. To that extent it was prepared to discuss not only the matter of a second front but also commercial policy and economic relief. But he reminded the Soviet diplomats that both Roosevelt and Hull were opposed to the introduction of frontier problems before the end of hostilities. Molotov promised to reconsider the American position as well as Eden's draft treaty, which contained no reference to frontiers. On the following day, Molotov informed Eden that he had recommended to Moscow the acceptance of the British draft. On May 26, Molotov received Kremlin approval and that afternoon signed an alliance pact with Britain. Washington had succeeded in diverting Soviet attention from the embarrassing question of frontiers to the more immediate and essential issue of maintaining an effective military collaboration against Germany.[16] To Hull the victory for principle remained paramount. It was preferable, he concluded in his *Memoirs*, "to take a firm attitude now, rather than to retreat and to be compelled to take a firm attitude later when our position had been weakened by the abandonment of the general principles."

It soon became apparent why the Soviets had receded from their territorial demands and accepted from Britain a simple treaty of alliance. By this act of cooperation, Molotov acquired for the U.S.S.R. the needed moral and physical support of the United States. Without an eventual victory over Germany, an allied agreement on territories would matter little. Soviet leaders, moreover, had not given up their long-range interest in an expanding sphere of influence. With Germany's defeat, the Kremlin would be in control of any territories it desired. Never again throughout the war would the United States gain the diplomatic advantage over the Soviet Union, for the more complete the allied conquest of Germany, the more complete would be the Soviet occupation of Eastern Europe. Hull's pursuit of self-determination for Eastern Europe could terminate in one of two possible situations. Either Americans who took his principles seriously would accept a settlement that they regarded immoral, or Russians who favored an enlarged Soviet sphere of influence would feel betrayed by the West. From such political penalties there was no apparent escape.

* * *

Undaunted by its profound disagreements over the future of Eastern Europe, the Grand Alliance embarked on its crusade to disarm Germany. To that end the Western Allies underwrote the Soviet war effort with military aid and coordinated strategies. When Churchill conversed with Stalin over strategy in Moscow during August 1942, Stalin again pressed Churchill for a second front. When Churchill informed him that there would be no second front in 1942, Stalin bluntly accused the British of being afraid to face the German armies. Churchill insisted that Britain and the United States had achieved all in their power and had not broken any promises.[17] Whatever the limited Western contribution in 1942, the collaboration had bound the American and Soviet armies together in a symbiotic relationship; both understood that neither would survive without the other.[18] By the spring of 1943 that military collaboration had delivered astonishingly successful results, most notably the Soviet victory at Stalingrad and the Soviet advances that followed. The United States, in the interest of victory, encouraged the U.S.S.R. to conquer and occupy those regions of Eastern Europe that had for generations comprised the ultimate political goals of Russian foreign policy. What mattered to those fighting Nazi Germany was the Soviet contribution to victory; for good reason Roosevelt repeatedly congratulated the Red Army on its successes.[19] Even before the United States actively entered the struggle for Europe, the ironies that beset the alliance were profound.

During the spring of 1943 the unforeseen Soviet-Polish conflict threatened to undo the Western commitment to allied unity, as a prelude to victory and to self-determination as embodied in the Atlantic Charter. Poland's exiled government, residing in London after June 1940, was officially at war with Germany. However, the Soviet occupation of eastern Poland up to the frontiers granted in the Nazi-Soviet Pact of August 1939, created a Polish state of war with the U.S.S.R. as well. Soviet occupation authorities proceeded to export perhaps a million Poles, most of whom simply disappeared. Then, in the spring of 1940, Soviet police targeted the Polish military with a view to eliminating the officer corp. The exiled Polish government was determined to free Poland of both German and Soviet occupation and reestablish the Polish frontiers that existed before August 1939.[20] Such goals required the elimination of both Germany and the U.S.S.R. as major factors in the postwar world.

Unfortunately for Poland, Stalin was determined to prevent the creation of another *cordon sanitaire* of anti-Soviet states along the Soviet Union's western periphery. Although allied to Poland in opposition to Germany, the Kremlin hesitated to negotiate any wartime accord with the London Poles, known to be intensely anti-Soviet, especially one that involved postwar borders. Finally in late July 1941 the Soviets, under Allied pressure, signed an agreement that recognized the exiled Polish government, granted amnesty to the Poles detained or incarcerated in the U.S.S.R., and offered the ambiguous statement that the

U.S.S.R. "recognizes that the Soviet-German Treaties of 1939 regarding territorial changes in Poland have lost their validity." Poland's prime minister, General Wladyslaw Sikorski, moved immediately to strengthen the exiled government's claims to nationhood by recruiting Polish forces to join the British in the Middle East and elsewhere.[21]

During his conversations with Eden, in December 1941, Stalin insisted that the Kremlin, in any postwar settlement, would accept no less than the Curzon line for Poland, roughly equivalent to the ethnic boundary defined in the Nazi-Soviet Pact. The Curzon line, proposed but rejected at the Versailles Conference, lay far to the west of the boundary that the victors imposed on Russia in the Polish-Soviet Treaty of Riga (1921). By the spring of 1943, the Kremlin was prepared to affirm its claims to the Curzon line. During April, it announced that Polish nationals found on territory claimed by the U.S.S.R. would be considered Soviet citizens.[22] This coercion of Polish nationals to accept Soviet citizenship, proclaiming the permanency of the new Soviet frontiers, created a crisis in Polish-Soviet relations. The exiled Polish government remained adamant, informing Washington and London that it had refused "even to discuss the question of Poland's Eastern territorial borders, which it regarded as finally settled by virtue of the [Riga Treaty] ... , and to accept no compromise in the matter of Polish citizenship."[23] The London Poles, openly rejecting Soviet demands while seeking support in the West, had ceased to be acceptable to Kremlin.

Washington and London, conscious of their repeated avowals of the Atlantic Charter, remained publicly reassuring but privately silent. Britain had neither the power nor the interest to confront the U.S.S.R. on the issue of the Curzon line. Eden informed Polish leaders that Britain would recognize no territorial changes imposed on Poland after August 1939. At the same time he advised the House of Commons that Britain would not guarantee the former Polish frontiers.[24] Privately British officials accepted Soviet territorial demands in Poland as the necessary price of preserving the Grand Alliance.[25] Washington faced the Soviet challenge to the Atlantic Charter's principle of self-determination, no less uncertain and divided. From Moscow, Ambassador William Standley admonished the administration to avoid the Soviet-Polish clash, especially since Sikorski had taken his case to Washington. State Department expert Elbridge Durbrow, harboring a deep distrust of the U.S.S.R., advised Washington that the United States would gain nothing by sacrificing its principle of self-determination. Joseph E. Davies, former ambassador to the Soviet Union, reminded Durbrow that the future of the Grand Alliance required a firm understanding with the

Kremlin on the question of postwar frontiers. Nowhere, he added, did Soviet demands threaten any Western strategic interests.[26] It was precisely such wartime controversies that Roosevelt and Hull had hoped to postpone until the end of the war.

Eden arrived in Washington, on March 12, for two weeks of conversations with Roosevelt, Hull, and other State Department officials. During his meetings in Washington, Eden emphasized the Western need to come to terms with the Soviet Union's probable future demands, especially in Eastern Europe. He reminded the president that even if the worst fears of Soviet expansionism proved to be correct, "we should make the position no worse by trying to work with Russia."[27] Roosevelt agreed with Eden on the need to sustain Soviet military cooperation by making boundary concessions in Finland, Rumania, and Poland. He acknowledged Soviet annexations of the Baltic States, hoping only that Stalin would render them more acceptable by holding plebiscites. Most threatening to Allied unity was Poland's unrealistic demands. Eden recalled for Roosevelt the utopian Polish notion that the war would eliminate both German and Soviet power as factors in European politics, enabling Poland to emerge from the war at once sovereign and victorious. The Poles, proud and patriotic, seemed temperamentally unable to come to terms with their predicament. Roosevelt assured Eden that he "did not intend to go to the Peace Conference and bargain with Poland or the other small states."[28] Without openly repudiating the principles of the Atlantic Charter, Eden and Roosevelt were prepared to make extensive concessions to Soviet power in Eastern Europe. Poland would soon test that resolve.

* * *

Polish-Soviet tension reached the breaking point on April 13, 1943, when Berlin radio announced the discovery of the remains of more than 25,000 Poles, including nearly 15,000 Polish officers whose bodies had been dumped in a mass grave in the forest of Katyn, near Smolensk. The Germans accused the Soviets of murdering the Poles. The Kremlin denied the charge, insisting that the Nazis had killed the officers after they occupied the area in 1941. The Polish government in London demanded an impartial investigation by the International Red Cross. Stalin complained to Churchill that any investigation in territory under German control would be fraudulent. Churchill agreed. He requested Sikorski to withdraw Polish approval of any German-sponsored investigation, admonishing Sikorski not to adopt a pro-Nazi posture. Under pressure, the exiled Poles paid their respects to Western demands, but they would never pay the Kremlin's price for satisfactory relations.[29] The Katyn incident presented Stalin the desired excuse to terminate his fruitless exchanges with the London Poles. Accusing the Poles of slander against the U.S.S.R., Stalin, on April 25, announced that the Kremlin had severed diplomatic relations with Poland. Several days later the Soviet leader proclaimed the establishment of the Union of Polish Patriots to inaugurate the process of creating a pro-Soviet government for Poland.[30] Churchill and Roosevelt advised Stalin that the Western powers would not recognize any Kremlin-instituted Polish regime.[31]

Lacking the needed support in Washington and London for its claims to the Riga frontiers, the exiled Polish government, with enthusiastic support from Polish émigrés in the United States, mounted a vigorous assault on the American mind. The Polish language press campaign against the U.S.S.R. gathered momentum during the spring of 1943 and reached the heights of vituperation with the break in Soviet-Polish diplomatic relations. At issue, declared Polish writers, was not merely Poland's eastern frontiers but the alleged Soviet threat to the entire region separating the U.S.S.R. from Germany. "Those who do not come out in defense of the boundaries of Poland, in defense of Lithuania, Latvia, and Estonia," warned Chicago's *Dziennik Zwiazkowy*, "are apostles of the world-capital in Moscow." Polish editors freely predicted a Western war against the U.S.S.R. following the defeat of Germany.[32] General Wladyslaw Anders, commander of the Polish army, was not alone in pinning his hopes for a free Poland on such a war. For Stalin, too many London and American Poles had become pro-German. He condemned his British and American partners for not controlling the verbal Polish crusade against the U.S.S.R. Actually the Soviets blunted the Polish challenge by enlisting their own Polish writers who were willing to argue that Poland's future rested on accommodation with the U.S.S.R., not Germany. Much of the American press took up the Soviet cause and condemned the Poles for feeding German propaganda that pictured the U.S.S.R., not Germany, as the enemy of the West.[33]

Polish attacks on the U.S.S.R. merely paralleled those in the German press. Joseph Goebbels, the Nazi propaganda minister, regarded the anti-German alliance a fraud, papering over immense tensions and incongruities. He observed as early as March that the Soviet-Polish quarrel over frontiers exceeded "by far the bounds usually respected by allies in wartime." Soviet gains along the Eastern Front vastly magnified the possibilities of the anti-Soviet crusade. Following the Katyn incident, Goebbels noted that the Poles would soon discover what a German defeat would mean to them. Goebbels confided to his diary on November 16: "I have ordered all our propaganda services at home and abroad to start a great, new anti-Bolshevik campaign. This will be based upon the military successes of the Soviets and is to give Europe and our enemies the creeps. I don't want them to stop being frightened about Bolshevism."[34] Ultimately, Goebbels predicted, both the Soviets and the Anglo-Americans would seek German support as they faced one another across a war-torn Europe. French writer Raymond Aron recalled that the more Goebbels proclaimed the hostility among members of the Grand Alliance, the more Washington and London were compelled to camouflage it.[35]

* * *

Amid the deepening conflict over Poland, the Western Allies, in August 1943, gathered in Quebec for the Quadrant Conference to determine strategy for the needed invasion of the European continent. Churchill had long believed peripheral assaults along Europe's Mediterranean coast preferable to a cross-Channel invasion, less likely to split Europe militarily through the middle along a north-south axis. In May, during the Trident Conference in Washington, U.S. General George C. Marshall had dismissed the Mediterranean operations as incapable of ending the war. Not until Quadrant did the American Joint Chiefs of Staff persuade the British to accept OVERLORD, the cross-Channel attack to come on May 1, 1944.[36]

At Quadrant, the British gained approval of the Italian campaign as a logical continuation of the successful Allied invasion of Sicily. Meanwhile, on July 25, a bloodless coup overthrew Italian dictator Benito Mussolini; General Pietro Badoglio, Mussolini's former Chief of Staff, became the new prime minister. When the Quadrant Conference opened, Badoglio announced his intention to take Italy out of the war, creating, as Roosevelt reminded Churchill, the first occasion for the Allies to establish their surrender and occupation policies. Thereupon the two Western leaders proceeded to exclude the U.S.S.R. from any role in the Allied Control Commission for Italy. Stalin was enraged. He addressed Roosevelt on August 22: "To date it has been like this: the U.S.A. and Britain reach agreement between themselves while the U.S.S.R. is informed of the agreement between the two Powers as a third party looking passively on. I must say that this situation cannot be tolerated any longer." At the surrender ceremony, in early September, American General Dwight D. Eisenhower, with

Stalin's approval, signed for the U.S.S.R. Stalin's exclusion from the Italian occupation assured Italy's postwar membership in the Western bloc; it also provided the Kremlin the perfect precedent to eliminate Anglo-American influence from the predictable Soviet occupations of Eastern Europe.[37]

* * *

When Soviet forces held back the dreaded *Wehrmacht* at Stalingrad in the winter of 1942–1943 and inaugurated the slow, costly process of driving Hitler's prime armies from Soviet territory, they presaged their country's escape from disaster as Europe's leading military power. Following Stalingrad, Italian and Japanese leaders urged Hitler to seek a compromise peace with Stalin. They doubted that Germany would ever recover from its stupendous losses. Throughout the autumn of 1943, Soviet armies, advancing on all sectors of the Eastern Front, assured the eventual elimination of German forces from Soviet territories. The continuing display of Soviet power and resiliency relegated the United States and Britain to the role of junior partners in the coalition. When Harry Hopkins arrived at the Quadrant Conference, he carried a high-level U.S. estimate of the Soviet strategic position. The document read in part: "Russia's postwar position in Europe will be a dominant one. With Germany crushed, there is no power in Europe to oppose her tremendous military forces. . . . Since Russia is the decisive factor in the war, she must be given every assistance and every effort must be made to obtain her friendship."[38] In conversation with New York's Cardinal Spellman at the White House, in early September, Roosevelt predicted that the Soviets would dominate Eastern Europe at the end of the war. The United States, moreover, would engage in no anti-Soviet maneuver to prevent it. "Be that as it may," ran his conclusion, " . . . the United States and Britain cannot fight the Russians." In time, the president predicted, the European peoples would adjust to Soviet domination.[39]

Big Three unity could scarcely survive the West's increasing reliance on Soviet power. Britain's alliance with the United States received formal status in December 1941, with the formation of the Anglo-American Combined Chiefs of Staff. Thereafter Churchill, in his uncompromising commitment to victory, had no choice but to rely on the goodwill and resolution of Roosevelt and the American people. The war had dealt Britain a poor hand. To conduct a war that quickly overwhelmed its capabilities, the United Kingdom liquidated overseas assets, abandoned markets, and borrowed billions of pounds within the sterling area.

The excessive demands on Britain's financial and material resources presaged, even in victory, not the elevation, but the diminution, of what remained of that country's historic power, position, and prestige. The promise of the Atlantic Charter undermined the global support for the British Empire. Only a firm partnership with the United States, one anticipating, possibly, even a common citizenship, could save Britain from financial ruin, the loss of empire, and descent to second-class status. For Churchill, the Anglo-Soviet pact of May 20, 1942, followed by the Soviet successes of 1943, served the British interest in victory over Germany. Yet for Churchill the collaboration with the U.S.S.R. was never complete. His distrust of Soviet intentions was profound. On August 25, 1942, he informed the War Cabinet that the "black spot at the present time is the increased bearishness of Soviet Russia." To preserve Britain's interests as well as its leadership role, Churchill maneuvered to create and direct an Anglo-American front against the U.S.S.R.[40] Churchill's relationship to Roosevelt was never as close as he wished it to be or as his wartime memoirs suggest. During 1943 the earlier special Anglo-American relationship evaporated under the impact of the Soviet Union's growing importance in the Allied war effort. With few exceptions, U.S. officials, no less than the American public, had long accepted the U.S.S.R. as a necessary and trustworthy ally. Not even the country's politically conservative elements offered resistance to closer ties with the Kremlin.[41] The country's remarkable wartime unity was a measure of its overwhelming satisfaction with the goals and performance of the Grand Alliance. But Roosevelt's growing appreciation for Stalin responded to a body of specific wartime necessities. Stalin, not Churchill, held the power to guarantee or prevent the triumph of the president's vision of the postwar settlement. Only the U.S.S.R. could assure total victory over Germany with the least possible loss of American life.

Having assigned to Stalin the power of life and death over the entire range of his wartime objectives, Roosevelt sought to build bridges to the Kremlin through unrestricted Lend-Lease and promises of postwar credits. Lend-Lease, Washington presumed, would sustain an effective Soviet effort on the Eastern Front. Because the *quid pro quo* of Lend-Lease was Soviet lives, Roosevelt made no effort to coerce the Soviets with threats of withdrawal.[42] He ordered the delivery of supplies to the U.S.S.R. without demanding the customary evaluation of Soviet needs or determining the ultimate disposition of Lend-Lease shipments. Ambassador Standley, in March 1943, condemned the Soviet refusal to acknowledge American Lend-Lease aid publicly or offer any accounting of its disposal. Similarly General John Deane, U.S. military attaché in Moscow, complained of unnecessary official secrecy and the misuse of American supplies. Such reporting had no influence on Roosevelt's quest for Stalin's cooperation. To strengthen his ties with the Kremlin, the president replaced anti-Soviet Standley with W. Averell Harriman to assure better U.S.-Soviet collaboration. In May 1943, he sent Joseph E. Davies to Moscow to suggest a private Stalin-Roosevelt meeting, free from the embarrassment of Churchill's presence. Stalin declined the invitation. When Churchill discovered the president's scheme, he informed Roosevelt that such divisive tactics should delight Hitler.[43]

Prompted by his pro-Soviet advisers, Roosevelt rejected every appearance of a special affinity for Britain, even refusing to acknowledge Britain's economic woes. His anti-British proclivities were highly acceptable to leading State Department officials, many of whom harbored a deep distaste for Britain and the British Empire. In their Lend-Lease negotiations of 1941 and 1942 with financially weakened Britain, they exerted their special wartime leverage to assure arrangements that would vastly restrict British exports and prevent the British from entering new markets at the expense of U.S. exporters. The basic Lend-Lease document insisted that the British provide access to raw materials, including oil, in return for aid. It demanded as well that the British abandon imperial preference and financial controls after the war. Churchill charged that the U.S. effort to terminate the principle of imperial preference in exchange for Lend-Lease was intervention in the affairs of the British Empire. The London government signed the agreement in February 1942 only after Roosevelt made necessary concessions on imperial preference.[44] Lend-Lease shipments to Britain were not a mark of friendship; Washington officials were never prepared to treat that country generously. As the war progressed, Churchill's fears of a Soviet hegemony in Eastern Europe had no effect on strategy or the cohesion of the Anglo-American alliance.

* * *

Determined to save Poland, Washington, by October 1943, had formulated a plan to bridge the growing dichotomy between the Kremlin's political designs on that country and the West's equal determination to protect its independence. For Hull the answer lay in another, more telling, Allied agreement on principles. The final draft of the State Department's carefully worded Declaration of Four Nations included a reaffirmation of principles of the Atlantic Charter: "[The signatory states] will not employ their military forces within the territory of other states except for purposes envisaged in the declaration and after joint consultation and agreement." The declaration, with its self-denying clause, received the approval of both Churchill and Eden at the Quebec Conference. In October, Hull managed to place the declaration on the agenda of the Moscow Foreign Ministers Conference. The apparent triumph for self-determination embodied in the Soviet signature of the document overwhelmed the incredulous secretary. But Hull found even greater assurance for Soviet-American unity in the Soviet promise to participate in a postwar United Nations organization. Contrasted to that prospect for future security, Stalin's designs on Poland seemed inconsequential. Anne O'Hare McCormick of the *New York Times* believed that Hull had found the formula that combined postwar security with self-determination for all. In his address to a joint session of Congress on November 18, the secretary predicted the triumph of American principles. "As the provisions of the Four Nation Declaration are carried into effect," he declared, "there will no longer be need for spheres of influence, for alliances, for balance of power, or any other of the special arrangements through which ... the nations strove to safeguard their security or to promote their interests." The Moscow agreements, he said, had laid the foundation for a cooperative effort that would enable the peace-loving nations, large and small, to live in peace and security.[45]

Privately Churchill and Roosevelt acknowledged their limited power to protect Polish interests. Churchill reminded the London Poles that they could not expect the Soviets to fight Germany to victory and then settle for boundaries dictated at Riga. Similarly Roosevelt informed Czechoslovakia's Eduard Benes that he regarded the Curzon line a fair solution of the Polish boundary question.[46] Publicly, however, the Western leaders avoided the boundary issue. When, in July, Hull sent to Moscow a series of proposals for a Soviet-Polish settlement, he made no reference to boundaries. With this policy Polish officials agreed; they knew that any territorial agreement acceptable to the Kremlin would be at Poland's expense. Shortly before Hull left for the Moscow Foreign Ministers Conference, Jan Ciechanowski, the Polish ambassador, urged him to avoid any decision on frontiers. The Four Nations Declaration evaded the question of specific postwar frontiers. Still Polish officials were not reassured. When Ciechanowski complained to Hull that the Moscow Conference had not guaranteed Poland's future, Hull responded in amazement, reciting to him the provisions of the Declaration of Four Nations. That statement, Hull added, meant everything to Poland. The reality was different. Hull confided to Roosevelt on November 23, "As the Russian Army approaches the Polish frontier the Polish Government is showing its extreme anxiety over the future of Poland."[47]

By the Teheran Conference of November 1943, the British War Cabinet and Foreign Office recognized Washington's lack of commitment to London's quest for Anglo-American solidarity in confronting Soviet power and expansionism. Unable to fight over everything, Churchill fought over less and less, the victim of his country's dwarfing by its two more powerful allies.[48] At Teheran, Roosevelt's pursuit of Stalin's approval was perceptible enough for all to see. The president held private meetings with Stalin, but refused to confer with Churchill alone. Roosevelt's faith in his ability to deal with Stalin was undying. He admonished Churchill as early as May 1942, "I know you will not mind my being brutally frank when I tell you that I think I can personally handle Stalin better than either your Foreign Office or my State Department. . . . He thinks he likes me better, and I hope he will continue to do so." At Teheran, to the dismay of Lord Alanbrooke, Roosevelt informed Stalin that Americans, being egalitarian and progressive in outlook, were able to understand the U.S.S.R. better than could the British. To Stalin's amusement, Roosevelt invited Churchill to dismantle the British Empire. The president made Churchill the butt of his jokes and was especially delighted when Stalin responded with a hearty laugh.

Churchill's declining influence became most apparent when, at the first plenary session, the Big Three turned to strategy. Churchill resumed his opposition to Allied concentration on OVERLORD to the exclusion of diversionary actions in the Mediterranean. Again, General Marshall, along with Soviet strategists, rejected Churchill's peripheral strategy as unpromising and wasteful. Some British observers attributed the final decision for OVERLORD to Soviet-American collusion.[49]

Many military analysts and historians, in retrospect, agreed with Churchill that the Western Allies might have eliminated Soviet as well as German power from the Balkans, perhaps even from much of East-Central Europe. For them the agreement on OVERLORD marked the central disaster of the war, because it assured the triumph of the old czarist dream of Russian hegemony over Eastern Europe. Isaac Deutscher, in his biography of Stalin, wrote of the OVERLORD decision: "This was a moment of Stalin's supreme triumph . . . . Europe had now been militarily divided in two; and behind the military division there loomed the social and political cleavage." The noted student of the Second World War, John A. Lukacs, agreed, declaring that the Teheran decision of November 30 set the stage for the massive invasion of Normandy and thereby delivered Eastern and Central Europe to the Soviet Union. Similarly, British General J. F. C. Fuller charged that Austria and Hungary were politically decisive areas and that the Soviet occupation of these countries ahead of the Western Allies was in itself sufficient to render the whole Western war effort futile, substituting Soviet for German control of Eastern Europe.[50] Still, it was by no means certain that the Western Allies possessed the military forces to execute Churchill's strategy by occupying vast stretches of the Balkans and Eastern Europe ahead of the Soviet forces. Europe was destined to be divided; it probably would not have served Western interests to have it fragmented in some other fashion.

OVERLORD's promise of Soviet military dominance of Eastern Europe in no way dampened Roosevelt's enthusiasm for his anti-German crusade. At Teheran he refused to compromise his goal of unconditional surrender. Stalin questioned that intention, observing that the Allies had not defined the terms of Germany's surrender. Under such circumstances, Stalin warned, unconditional surrender would merely unite the German people behind the Nazi war effort. Churchill responded to Stalin's doubts by stating his conditions for unconditional surrender in a cabinet note of January 14, 1944, and then in the House of Commons on February 22. In early April, Hull expressed his doubts by advising Roosevelt to modify his views on unconditional surrender. Again the president refused.[51] Unfortunately, Roosevelt's emergence from Teheran with a sure strategy for victory could not surmount the profound inequality of effort in the Allied war against Germany. The reality was that the United States could command the design of the postwar order only if it won that right on the battlefield.

At Teheran, Roosevelt searched for some accommodation with Stalin on matters of Eastern Europe. In a private meeting with the Soviet leader on December 1, Roosevelt approved the Curzon line as Poland's postwar boundary with the U.S.S.R., but he preferred that Lwow and the Galacian oil districts remain in Poland. The president explained the privacy of this concession. The probable continuation of the war, he said, might compel him to run for the presidency again in 1944. As a practical politician he did not wish to lose the votes of six or seven million Americans of Polish extraction. Thus for political reasons he could not participate in any decisions at Teheran on the future boundaries of Poland. Stalin replied that he understood. At Teheran the Big Three agreed implicitly on Poland's future borders; beyond that they agreed on nothing. "The Polish frontiers," Churchill concluded, "exist only in name, and Poland lies quivering in the Russian-Communist grip." Roosevelt acknowledged that the Baltic States had long been part of the U.S.S.R.; he would not, therefore, challenge Stalin's determination to remove these states from further international discussion. But he reminded the Soviet leader that Americans of Baltic extraction would favor some public expression of approval on the question of reannexation to the Soviet Union. Stalin replied that the Baltic States had received no choice under the last Czar, Nicholas II, and the Western powers had not raised the question of public opinion. When Roosevelt replied that "the public neither knew nor understood," Stalin suggested that the president proceed to inform them.[52]

Officially, the Teheran Conference was a demonstration of Allied harmony. The Teheran communiqué closed with the assurance: "We came here with hope and determination. We leave here, friends in fact, in spirit and in purpose." Stalin proclaimed Teheran a measure of Allied solidarity on matters of war and peace. For Roosevelt the perpetuation of the Grand Alliance demanded continuing concessions to Stalin. Still he could never acknowledge to either the Polish government or the American people that the Soviet ascendancy gave him no choice but to trust future Soviet behavior. He reassured the American people in the days following Teheran: "I believe that we are going to get along very well with [Stalin] and the Russian people—very well indeed."[53] Shortly thereafter Roosevelt's old friend, William Bullitt, warned him that Stalin intended to dominate postwar Europe. The president replied:

I just have a hunch that Stalin isn't that kind of a man. Harry [Hopkins] tells me he's not and that he doesn't want anything but security for his country. I think that if I give him everything I possibly can and ask for nothing from him in return, *noblesse oblige*, he won't try to annex anything and will work with me for a world of democracy and peace.[54]

Roosevelt's faith in Stalin was apparently boundless.

CHAPTER 2

The Road to Yalta

The fateful year of 1944 opened with a growing Allied crisis over Poland. On January 4, Soviet forces crossed the prewar Polish border. Several days later Moscow warned the Polish émigré government in London that Poland's eastern frontier would conform to the Curzon line. Despite the looming, inescapable crisis in Soviet-Polish relations, Churchill advised Roosevelt to avoid any meeting with Stanislaw Mikolajczyk, Premier of Poland since Sikorski's death in July 1943. If Mikolajczyk visited the United States without a Polish-Soviet agreement, Churchill feared, his presence would set off a wave of anti-Soviet sentiment that would damage Polish interests irreparably.[1] Churchill suggested that Mikolajczyk seek Soviet recognition and negotiate a settlement with the Kremlin, based on the Curzon line. Britain, Churchill acknowledged, had gone to war in 1939 for the sake of Poland, but not for any particular frontier. Unless the émigré government admitted its evaporating military and diplomatic position and accepted a new boundary, Churchill warned, it would have difficulty even in protecting Poland's political independence.[2] The Poles rejected Churchill's advice. A Polish broadcast of January 5 announced that the Polish government intended to stand firm on the boundary issue.

In Washington, Ambassador Ciechanowski acknowledged that the Soviet advance threatened all Polish rights, not merely Poland's claims to its prewar frontiers. State Department officials listened to him, but offered neither advice nor guarantees against Soviet domination. When Ciechanowski announced his plan to visit Washington in February, the president refused to see him. He instructed the State Department to warn the ambassador against any Polish effort to press the frontier issue and to remind him that Stalin had long demanded the elimination of all anti-Soviet ministers from the émigré government. The Polish government might relieve Soviet suspicions by promising an election and retirement at the end of the war.[3] Roosevelt assured Ciechanowski in February that the United States would continue to do all that was proper "within the framework of our interest in the larger issues involved."[4]

When Ciechanowski returned to Washington in March, he brought Mikolajczyk's statement on Polish policy. Without the support of the United States, Mikolajczyk reminded Roosevelt, Poland had no future. Poland, he wrote, "looks upon you as the champion of the principles which you have proclaimed with such deep faith and conviction. . . . On behalf of the Polish Nation and Government I appeal to you, Mr. President, to do all in your power . . . to safeguard the sovereign rights of the Polish State and of its lawful authorities." On the question of the Polish government's composition, Mikolajczyk admitted no right of foreign intervention. His government would accept the Curzon line as part of a general settlement, but would not concede Lwow or Vilna with their large Polish populations. Any announced retreat from the Riga line in advance of a general settlement would merely invite the repudiation of the Polish people.[5]

Early in April, Churchill advised Roosevelt to confer with Mikolajczyk in Washington, demonstrating thereby the American concern for Poland's future. State Department advisers warned the president that further postponement of Mikolajczyk's visit would create the impression that the administration had abandoned Poland for the sake of placating Moscow. Roosevelt now invited the Polish premier to visit him in early June. Edward R. Stettinius at the State Department assured the inquiring Soviet ambassador, Andrei A. Gromyko, that the president contemplated no new policy proposals for Poland, nor would he issue any communiqué at the conclusion of the conversations. Ambassador W. Averell Harriman repeated these assurances to the Kremlin in Moscow.[6]

On June 7, Roosevelt, revealing none of his private agreements with Stalin at Teheran, promised the visiting Mikolajczyk that he could rely on the moral support of the United States government. Poland, said Roosevelt, must be free and independent. He had not acted openly on the Polish question, he informed the premier, because 1944 was an election year. Eventually, he assured Mikolajczyk, he would act as a moderator in defending Polish interests. But he advised the premier to seek an understanding with the Soviets. "On your own," he said, "you'd have no chance to beat Russia, and, let me tell you now, the British and Americans have no intention of fighting Russia. But don't worry," he added, "Stalin doesn't intend to take freedom from Poland. He wouldn't dare do that, because he knows that the United States

Government stands solidly behind you. I will see to it that Poland does not come out of this war injured."[7] Before he departed for London, Mikolajczyk asked Stettinius, Charles Bohlen, Chief of the Division of Eastern European Affairs, and other State Department officials what Roosevelt meant by his promise of moral support. Bohlen replied simply that the time and manner of American support must be left to the president.[8] Eden shared Mikolajczyk's doubts that Washington was prepared to underwrite its promises to Poland. "The president," he recorded, "will do nothing for the Poles, any more than Mr. Hull did at Moscow or the president did himself at Teheran. The poor Poles are deluding themselves if they place any faith in these vague and generous promises."[9]

Churchill joined Roosevelt in urging Mikolajczyk to seek an understanding with Stalin in Moscow. "Meanwhile," he wrote to Roosevelt, "it is of utmost importance that we do not desert the orthodox Polish Government." Unfortunately the two Western leaders could mount no defense of the Polish government beyond upholding its legitimacy. To save the London regime from the Kremlin's political encroachments,

Figure 2.1
(L to R) Roosevelt, Secretary of State Cordell Hull and Truman's future Secretary of State James Byrnes (Courtesy: National Archives)

Roosevelt and Churchill advised Mikolajczyk to force the resignation of persons known to be objectionable to Moscow and to accept a boundary settlement, effective at the conclusion of the war, on which all Allies could agree.[10] What troubled Roosevelt and Churchill was less Stalin's continued rejection of the Polish demands for Lwow and Vilna than his power to determine the composition of the Polish government. Stalin announced, early in July, that the Soviet advance demanded a more cooperative and effective Polish administration; the Polish-Communist Committee of National Liberation, he declared, was the only group capable of taking control. On July 25 Soviet forces occupied Lublin, the temporary residence of the Committee. Churchill again warned Stalin against recognizing one body of Poles while the Western allies recognized another. Such a decision would lead to friction and hamper the work of postwar reconstruction.[11]

* * *

On July 27, Mikolajczyk, accompanied by two other Polish officials, left London for Moscow. On that day Soviet newspapers announced the Lublin Committee's authority to direct all civil affairs in the liberated regions of Poland. Harriman reminded Mikolajczyk upon his arrival that the Soviet government had consistently refused to recognize the Polish government-in-exile because it contained members known to be irreconcilably antagonistic toward the Soviet Union. Mikolajczyk admitted that he might secure some resignations, but only as part of a concrete Polish-Soviet agreement.[12] To Stalin, Mikolajczyk was not the spokesman of a Polish government but merely the representative of an émigré regime that Moscow did not recognize. He invited a delegation of Lublin Poles to confer with Mikolajczyk; that group proposed a fusion government comprised of 14 Poles from the Lublin Committee and four members from the London group, with Mikolajczyk holding the premiership. To Mikolajczyk the suggestion was preposterous. He rejected it and countered instead with a proposal based on equal representation. On leaving Moscow, Mikolajczyk reported that his conversations with Stalin and Foreign Minister Vyacheslav M. Molotov had been more cordial than he had anticipated. But the necessary agreement with the Committee of National Liberation remained elusive. Stalin gave Mikolajczyk the simple choice of eliminating the anti-Soviet elements from his government or losing to the Lublin Poles. Molotov complained to Harriman that the London Poles had avoided an agreement for too long. "Now they must make up their minds quickly," he said, "or it will be too late."[13]

As the Soviet armies approached Warsaw in July 1944, the Polish Underground detected one final opportunity to salvage the London government. By holding the capital, it might create a seat to which the London regime could return. Pro-London Poles, who had earlier had looked to Germany for their salvation, would now use Soviet power to free Warsaw of German occupation. In time, they confidently believed, Western strategies would free Warsaw of Soviet domination. On August 1, the underground launched a fierce, but futile, assault on the Nazi forces occupying the city, expecting active support from the Soviet army advancing toward Warsaw. Stalin had promised Mikolajczyk that he would send aid to the underground, but, following the Polish leader's departure, he refused to do so. Declaring that the underground had acted without consulting Soviet officials, the Moscow government distanced itself from "the Battle of Warsaw," as it was first known, and refused to assume any responsibility for the assured destruction of the Polish resistance. The Warsaw uprising, ran the official Soviet rationale, "represents a reckless and terrible adventure which is costing the population large sacrifices."[14]

On August 14, Harriman sent Molotov an urgent message, asking permission for American bombers to drop arms to the resistance forces in Warsaw, and then proceed to Russian air bases. The Kremlin denied the request with the argument that the Polish uprising was a "purely adventuristic affair and the Soviet Government could not lend its hand to it." Newspaper and radio accounts, Molotov added, revealed that the leaders of the Polish underground were antagonistic toward the Soviet Union. The Soviet government, therefore, would countenance no external association with their actions. Harriman, joined by British Ambassador Sir Archibald Clark Kerr, advised Soviet officials that their decision would have serious repercussions in Washington and London. With the bargaining power of the London Poles approached the vanishing point, Roosevelt advised Mikolajczyk to frame a reasonable proposal to the Lublin Poles before the Polish situation disintegrated completely.[15] Mikolajczyk accused Britain and the United States of watching passively while Poland moved under Soviet control. Roosevelt reminded the Polish premier that he and Churchill had urged Stalin to permit the dropping of supplies to the Polish underground. "I have not given up hope," he wrote, "that our intervention will have the desired results."[16] By September 5, the Germans had regained complete possession of Warsaw. Some 200,000 Poles and 17,000 German soldiers died in the uprising.

For Harriman the Soviet behavior toward the Warsaw uprising illustrated dramatically the growing divergence of interests and objectives between the Soviet Union and the Western allies. The ambassador reported his dismay to Roosevelt. "For the first time since coming to Moscow," he wrote, "I am gravely concerned by the attitude of the Soviet Government in its refusal to permit us to assist the Poles in Warsaw. . . . If [Andrei] Vyshinski correctly reflects the position of the Soviet government, its refusal is based not on operational difficulties . . . but on ruthless political considerations."[17] Harriman retained little confidence in Poland's future. Finally, on September 10, he asked Roosevelt's permission to return to Washington to report personally on his clash with the Kremlin. Harriman advocated no drastic action that would upset American-Soviet relations. Roosevelt, however, preferred to avoid public acknowledgement of any disagreements between the United States and the Soviet Union over Poland; he instructed Harriman to remain in Moscow.[18]

* * *

During the summer of 1944 the Balkan states faced the dilemma of preventing Soviet power from filling the vacuum created by Germany's retreat. Bulgaria had joined the Axis in December 1941, declaring war on the United States and Britain, but not on the U.S.S.R. Thereafter Bulgaria seized Thrace and Macedonia, thereby easing the German conquest of Greece. Otherwise Bulgaria played a minimal role in German strategy. While Bulgarian leaders sought arrangements under which their country might join the Allies without inviting a Soviet occupation, German officials warned them that, with Germany's withdrawal, no country could save them from Bolshevism. Roosevelt acknowledged that neither the United States nor Britain could participate in the postwar occupation and control of Bulgaria.[19]

Rumania, unlike Bulgaria, joined Hungary and Italy in the Nazi invasion of the U.S.S.R. with enthusiasm. With its German allies, Rumania lost heavily at Stalingrad. During March 1944 the Rumanian government asked Washington and London for guarantees against a Soviet occupation. Western leaders advised the Rumanians to discontinue any resistance to the Soviet advance and join the Kremlin in its fight against Germany. For reasons of their own the Rumanians rejected that advice. Early in April, the Soviets, as they prepared to enter Rumania, informed the Western Allies that they intended to recover the former Russian provinces of Bessarabia and Bukovina, but otherwise would seize no other Rumanian territory or attempt to impose a government on that country.[20] On May 8, as Soviet forces entered Czech territory, Soviet and Czech officials in London signed an agreement that promised Czechoslovakia a high degree of self-determination at the end of the war.[21]

For Churchill the Soviet advance to the Balkans was especially dangerous. Its perceived threat to historic British interests in Greece and the eastern Mediterranean required a showdown with the Kremlin over the region's future. Churchill penned a note to Eden on May 4, recommending that London set forth "the brute issues between us and the Soviet Government which are developing in Italy, in Rumania, in Bulgaria, and above all in Greece." Churchill foresaw a possible British-Soviet clash in Italy, Yugoslavia, and Greece—countries within reach of British forces. On May 18, Soviet Ambassador Ivan Maisky informed the Foreign Office that the U.S.S.R. was prepared to accept a temporary arrangement whereby the British received primacy in Greece while the Soviet Union gained a corresponding role in Rumania.[22] For such an agreement London required Washington's approval.

On May 30, British Ambassador Lord Halifax approached Hull for U.S. approval of an Anglo-Soviet agreement on the occupation of Rumania and Greece. Hull replied brusquely that the United States was not prepared to depart from its established principles. "I was, in fact," he noted in his diary, "flatly opposed to any division of Europe or sections of Europe into spheres of influence. I had argued against this strongly at the Moscow Conference."[23] On the following day Churchill repeated the request in a note to Roosevelt. The president deferred to Hull who replied that any agreement, however temporary, "would inevitably conduce to the establishment of zones of influence." On June 8, Halifax handed Hull another note that added Bulgaria and Yugoslavia to the list of Balkan states whose future status required some agreement with the Kremlin. When Roosevelt again demurred, Churchill reminded him that the Soviets were about to enter Rumania with great force, placing them in a position to deal with that country as they pleased. Britain, he added, had demonstrated its primary interest in Greece by sacrificing 40,000 men in its defense.[24]

Churchill now proposed a three-month trial arrangement, to be reviewed thereafter by the three Allies. This request reached Washington while Hull was resting at Hershey, Pennsylvania. State Department officials, in defense of Hull's principles, argued that any arrangement suggestive of spheres of influence would simply substitute unilateral for collaborative action in the Balkans. Without consulting the State

Department, Roosevelt agreed to the three-month trial, but admonished Churchill that the U.S. government opposed any postwar spheres of influence. Troubled by Washington's continued reluctance to accept British initiatives in the Balkans, Churchill and Stalin postponed their quest for a Balkan settlement.[25]

* * *

With the Allied invasion of Normandy on D-Day—June 6, 1944—the Soviet Union finally received its second front.[26] For many Americans, the Normandy invasion assured the defeat of Germany as a triumph for democracy and humane values. Historian David Eisenhower defined the invasion a demonstration of "the inherent toughness of free peoples when called to arms. . . . [I]t was a victory of the citizen soldier."[27] Actually, the Normandy invasion scarcely diminished the primacy of the war on the Eastern Front. Already the battles in the East had engaged as many as 1.5 million soldiers, leaving tens of thousands dead. Stalin, at Teheran, had promised to launch a massive Soviet offensive simultaneously with the Anglo-American landing in France. The Soviet advances of early 1944 had been persistent, but restrained. With the Allied invasion of Normandy, Stalin discarded his previous caution, assuring Roosevelt, in mid-June, that the Soviet Union would quickly unleash an offensive with 130 divisions.[28] Soviet Operation Bagration, that summer, comprised the major ground operation of the war, as General Zukov drove his men with absolute indifference to losses. So horrible and deadly were the massive engagements in the East that death became a relief from the continuing atrocities.

Such ruthless warfare eventually brought down the German army. After D-Day, two-thirds of German soldiers remained on the Eastern Front; there Soviet forces would account for 88 percent of German military deaths. Churchill lauded OVERLORD'S success, but recognized the price. "Good God," he exclaimed in August to Lord Moran, his personal physician, "can't you see that the Russians are spreading across Europe like a tide; they have invaded Poland, and there is nothing to prevent them from marching into Turkey and Greece."[29] The unfolding triumphs of U.S. strategy on the Western Front, following the Normandy invasion, scarcely eased Churchill's doubts regarding the future of Europe. Years later he recalled that OVERLORD caused him the greatest pang of the war.

Following Normandy, Churchill continued to press for a concerted Western drive through Istria and the Ljubljana Gap into the Danubian basin, thereby winning support from U.S. Generals Mark Clark and

Walter Bedell Smith. For Clark, the U.S. decision to invade southern France in August, rather than push into Yugoslavia, was one of the great military mistakes of the war. But in Washington the prime minister's preference for a Western invasion of the Balkans faced obdurate rejection, even as he persisted to the end. As late as August, recalled Harry C. Butcher, Churchill expressed his continuing doubts concerning American strategy to U.S. commander in Europe, General Dwight D. Eisenhower: "The PM [prime minister] wants ... to continue into the Balkans through the Ljubljana Gap, in Yugoslavia, to reach Germany through Austria."[30] U.S. Military expert Hanson W. Baldwin acknowledged that Churchill's strategy would have presented major challenges; yet, he concluded, "there is no doubt in my mind that such a strategy could have succeeded had sufficient sea and air power been allocated to it and had the same number of ground troops been employed that were actually used in Italy and the invasion of Southern France."[31]

During August and September the rapid Soviet advances created a burgeoning crisis in the Balkans, especially as the German forces prepared to withdraw. Churchill informed Roosevelt on August 1 that Britain would occupy Greece to prevent that country's seizure by the Communist-led Greek guerrillas.[32] Unable to obtain Western support, Rumania surrendered to Soviet forces on August 23 and declared war on Germany. The German forces retreated rapidly, yet the Soviets, in that successful engagement, lost more men than the British and Canadian armies lost in the entire northwest Europe campaign. The Soviet advance through Rumania brought the Red Army to the Bulgarian border on September 1. When the government in Sophia refused to break with Germany, the Soviet Union declared war on Bulgaria and invaded the country. On September 9, a new Communist-led regime in Sophia asked the Soviets for armistice terms, bringing the brief and bloodless war to an end. On September 12 Rumanian leaders signed their Soviet-dictated armistice. Several days later, Soviet troops entered the Bulgarian capital to take control of the country. With Bulgaria in possession of Macedonia and Thrace, no power could prevent a Soviet thrust into Greece. To avoid that disaster, Churchill and Eden prepared to recognize Soviet primacy in Bulgaria, hoping that Moscow would send no forces into Greece except by agreement with London. British forces landed in Greece on October 4 and reached Athens 10 days later.[33]

* * *

When Stalin continued to reject a Big Three meeting because of the
Red Army's intense engagements along the Eastern Front, Churchill
decided to seek a bilateral Balkan agreement with Stalin in Moscow.
Roosevelt responded by denying Churchill permission to negotiate
for the United States; Harriman would be available only for advice
and consultation.[34] Despite the Soviet Union's predominant contribution to Germany's defeat and its total control of Rumania and Bulgaria,
Roosevelt refused to grant the U.S.S.R. a status commensurate with that
of the United States in arranging the postwar settlement for Europe.
At no time did Roosevelt acknowledge equal Soviet rights in Italy.
Although the president had long decided that the United States would
avoid all military action in Europe east of Italy, he warned Stalin, on
October 4, against any arrangements for the Balkan states that denied
the United States an equal voice in determining that region's future.
Stalin reacted bitterly to Roosevelt's letter, complaining to Churchill
that the president "seemed to demand too many rights for the United
States leaving too little for the Soviet Union and Great Britain."[35]
Roosevelt's absence did not prevent the Churchill-Stalin meeting,
code-named TOLSTOY, from becoming the most important of the
wartime conferences.

During their first private conversation on October 9, Stalin and
Churchill agreed to postpone any discussion of the Polish question
and turned to the Balkans. Churchill hoped to protect Greek and
Yugoslav independence against possible Soviet encroachments from
Bulgaria, as well as Britain's historic primacy in Greece and the eastern
Mediterranean.[36] He acknowledged that the Soviet advance into
Rumania and Bulgaria demanded an agreement to prevent later
Soviet-British conflicts of interest. Churchill noted on a half sheet of
paper that the U.S.S.R. would have 90 percent predominance in
Rumania and 75 percent in Bulgaria, the British 90 percent control in
Greece. In Yugoslavia and Hungary, the two countries would divide
responsibility equally. When the Prime Minister pushed the paper
across the table to Stalin, he recalled, "There was a slight pause. Then
he took his blue pencil and made a large tick upon it, and passed it back
to us. It was all settled in no more time than it takes to set it down."
Molotov later revised the Hungarian formula to 75–25, the Bulgarian
to 80–20, all to Russia's benefit.[37]

Thereafter Stalin and Molotov set severe limits on future Anglo-
American influence in the Balkans. Eden came to Moscow determined
to challenge Soviet domination of the Allied Control Commission for
Bulgaria. The Soviets steadfastly refused to consider any armistice

terms for Bulgaria that granted the United States and Britain equal authority in that country—until three years after the war. Despite British and American objections, Bulgaria, in late October, signed a Soviet-dictated armistice.[38] Britain managed to obtain the removal of all Bulgarian forces from prewar Greece and Yugoslavia. Churchill explained to the War Cabinet, on October 12, that the Soviet Union would take the lead in Hungary because its armies would be in control. In Yugoslavia, Churchill anticipated joint action with the Soviets, but even there Soviet military operations, as well as the Kremlin's strong ties to Communist Marshal Tito and his Yugoslav Partisans, suggested that Yugoslavia would emerge, at best, as an area of East-West conflict.[39] Churchill accepted Stalin's request for revisions in the 1936 Montreux Convention, which assigned Turkey control of the straits between the Black and the Aegean seas. He explained his concessions to Roosevelt:

It is absolutely necessary [Stalin and I] should try to get a common mind about the Balkans, so that we may prevent civil war breaking out in several countries when probably you and I would be in sympathy with one side and [Stalin] with the other. . . . [N]othing will be settled except preliminary agreements . . . subject to further discussion and melting down with you.

A week later Churchill acknowledged that he could save Greece and some access to Yugoslavia, nothing more. Roosevelt accepted the Churchill-Stalin agreements on spheres of influence as the best solution available.[40] To resolve the critical question of Poland's political future Churchill pressed Stalin to permit Mikolajczyk's return to Moscow. Despite Poland's reverses of previous months, the premier came to Moscow in a demanding mood. He insisted not only on his earlier formula for equal Lublin-London membership in the postwar Polish government, but also on a future Poland as large as that of 1939 and in possession of all Polish cultural centers, even those east of the Curzon line. Such inflexibility reflected Mikolajczyk's conviction that he could rely on the full support of the United States. Sensing this, Molotov turned to Churchill and Harriman, reminding them that the Big Three had settled the Polish frontier question at Teheran. When Mikolajczyk demanded details of Teheran, Molotov continued, with his eyes on Churchill and Harriman, "If your memories fail you, let me recall the facts to you. We all agreed at Teheran that the Curzon line must divide Poland. You will recall that President Roosevelt agreed to this solution and strongly endorsed the Line. And then we agreed it would be best not to issue any public declaration about our agreement."

Recalling Roosevelt's personal assurances delivered at the White House, Mikolajczyk stared at Harriman and Churchill. "Harriman looked down at the rug," he recalled. "Churchill looked straight back at me. 'I confirm this,' he said quietly." Any acceptance of the Curzon line, Mikolajczyk predicted, would produce his repudiation in London. With Boleslaw Bierut, leader of the Lublin Committee, he could reach no agreement at all.[41]

* * *

Soviet advances across the heart of Europe during the summer and autumn of 1944 sustained the power revolution that underlay the massive Soviet-German confrontation on the Eastern Front. The Kremlin's military successes were not lost on American observers. Admiral William D. Leahy observed as early as May 1944 that the expansion of Soviet military power "seems certain to prove epochal in its bearing on future politico-military international relationships." In September, Kennan wrote from Moscow that 200 million Russians, "united under the strong and purposeful leadership of Moscow ... constitute a single force far greater than any other that will be left on the European continent when this war is over."[42] That Europe faced the most dramatic power revolution since Napoleon scarcely troubled Western leaders—and for good reason. The fundamental military decisions demolishing Europe's traditional equilibrium had been made in Berlin, not Moscow. It was Hitler's initiation of a two-front war that unloosed the forces now closing in on Germany. It was the savage Nazi assault on the U.S.S.R. that motivated the Kremlin's determination to prevent the recurrence of that disaster—a purpose with which few Americans cared to quarrel.

Thus Soviet advances into Eastern Europe flowed from the pursuit of victory and the opportunities afforded by Germany's self-destruction. On April 3, 1944, Anne O'Hare McCormick observed in the *New York Times*, "The Soviet Government is taking the tides of fortune at the flood. ... But nowhere is she moving ideologically. ... She is acting as a Great Power, ... more determined than Imperial Russia was to seize every opportunity offered by the war to further her national interests." To Kennan, the Kremlin was determined to "increase the relative power and prestige of the Russian state," not to communize the countries that the Red Army was overrunning—unless expediency demanded it.[43]

Those who knew the Kremlin well discovered that Soviet attitudes toward the Allies seemed to parallel the Soviet Union's expanding power and growing sense of security. Soviet officials, Harriman complained repeatedly after Teheran, were becoming less forthright and responsive.[44] For him Soviet action during the Warsaw uprising of August 1944 revealed dramatically the Kremlin's burgeoning disregard for American and British opinion. "I am disappointed and discouraged," he reported on September 9. "It is going to be more difficult than we had hoped to get the Soviet government to play a decent role in international affairs." Two days later he warned the president: "Unless we take issue with the present policy, there is every indication that the Soviet Union will become a world bully wherever their interests are involved."[45] State Department planners reminded the administration that it could not assume postwar Soviet cooperation when the demands of war could not assure it.[46] Hull asked Harriman to explain Soviet behavior. "I need not tell you," he wrote, "that questions of the highest import to the future peace of the world are involved." The ambassador acknowledged that he could not explain Soviet attitudes fully, but he warned the secretary that the Soviets seemed determined "to put into practice the policies they intended to follow in peace.[47]

Moscow's ambitions in Eastern Europe and the Balkans expanded in response to the opportunities that flowed from the progress of Soviet arms. After 1941 the Kremlin sought essentially Western recognition of the country's annexations under the Nazi-Soviet Pact, lands to which the U.S.S.R. had some ethnic or historic claims. In the absence of any restrictive agreements or countervailing power, the U.S.S.R., by 1944, was free to act in accordance with its widening interests and ideological preferences. The dynamics of a changing Europe, not some expansionist blueprint, determined what occurred.[48] The necessary Western reliance on the U.S.S.R. to deliver it from Germany was carrying a potentially heavy penalty. Stalin proclaimed his country's expanding intentions toward the regions, then coming under Soviet occupation, at a Kremlin dinner on June 5, 1944, "This war is not as in the past; whoever occupies a territory also imposes on it his own social system. Everyone imposes his own system as far as his army can reach."[49] Roosevelt and Churchill understood that the needed Soviet victories would come with a price. They never contested the Soviet annexations under the Nazi-Soviet Pact. Nor did Roosevelt ever challenge the Churchill-Stalin division of Eastern Europe into spheres of influence.

State Department planners faced the need to explain the growing chasm between the promises and the realities of the Atlantic Charter.

Under duress, they simply denied any contradiction between the administration's clear acceptance of spheres and its continued public adherence to the Charter's principles. They presumed that the Soviets would wield, in the border states, only the authority required to protect regional security interests, much as the United States had done in the Caribbean. State Department experts predicted that Kremlin-supported popular-front governments "would accept some degree of Soviet supervision in foreign affairs, but be free to conduct their domestic affairs without interference."[50] They explained that the Atlantic Charter required only that the U.S.S.R. exercise no *exclusive* influence in any region. In March 1944, James C. Dunn of the State Department's European section called for a formula that would recognize legitimate Soviet interests in Eastern Europe, but would protect the area from "complete dependence on the Soviet Union." Similarly, the Interdivisional Committee on Russia and Poland, in its advocacy of self-determination, advised Washington that "it would be contrary to the spirit of the Atlantic Charter and the Four-Power Declaration for any one power or group of powers to exercise *exclusive influence* in any region."[51]

Washington officials presumed as well that they possessed the ultimate power to compel some Soviet compliance with the principle of self-determination. Elbridge Durbrow, chief of the State Department's Eastern European Division, argued, in a long memorandum, that Soviet economic weakness offered U.S. aid and cooperation the leverage to discourage the Soviets from "taking unilateral actions which are not in conformity with . . . [our] basic principles." Harriman agreed that the weapon of economic assistance, enhanced by a continuing display of American concern for the problems of Eastern Europe, could temper Soviet domination and encourage acceptable behavior.[52] It remained only for the United States to be firm, avoiding compromise and indecision. Whenever Soviet behavior failed to conform to U.S. principles, Harriman concluded, they must be made to feel "specific results from our displeasure."[53]

Unfortunately, the only effective leverage available to the Western Allies lay in economic and military impositions on the Soviet capacity to wage war, an option demonstrably absent in 1944. Stalin's observation that the Soviet Union intended to impose its system as far as the reach of the Red Army proved to be accurate. Harriman, in Washington to report on the TOLSTOY negotiations, warned the State Department's Policy Committee that the Kremlin's encroachments in Eastern Europe's political affairs bordered on imperialism. Unless effectively opposed, the Soviets would impose their political system, with its horrors and repressions, on the entire region of occupation. "What frightens me," Harriman averred, ". . . is that when a country begins to extend its influence by strong arm methods beyond its borders under the guise of security it is difficult to see how a line can be drawn." Kennan advised Washington that a Soviet sphere meant, not limited self-determination, but political domination. National leaders in Washington, he feared, "had no idea at all . . . what a Soviet occupation, supported by the Russian secret police . . . , meant for the peoples who were subjected to it."[54] On November 30, Burton Y. Berry, U.S. minister to the new government of Rumania, reported that the Soviets were "quietly preparing to sweep away the democratic government and install a puppet Communist government with the aid of the Red Army."[55]

Such ubiquitous warnings that the Soviet sphere was becoming exclusive touched off no reaction in Washington; the Churchill-Stalin agreements had apparently settled the future of Eastern Europe. But Harriman worried that Washington refused to define the country's interests in Eastern Europe. Kennan complained to Bohlen: "We have consistently refused to make clear what our interests and our wishes were, in Eastern and Central Europe. We have refused to name any limit to Russian expansion."[56] On November 20, Ambassador-designate to Poland, Arthur Bliss Lane, reminded Roosevelt that if the United States, backed by its vaunted military power and his recent electoral mandate to protect the interests of Poland, could not maintain that country's independence, it would never succeed in doing so. The president replied sarcastically, "Do you want me to go to war with Russia?" On January 11, 1945, Roosevelt explained to a group of Senators privately that the United States had been unable to avoid the question of spheres. The Soviets, he said, had the power in Eastern Europe, and since it "was obviously impossible to have a break with them . . . the only practical course was to use what influence we had to ameliorate the situation."[57]

* * *

By the autumn of 1944, German lines were collapsing along the entire Western Front. Only shortages of fuel slowed the Allied advance. Brussels, Antwerp, and Le Havre fell during the first days of September, simultaneously with American crossings of the German frontier. British and American bombers poured destruction on German cities almost at will. Few expected the struggle for Europe to continue much longer; the time had arrived to contemplate the challenges of peace. Robert Sherwood recalled: "The Allies were well prepared for war to the death in Europe, but they were very ill prepared for the cataclysm of total victory."[58] With victory over Germany apparently in the offing, the Grand Alliance could no longer postpone the necessity, derived from the lessons of the interwar years, of eliminating the danger of aggressive totalitarianism, restructuring the world's economy with mechanisms to stabilize international currencies, facilitate the flow of capital and trade, and forestall the recurrence of destabilizing economic conditions, and, finally, to institutionalize the peace with an effective system of collective security. These internationalist objectives, all embraced in Roosevelt's Grand Design for the postwar world, were assured the support of the American people. Unfortunately, the successful pursuit of any postwar economic and security program hinged on the Grand Alliance's capacity to eliminate its internal conflicts and tensions that emanated from the war itself.[59]

For Allied leaders postwar peace hinged primarily on the defeat and occupation of Germany. Beyond the pursuit of unconditional surrender, the Big Three had formulated no program to guarantee Germany's postwar peaceful disposition. Stalin raised the issue of Germany's dismemberment in 1943. At the Quadrant Conference, both Hull and Eden opposed dismemberment as impracticable. Roosevelt, at Teheran and after, paid lip service to dismemberment, but recommended no decision.[60] In January 1944, the Allies established the European Advisory Commission to prepare joint Allied policies to govern Germany's surrender and post-surrender treatment. Roosevelt appointed John G. Winant, ambassador to London, as the U.S. delegate, with George Kennan as adviser. The British immediately presented a draft of a surrender document with detailed proposals for Allied zones of occupation—which proved to be acceptable to all. On the more fundamental question of Germany's future, many in Washington, led by Secretary of War Henry L. Stimson, favored Germany's rapid reconstruction and reentry into the international community. For the British Chiefs of Staff, troubled by the Soviet Union's changing role in continental affairs, postwar European stability would, of necessity, rely on Germany.[61] Amid such warnings against the total destruction of German power, the German question continued to drift.

Quebec's Octagon Conference, of September 1944, was ostensibly a military gathering to determine the final strategies for victory in Europe. It quickly succumbed to the proposal, submitted by Secretary of the Treasury Henry Morgenthau, for the dismemberment, denazification, and deindustrialization of Germany. Determined to uproot Germany's military potential once and for all, Roosevelt and Stalin embraced the Morgenthau solution of the German problem.[62] For Roosevelt, a harsh policy toward Germany would solidify his relations with Stalin. Such a policy, he wrote, "would convince the Russians that Americans really wanted to cooperate with them."[63] Churchill accepted what became the Morgenthau Plan—a program for dismantling Germany's metallurgical, chemical, and electrical industries to advance its conversion into a primarily agricultural and pastoral country. Those who saw some merit in Germany's economic recovery were dismayed at the Morgenthau program.

Kennan assumed the lead in arguing against the creation of disputable and artificial categories of Germans to be eliminated from the postwar German government. Most competent Germans, he advised the State Department, were nationalists by nature and probably involved in Nazi affairs. Germany's political evolution, Kennan added, should be conditioned by its national experience, not by foreign manipulation of its internal affairs.[64] On September 22, the Joint Chiefs of Staff in Washington submitted their ambiguous directive on occupation policy, JCS 1067. Among its guidelines for the administration of occupied territories were prohibitions against the employment of Germans, as executives and skilled workmen, who had been more than nominal members of the Nazi Party.[65] The document's combination of harsh and lenient objectives toward Germany merely fueled the ongoing debate between the State and Treasury departments. Both groups favored some form of German reparations, either from current production or from removals of capital equipment.[66]

For Hull, the key to postwar peace and prosperity lay in the expansion of international trade, based on tariff reduction and multilateral nondiscriminatory commercial relations. Free global markets, he believed, would raise living standards and, in the process, serve the U.S. economy. To secure Soviet and world adherence to its program of world economic expansion, Washington called the Bretton Woods Conference, which met at the Mount Washington Hotel in New Hampshire during July 1944. Lord Maynard Keynes, who led the British delegation, arrived with a program of his own. Whereas Hull favored fixed exchange rates and open trade, Keynes advanced an autonomous economic program for Britain and the Empire, with moveable exchange rates, trade controls, and preferential tariffs, especially within the British Commonwealth. For Keynes, the international economic order required a compromise between open commerce and the quest for full domestic employment. He advocated a well-financed central bank that would enable debtor countries to obtain credit and thus avoid the necessity of more stringent monetary and fiscal policies.

Keynes's restrictive program failed to capture the mood of the conference's thousand delegates, from 44 countries, who adopted the American formula to rescue the world economy from the monetary instability, excessive trade barriers, and trade and exchange restrictions of the interwar years, and to prepare the world for a new era of international prosperity. In essence, the Bretton Woods agreement proposed a system of reasonably stable exchange rates within a structure of multilateral credit, centered in the World Bank and the International Monetary Fund. Despite the Soviet Union's isolation from foreign monetary markets, the Soviet delegates remained actively engaged in the work of the conference, mindful of the credits available from the contemplated banking institutions.[67]

What troubled Churchill after Bretton Woods was the looming collapse of the British economy. Britain's minister of state, Richard Low, reminded Washington in July of the precarious state of British finances. Upon his return from London shortly thereafter, Morgenthau reported that only the United States could prevent Britain's bankruptcy. "Now we have got to help her," he informed the president. "She is a good credit risk, a good moral risk, and we have to put her back on her feet ... for a permanent world peace." Roosevelt, long convinced that Britain suffered only from a lack of nerve, confessed to Morgenthau, "I had no idea England was broke."[68] Many State Department officials now advocated a U.S. effort to reestablish Britain's economic health as quickly as possible. Others, led by Hull, argued that Phase II of Lend-Lease required Britain to implement the Bretton Woods agreement by reducing its trade barriers. Roosevelt accepted Morgenthau's advice to avoid any *quid pro quo* for aid to Britain. On September 14, he informed Churchill in Quebec that Lend-Lease would continue without conditions that might impede Britain's commercial recovery. Roosevelt's generous offer delighted the British War Cabinet; Hull recalled that nothing, while secretary of state, angered him more.[69]

Frustrated by Roosevelt's perennial success in placing others between him and the White House on important policy matters, Hull resigned in late November 1944. The secretary received praise from friends in government and the press, but *Life* noted his departure by recalling his promise, in November 1943, of an end to spheres of influence, alliances, and balance of power—something believed by no government in the world. *Life* observed the widening chasm between the limited possibilities of international diplomacy and the principles of the Atlantic Charter.[70]

Roosevelt's ultimate quest for postwar peace and security lay in a new international security organization wherein the smaller states would join the major powers in managing international affairs. Recalling Woodrow Wilson's failure to obtain Senate approval for the League of Nations, Roosevelt, as early as 1943, involved both Republican and Democratic members of Congress with State Department planners in the evaluation and design of alternative organizational drafts.[71] Roosevelt outlined his early plans for an international organization at the Teheran Conference, including his concept of the "Four Policemen" in which the U.S.S.R., the United States, Great Britain, and China would take responsibility for maintaining the peace. Stalin committed his country to membership in the new organization, but doubted that the smaller states would tolerate domination by four policemen, or that China would be an effective participant.[72]

At Dumbarton Oaks, the Georgetown mansion of the former U.S. ambassador to Argentina, Robert Woods Bliss, the powers convened on August 21, 1944, with a second session opening on September 29, to formulate a more precise structure for the new security organization, with its General Assembly and Security Council. Stalin proposed that 16 Soviet republics receive seats in the General Assembly, then agreed to postpone a resolution of that divisive issue. The Big Three readily accepted the need for unanimity among the major powers, based on their right of veto in the Security Council. But the Soviets, anticipating the presence of an opposing bloc in the Council, demanded that the great powers receive the right of veto on issues that directly touched their interests.[73] To Roosevelt and Churchill such veto power would paralyze the organization. South African Prime Minister Jan Smuts reminded Churchill that Stalin gave the Western powers little choice. "If a world organization is formed with Russia out of it," he wrote, "she will become the power centre of another group and we shall be heading for World War III." Smuts observed that the Soviets were obsessed by their standing among the powers. Roosevelt agreed that an international security organization without the U.S.S.R., as a full and equal member, would achieve little.[74] The troublesome veto issue remained unresolved.

Whether the forthcoming United Nations Organization, with or without the U.S.S.R., could eliminate the inescapable tendencies toward future conflict was questionable. Underlying the popular confidence in the United Nations was the assumption that the preservation of the prewar international order would automatically eliminate the danger of future wars. Unfortunately, the *status quo* embodied in the Atlantic Charter did not guide Soviet policies and intentions. No international organization, in itself, could prevent a great power from dominating a smaller one; thus the evolving challenges of 1944 could find no solution in legalistic mechanisms for the regulation of international politics. A new security organization could not reinstitute the former European equilibrium or protect Eastern Europe from the Kremlin's burgeoning domination. Any defense against the Kremlin's surging dominance lay elsewhere. Traditional power politics would continue to rule the world.

* * *

By December 1944, Poland had become the litmus test of East-West cooperation in the emerging postwar world. Roosevelt and Churchill had long come to terms with Stalin on the Curzon line and acknowledged the legitimacy of his demands for the elimination of anti-Soviet elements from the exiled Polish government. But for political and historical reasons, London and Washington refused to countenance the exclusion of London Poles from any postwar Polish government. Condemned in London for his repeated failures to establish the rights of exiled Poles in a new Polish government, Mikolajczyk resigned on November 24. His successor, the aged socialist, Franciszek Arciszewski, was clearly too intransigent to come to terms with Moscow. For Churchill, addressing the House of Commons on December 15, Mikolajczyk alone could bring the necessary reconciliation between the exiled Poles and the Lublin Committee, based on compromises reached in Moscow. Meanwhile, he assured Parliament, Britain would continue to recognize the Polish government-in-exile. Roosevelt informed Stalin that the United States also stood "unequivocally for a strong, free, independent and democratic Poland," with boundaries based on mutual agreement.[75] On December 18, *Pravda* published an article in Moscow in which the Lublin Poles demanded a western Polish boundary along the Oder-Neisse rivers, assigning lower Silesia to Poland. Such a boundary, Kennan noted, would compel Poland to rely on the U.S.S.R. for the defense of its German border. Churchill and Roosevelt rejected the Oder-Neisse line as a potentially dangerous imposition on Germany. Prodded by Churchill, Roosevelt implored Stalin not to recognize the Lublin Poles as the Provisional Government of Poland. On December 27, Stalin informed the Western allies that he could no longer delay the recognition of the Lublin Committee; that regime alone could give the Soviet forces in Poland their required security. Roosevelt made a final effort to assure some measure of self-determination for Poland. "I am more than ever convinced," ran his appeal to Stalin on December 30, "that when the three of us get together, we can reach a solution of the Polish problem, and I therefore still hope that you can hold in abeyance until then the formal recognition of the Lublin Committee as the government of Poland."[76]

Early in January 1945, a Moscow broadcast announced that the Soviet Union had recognized the Communist-led Lublin Committee as the Provisional Government of Poland. England's *Manchester Guardian* observed realistically that the Lublin Committee would win any contest with the London Poles because the Soviets controlled Poland.[77] Undaunted, the Polish-American Democratic Organization of Chicago, on January 4, reminded Roosevelt that in his 1944 presidential campaign for reelection he had assured Polish voters that the United States government "would not let the Polish people down and would restore Poland as a free sovereign nation." Prime Minister Arciszewski pleaded with Roosevelt to prevent any decision that might jeopardize legitimate Polish rights at the coming Big Three Conference at Yalta.[78] Members of Congress took up the Polish cause. On January 10 Senator Arthur H. Vandenberg of Michigan, reflecting the views of his large Polish constituency, condemned the president's apparent dismissal of the Atlantic Charter. Responding to such pressure, the State Department advised Roosevelt to seek, at Yalta, "the emergence of a free, independent, and democratic Poland [based on] an interim government which would be broadly representative of the Polish people and acceptable to all the major allies."[79]

Unfortunately, such recommendations ignored both known Soviet ambitions and the recent Soviet military advances. Early in January, Churchill pleaded with Stalin to unleash a powerful Soviet offensive to relieve pressures along the troubled Western Front. Stalin responded with a crushing Soviet advance.[80] By February 1945 Soviet forces had disposed of Finland, occupied Rumania and Bulgaria, and driven deeply into Hungary, Czechoslovakia, and Yugoslavia. From the region south of Warsaw, the Red Army had swept westward to the Oder and liberated almost all of Poland. Altogether, the Soviet assault eliminated another 400,000 German soldiers from the war.[81] Writers joined U.S. officials in lauding the Russian victories and the looming collapse of Germany. *The Nation* termed the Soviet midwinter offensive "one of the great achievements of the war."[82] Many writers saw the significance.

Time asserted that the Soviet Union had emerged as the greatest power in Europe, able and willing to fill the political void left by the crushing of Germany. Stalin now ruled an empire "spilling across Europe and Asia, from Poland to the Pacific Ocean, and threatening to spill further." James Reston observed in the *New York Times*, "the American people do not know what this terrific power is or where it is going or what it intends to do with victory."[83]

Some State Department realists reminded the administration what the Soviet advance meant for Eastern Europe. On January 8, John D. Hickerson, Deputy Director, Office of European Affairs, advised Edward R. Stettinius, secretary of state since November 1944, that much of Eastern Europe had slipped irretrievably beyond Western control. To contest the Soviets in Poland or the Balkans would merely return Europe to the diplomacy of the jungle. Hickerson suggested that Washington prepare the American people for the only Eastern European settlement available. "We must have the cooperation of the Soviet Union to organize the peace," he wrote. "There are certain things in connection with the foregoing proposals which are repugnant to me personally, but I am prepared to urge their adoption to obtain the cooperation of the Soviet Union in winning the war and organizing the peace."[84] For Hickerson, the West would not regain in Eastern Europe what it conceded to others when it failed to protect Czechoslovakia and Poland against the combined Nazi-Soviet advances of 1939.

For columnist Walter Lippmann, Washington was paying the price of postponement, having nullified whatever wartime influence it might have exerted in Moscow. Similarly Kennan, in a letter to Bohlen, argued that since the United States could not control Soviet decisions in Eastern Europe, it should accept the limits of its reach and recognize the Soviet sphere. Bohlen rejected Kennan's willingness to capitulate. Practically, he responded, a democracy could not make such a decision. To recognize the existence of a Soviet sphere would not relieve the U.S. of responsibility but would compound its dilemma by unleashing an outcry of anguish from Poles and Czechs everywhere. "In short," Bohlen wrote, "foreign policy in a democracy must take into account the emotions, beliefs, and goals of the people. . . . The great leader in foreign affairs formulates his policy on expert advice and creates a climate of public opinion to support it."[85] Unfortunately, American opinion, as Bohlen defined it, was not the controlling element in U.S.-Soviet relations.

* * *

At Yalta near the Black Sea, Roosevelt and Churchill sought for eight days, February 4–11, 1945, to counter the burgeoning unilateralism in Soviet policy toward the regions of Soviet occupation. The formal meetings at Yalta were held in the Grand Ballroom of the Livadia Palace, the summer home of Nicholas II and Roosevelt's residence at the conference. Fundamentally the two Western leaders faced the task of reaffirming the Teheran and TOLSTOY decisions in a series of specific arrangements that would deny the U.S.S.R. a monopoly of political influence where the Red Army controlled. No agreement at Yalta, however, could gain more for self-determination than Churchill had achieved in Moscow.[86] On the central question of Poland, the Big Three, before Yalta, had negotiated no final settlement at all. The exiled Polish government in London had little authority in Poland; yet to Roosevelt and Churchill it possessed the sole claim to legitimacy. That regime continued to resist any political or territorial infringements on the Polish state. Compelled to negotiate for an absent and intransigent Polish government, the Western leaders at Yalta accepted the Curzon line, with digressions up to eight kilometers in favor of Poland. Roosevelt and Churchill favored the Oder River as Poland's western boundary, believing that the Neisse, favored by Moscow, would stir irredentist feelings in Germany. So great was the Western opposition to the Oder-Neisse line that Stalin agreed to leave Poland's western frontier undefined until a peace conference.[87]

What troubled Roosevelt and Churchill far more than the boundary question was the future of the Polish government. Whereas the Western leaders faced adamant Polish resistance to Soviet political encroachments, their acceptance of the Soviet Union's right to a friendly postwar Polish government eliminated any attempt to return the exiled regime. At Yalta, Roosevelt and Churchill sought enough Soviet concessions to legitimize Poland's Communist-dominated government. Churchill argued at the third plenary session on February 6 that British honor required a free and independent Poland based on a new government, not merely the Soviet-backed Provisional Government with the inclusion of some London Poles. Stalin retorted that "throughout history Poland has been the corridor for attack on Russia. . . . It is not only a question of honor but of life and death for the Soviet State." Following that session, Roosevelt sent a note to Stalin, deploring the failure of the allies to reach a settlement of the Polish question. "It seems to me," he wrote, "that it puts all of us in a bad light throughout the world to have you recognize one government while we and the British are recognizing another in London. . . . Surely there is a way to reconcile our differences."[88]

Figure 2.2
Premier Josef Stalin, Roosevelt, and Churchill at Yalta, 1945 (Courtesy: National Archives)

On February 9, the American delegation recommended a compromise that would transform the Polish Provisional Government into a representative government, largely through free elections. The final Declaration on Poland proclaimed that the "Polish Provisional Government of National Unity shall be pledged to the holding of free and unfettered elections as soon as possible on the basis of universal suffrage and secret ballot." When the Polish government fulfilled these requirements, it would receive the recognition of Britain and the United States. The Polish agreement authorized Molotov, Harriman, and Clark Kerr, acting as a commission, to consult in Moscow with members of the Provisional Government, as well as Polish democratic leaders, to reorganize the present government in accordance with established procedures.[89] This agreement, in some measure, accepted the Soviet position that the Lublin regime must form the basis of the new Polish government.

In the Balkans the British and Soviet occupations continued to fulfill the Moscow percentages agreement. Greece remained firmly in British hands as the Soviets refrained from aiding the Communist-led EAM/ELAS, fighting to prevent the return of King George II. The British, under intense U.S. pressure, established a regency until the Greek people could decide the question of the monarchy. Before the end of

December, the British were able to stabilize the situation in Greece.[90] But Harriman reported on January 10 that the Soviet occupation of Rumania, Bulgaria, and Hungary continued to follow a largely repressive and exclusive pattern. The Soviets, he warned, were employing the wide variety of means at their disposal—occupation troops, secret police, local Communist parties, labor unions, sympathetic leftist organizations, sponsored cultural societies, and economic pressure— to "assure the establishment of regimes which, while maintaining an outward appearance of independence ..., actually depend for their existence on ... the Kremlin."[91]

Confronted by such realities, Roosevelt made no effort to weigh Harriman's plea that he define the minimum interests of the United States in Eastern Europe and the Balkans, or Hickerson's advice that he acknowledge the absence of important interests at stake and recognize the Soviet sphere of influence. The potential military or political costs in either decision were too high. Instead Roosevelt hoped to retain some cost-free Western influence in the region by fixing Stalin's signature to another statement of principles in the final protocols. Under the Declaration on Liberated Europe, the Big Three pledged to assist the former Nazi satellites "to solve by democratic means their pressing political and economic problems [and to acknowledge] the right of all people to choose the form of government under which they will live."[92] The declaration could not govern the future of the regions under Soviet occupation; it suggested only that the Western powers expected the Soviets to observe certain minimal standards of behavior.

Toward Germany the Big Three's objectives seemed clear enough. "It is our inflexible purpose," ran the Yalta agreement, "to destroy German militarism and Nazism and to ensure that Germany will never again be able to disturb the peace of the world." But Roosevelt and Churchill, in the interest of wartime unity against the common enemy, made no effort to convert allied intentions into concrete arrangements. Roosevelt, unlike the British, was little concerned with France's return to an active role in European politics, but he urged Stalin to accept an occupation zone for the French.[93] Stalin denied that the French deserved a zone or any voice in occupation policy, but eventually he accepted a French zone, carved out of the British and American zones.[94] Stalin pressed for a decision on German dismemberment. Roosevelt and Churchill accepted dismemberment in principle, but avoided any specific commitment to that objective. The Western leaders agreed with Stalin to a ten-year program of reparations from Germany in kind, based partially on the removal of heavy industrial equipment, partially on the productions of surviving German industries. The Soviets preferred a fixed sum for reparations, suggesting $20 billion, half for the U.S.S.R. Churchill regarded the amount outrageous; he feared that the drain on German production might compel the West to finance and feed the country. Roosevelt believed the Soviet program dangerous to Europe's postwar recovery. Under Hopkins's prodding, however, the president conceded, permitting Stalin to enter a figure, but only as the basis of discussion. A reparations commission would establish the extent and method of German compensation for damages inflicted by German forces. In creating no policy for Germany on surrender, denazification, demilitarization, or reparations, Yalta presaged that country's ultimate division into spheres of influence.[95]

At Yalta, Churchill, Roosevelt, and Stalin recommitted their countries to close military cooperation as they launched their final air and ground assaults against the German enemy. They appealed to the German people to ease the burden of defeat by terminating their hopeless resistance. At Yalta, Roosevelt and Stalin completed the arrangements for Soviet entry into the Pacific war. At the Moscow Conference of October 1943, and again at Teheran, Stalin assured Washington that Russia would enter the war against Japan after Germany's defeat. To encourage Stalin to fulfill that promise, Roosevelt and Churchill agreed to return the Manchurian port of Dairen and, in addition, offered the Soviets the southern half of Sakhalin and the Kuriles, as well as a free hand in Manchuria and Outer Mongolia. They asked only that the Kremlin seek the approval of the Chinese government. Stettinius defended the concessions of Chinese territory: "What, with the possible exception of the Kuriles, did the Soviet Union receive at Yalta which she might not have taken without any agreement?" The Soviets now formally agreed to enter the war three months after Germany's surrender. Roosevelt's military advisers believed the Russian entry into the Pacific war essential before the United States could contemplate any invasion of the Japanese home islands.[96]

Again on matters of war and peace the negotiations at Yalta took up the questions of membership and great-power unity in the United Nations left unresolved at Dumbarton Oaks. Stalin neutralized the veto controversy by accepting a proposal that seven of the eleven votes could bring an issue before the Security Council. Roosevelt and Churchill then agreed to Stalin's demand that Byelorussia and the Ukraine receive membership in the organization. They announced a meeting at San Francisco on April 25, 1945, to prepare the UN charter in accordance with the agreements reached at Dumbarton Oaks and Yalta.[97]

Yalta did not divide Europe into zones of influence; no text provided for Soviet rule in the East and liberal democracy in the West. But Yalta could not nullify Soviet occupations that the West had encouraged for so long in the interest of victory—or Stalin's power to exploit them.[98] Churchill, as well as some observers and scholars, believed that the two democracies, had they stood together, might have forced a showdown at Yalta that would have limited Stalin's impositions on Europe. Roosevelt made little effort to reach agreement with Churchill on such issues before or during the conference. To British delegate Gladwyn Jebb, Roosevelt's entire conduct at Yalta, including his occasional aspersions on the British Empire, revealed a persistent effort to placate the Soviet leader. Stettinius acknowledged that the president sought, in every way, to reassure Stalin that the United States had entered no bargains with the British. Lord Moran complained that Roosevelt's American advisers, in supporting his partiality, did not seem to "realize how the president had split the Democracies and handcuffed the P.M. in his fight to stem Communism."[99] During the Yalta deliberations Stalin appeared exceedingly cordial. Sir Alexander Cadogan reported that the Soviet leader was "more congenial and more reasonable than I have ever seen him."[100] That cordiality did not reflect Stalin's relations with Roosevelt, but the position of his armies. The assurance of ultimate control permitted him the luxury of accepting cost-free agreements that he could later break with impunity.

Yalta produced a variety of reactions across the Western world. The London Poles denounced the Yalta communiqué as a violation of the principle of self-determination. Prime Minister Arciszewski informed Roosevelt that the Yalta decisions "are received by all Poles as a new partition of Poland leaving her under Soviet protectorate." Charles Rozmarek, president of the Polish-American Congress, declared: "It is with sorrow, dismay, and protest that we greet the decision of the Big Three to give all land east of the so-called Curzon line to Russia in direct contradiction to all sacred pledges of the Atlantic Charter." The *Chicago Tribune* observed simply that American morality and diplomacy reached a new low at Yalta. On February 16, the *Wall Street Journal* predicted the disintegration of American-Soviet relations.[101]

Much of the press, however, accepted the Yalta accords at face value. The *Manchester Guardian* editorialized on February 16, "The results of the Yalta meeting of the Big Three justify nearly all our hopes." *Newsweek* asserted on February 19 that Roosevelt's leadership at Yalta had assured satisfactory compromises on all issues. The *Washington Post* added that the president "is to be complimented on his part in this all-encompassing achievement." The *New York Times* declared the conference "a milestone on the road to victory and peace." For the *New York Herald-Tribune* the Big Three meeting at Yalta was simply "another great proof of allied unity, strength and power of decision."[102]

Privately and publicly U.S. and British officials shared the euphoria. Churchill expressed his conviction before the House of Commons that Stalin and the Soviet people wished "to live in honorable friendship and equality with the Western democracies." State Department spokesmen assured the American public that the principles of the Yalta Declaration would prove effective in practice, eliminating any danger of competing spheres in Europe. The Big Three, declared James Dunn over NBC, "are pledged to consult with each other constantly in every part of liberated Europe." On March 1, Roosevelt assured Congress that the Yalta Conference had found a common ground for peace in its elimination of alliances, spheres of influence, and balances of power. "We propose," he concluded, "to substitute for all these a universal organization in which all peace-loving nations will finally have a chance to join." So cordial were the outward exchanges at Yalta that Harry Hopkins recalled: "We really believed . . . that this was the dawn of a new day. . . . We were *absolutely certain* that we had won the first great victory of the peace." Former Senator James F. Byrnes, who attended the conference, joined the chorus, "There is no doubt that the tide of Anglo-Soviet-American friendship had reached a new high."[103] The world would discover soon enough that appearances could be deceiving.

CHAPTER 3

A Troubled World at Peace: 1945

Despite the myriad of thorny issues that confronted Franklin D. Roosevelt, Winston Churchill, and Josef Stalin at Yalta, the three Allied leaders succeeded in burying their accumulating disagreements in declarations that clouded their transparency, enabling the Grand Alliance to survive the conference apparently unscathed. The astonishingly effective ground and air war against both Germany and Japan assured an ultimate victory.[1] Still, as late as Yalta, Roosevelt continued to rely on the Soviet Union to carry the major burden of the European war. That heavy contribution to the anticipated triumph of the Grand Alliance required a price and Roosevelt was willing to pay it in the form of superficial, nonenforceable agreements with the U.S.S.R. Roosevelt accepted a flawed Eastern European settlement, persuaded that the Soviets would command the region's future, whatever the phraseology of the agreement.[2] Clearly the future of the Grand Alliance rested on the willingness of Britain and the United States to accept the Soviet definition of the Yalta agreements and not contest the burgeoning Soviet control of East-Central Europe and the Balkans.

Within days of Yalta the Kremlin revealed its own interpretation of the Yalta accords by confirming its established occupation policies in Rumania, Hungary, Bulgaria, and elsewhere. Throughout the war zone of Eastern Europe, Soviet officials acted unilaterally, ignoring the Western members of the Allied Control Commissions as they tightened their control. In late February Andrei Vyshinski, Deputy Commissar of Foreign Affairs, arrived in Bucharest and ordered King Michael to form a new government. On March 6, the king dismissed General Radescu, the Rumanian prime minister, and installed a Communist-controlled regime under Petra Groza. The Soviets then signed a five-year treaty with the new government.[3] In Budapest,

Soviet leaders, backed again by huge occupation forces, dismissed Hungary's Allied Control Commission and proceeded to exercise predominant political and economic power. Moscovite Hungarians—the hard core of the Communist Party—readily accepted Soviet political domination as well as economic measures that quickly undermined Hungary's market economy. Thereafter Soviet officials revealed nothing to U.S. and British representatives on the status of Hungary's economic conditions. Through similar procedures the Kremlin solidified its domination of Bulgaria and the other states under Soviet occupation.[4]

Ambassador W. Averell Harriman warned Washington from Moscow that such Soviet behavior, unless countered effectively, would nullify the Yalta Declaration on Liberated Europe, with its promise of self-determination. He pressed Roosevelt to challenge Moscow's flagrant defiance of the Yalta accords.[5] At issue was Roosevelt's willingness to avoid a confrontation with the U.S.S.R. in the areas of occupation. James F. Byrnes, Roosevelt's official interpreter of the Yalta agreements, boasted to the American press that they comprised a triumph of American democratic principles. For Washington generally the Declaration on Liberated Europe quickly lost its tentative quality; the United States would expect full and unquestioning Soviet compliance.[6] Roosevelt, however, had no intention of contesting Soviet policy in the Balkans. He responded to King Michael's appeals for help with verbal protests, nothing more. Churchill accepted Roosevelt's decision. For him the TOLSTOY accords of October 1944 still governed British-Soviet relations in the Balkans. The Soviets had not interfered in Greece, Churchill reminded Foreign Secretary Anthony Eden on March 5, and thus Britain would not intervene in Rumania. A week later Churchill reaffirmed that decision, informing Eden that the London government "accepted in a special degree the predominance of Russia in this theatre [Rumania]."[7]

Poland was always going to be another matter. Britain had chosen war in September 1939, in part, due to the imperative of a special obligation to Poland. At Yalta, Churchill sought above all to protect the authority of the exiled London Poles in the postwar reconstruction of their country. The Declaration on Poland, adopted at Yalta, provided for three-power involvement, operating under democratic procedures, in the creation of Poland's postwar provisional government. Unfortunately for London, the Soviet-backed Lublin Poles were firmly in control of the existing government in Warsaw. After Yalta the Kremlin ignored Britain's known commitment to the London Poles and refused to expand the Provisional Government with members of either the Polish underground or the exiled government. The Soviets jailed the chief leaders of the wartime Polish resistance and denied the London Poles the benefit of a Western presence in Poland.[8] With British elections approaching, Eden acknowledged to Lord Halifax that unless Britain and the United States could guarantee fair treatment for the London Poles, they would properly stand accused of subscribing to an unworkable formula at the Crimea Conference. The Churchill cabinet wanted to avoid accusations of another Munich because it failed to defend another victim of aggression to which Britain was committed.[9]

Britain remained powerless to mount an anti-Soviet offensive without Washington's strong support. When as early as February 20 New Zealand's prime minister chided London for its failure to honor its pledges to Poland, Churchill explained that Britain and the Commonwealth possessed no power to enforce its point of view. "We cannot," he wrote, "go further in helping Poland than the United States is willing or can be persuaded to go."[10] During the war, Churchill saw clearly that Britain's postwar standing in global politics required both strong ties to the United States and the containment of Soviet influence where it endangered Britain's historic interests. On March 8, Churchill approached Roosevelt on the necessity of Anglo-American unity in opposing Soviet domination of Poland. "I have based myself in Parliament," he wrote, "on the assumption that the words of the Yalta declaration will be carried out in the letter and spirit. . . . [I]f we do not get things right now, it will soon be seen by the world that you and I by putting our signatures to the Crimea settlement have underwritten a fraudulent prospectus." For Churchill, Poland had become Yalta's crucial test. To halt the Kremlin's attachment to the Lublin Poles, he asked Roosevelt to join him in sending personal messages to Stalin; otherwise, he would acknowledge the dishonesty of Yalta before Parliament.[11]

* * *

Roosevelt could not ignore the Soviet impositions on Poland. He had demanded the Declaration on Poland in part to assuage the fears of Polish Americans in the United States. Byrnes, moreover, had warned the country that the Declaration comprised the measure of postwar Allied unity. He assured concerned Americans that the administration's attachment to the Grand Alliance did not include the acceptance of a Soviet sphere in Eastern Europe.[12] Roosevelt, like Churchill, presumed that the tripartite commission meeting in Moscow would, in time, terminate the burgeoning clash over Poland by designing a Polish government acceptable to all. Indeed, the commissioners moved steadily toward agreement until they faced the task of designating what Poles the commission would invite for consultation. Molotov argued that the Lublin Poles had the right to accept or reject whomever they wanted in the formation of a new Polish government. The British demanded free elections supervised by Western observers. The State Department, on March 3, instructed Harriman to accept the British position of postponing consultations until the commission could name non-Lublin representatives.[13] While Molotov resisted every effort to broaden the base of the Lublin regime, Harriman advised Washington that Soviet support assured Lublin predominance in Poland.[14]

For Roosevelt the Grand Alliance took precedence over Poland. During March he informed the departing diplomat, Robert Murphy, "to bear in mind that our primary postwar objective was Soviet-American cooperation—without which world peace would be impossible."[15] Roosevelt rejected Churchill's appeal for a strong message to Stalin. "In my opinion," he wrote, "... we should leave the first steps to our Ambassadors from which we hope to obtain good results."[16] For Churchill and Eden, the Grand Alliance had reached the point of collapse; only firm Anglo-American cooperation could set limits to Soviet behavior and thereby save the alliance. On March 24 Eden caught Churchill's attention by observing that Big Three disagreements over Poland endangered the San Francisco UN Conference, scheduled to open in late April. Churchill saw immediately that nothing could bring Washington into line more assuredly than the possible imperiling of the San Francisco Conference. On March 27, Churchill asked Roosevelt whether a world peace organization could function without great power unity. That simple message brought the response that Churchill had sought for almost a month. "[T]he time has come," Roosevelt agreed, "to take up directly with Stalin the broad aspects of the Soviet attitude." Even then Roosevelt reminded Churchill that the Yalta agreement on Poland placed greater emphasis on the Lublin Poles than on other Polish factions.[17]

In his letter to Stalin, Roosevelt characterized the Polish Provisional Government as little more than a continuation of the former Lublin regime. "I cannot," he concluded, "reconcile this either with our agreement or our discussions [at Yalta]. While it is true that the Lublin Government is to ... play a prominent role [in a reorganized government] it is to be done in such a fashion as to bring into being a new Government. ... I must make it quite plain to you that any such solution which would result in a thinly disguised continuance of the present Warsaw regime would be unacceptable and would cause the people of the United States to regard the Yalta agreement as having failed."[18] During subsequent days Roosevelt was torn between his acceptance of London's hard-line stance and his refusal to face the consequences of a total break in U.S.-Soviet relations. Conscious of the steady advance of Soviet forces across Europe, Churchill reminded the president on April 5 that the Western powers must establish a point beyond which they would accept no Soviet repression. Roosevelt agreed.[19]

Roosevelt's reluctant message gave Stalin the golden opportunity to restate the Soviet case for Poland. In his reply of April 7, he reminded Roosevelt that the three powers at Yalta had accepted the existing Polish Provisional Government as the core of a new Provisional Government of National Unity. But the American and British ambassadors in Moscow, he complained, had ignored the Warsaw regime in their attempt to create a new government. "Things have gone so far," Stalin continued, "that Mr. Harriman declared in the Moscow Commission that it might be that not a single member of the Provisional Government would be included in the Polish Government of National Unity." Harriman and Clark Kerr, he added, demanded the right to invite Polish leaders from London and Poland for consultation without regard to their attitudes toward Yalta and the U.S.S.R.—all in direct violation of the Yalta Declaration on Poland. The Soviet Union, Stalin concluded, proceeded on the assumption that those invited for consultation should be Polish leaders who understand the Yalta decisions and "actually want friendly relations between Poland and the Soviet Union."[20]

Stalin launched a bitter dispute with Roosevelt when he discovered early in April that Nazi General Karl Wolff had met British officers near Bern, Switzerland. Stalin feared that Germany was seeking easy terms in the West so that it could transfer additional divisions to the Eastern Front. Roosevelt assured Stalin that the Bern meeting was designed to make contact with competent German officers and not inaugurate negotiations of any kind.[21] Then Roosevelt addressed Stalin's accusations:

[I]t would be one of the greatest tragedies of history if at the very moment of the victory, now within our grasp, such distrust, such lack of faith should prejudice the entire undertaking.... Frankly I cannot avoid a feeling of bitter resentment toward your informers, whoever they are, for such vile misrepresentations of my actions or those of my trusted subordinates.

Stalin reminded the president that the war still raged on the Eastern Front. The Germans, he lamented, continued to fight savagely over every crossroad in Czechoslovakia, but surrendered to Western forces without resistance. "Don't you agree," Stalin asked, "that such a behavior of the Germans is more than strange and incomprehensible." With Stalin's expression of concern over German resistance the matter ended. Roosevelt refused to the end to adopt an adversarial posture toward the Kremlin. Shortly before his death on April 12, he answered Churchill's request for guidance in responding to Stalin's apology for the Bern incident: "I would minimize the general problem as much as possible, because these problems, in one form or another, seem to arise every day and most of them straighten out."[22]

As Allied armies closed in on Germany during the early days of April, Churchill advised Roosevelt that the advancing British and American forces might enable the Western powers to limit the forward movement of Soviet influence across Central Europe. Churchill hoped especially that Western forces would capture Berlin before the Soviets arrived. He warned Roosevelt on April 1 that, should the Soviets take Berlin, they would thereafter behave as if they had been the overwhelming contributors to the common victory. "[M]ay this not," Churchill added, "lead them into a mood which will raise grave and formidable difficulties in the future?" It was essential, Churchill repeated on April 5, "that we should join hands with the Russian armies as far to the east as possible and if circumstances allow, enter Berlin."[23] Churchill favored the capture of Prague as well. But General Dwight D. Eisenhower, U.S. commander in Europe, preferred to concentrate his forces rather than compete with the Soviets for Czech territory. He professed disbelief that the prime minister would intermingle political and military considerations in the advocacy of an anti-Soviet strategy. On April 14 he ordered General William H. Simpson, whose Ninth Army had crossed the Elbe, to withdraw to the west bank of the river.[24] Two days later Soviet forces numbering a million men launched their final assault on Berlin. Roosevelt, no more than Eisenhower, had no intention to contest the Kremlin's wish to crush German power within its designated zone.

* * *

Harry S. Truman entered the White House amid State Department efforts to assess the state of U.S.-Soviet relations. On April 3, Secretary of State Edward R. Stettinius asked Harriman for a detailed report from Moscow. In his long response three days later, Harriman averred that a full analysis required his return to Washington. The Soviets, he wrote, would continue to act unilaterally in the border states to assure their absolute control. No longer, he warned, did the Kremlin merely seek a security ring of totalitarian governments in Eastern Europe; now it sought stronger ties with Communist-controlled parties elsewhere to create a broader "political atmosphere favorable to Soviet policies." To Harriman, Soviet leaders interpreted Western generosity as a sign of weakness; the time had come to demonstrate that they could not "expect our continued cooperation on terms laid down by them."[25] Brought to Washington in mid-April by Roosevelt's death, Harriman confessed to Truman that Soviet behavior had become intolerable. From its occupied border areas, he warned State Department officials, the Soviet Union "would attempt to penetrate the next adjacent country," suggesting that Soviet occupations were dangerous as well as oppressive.[26] U.S. security demanded that Washington make the Soviets understand "that they cannot continue their present attitude except at great cost to themselves." Unfortunately, U.S. and Soviet interests and strategic advantages in occupied Europe and the Balkans were not sufficiently symmetrical to permit policies that would levy the necessary costs.

After mid-April, the Kremlin's unilateral action in Eastern Europe created a crisis mood in Washington. On April 13, Stettinius briefed Truman on the situation. Nowhere in liberated Europe, ran his troubling summary, would the Soviets acknowledge that their actions justified any appeal to the Yalta agreements. Four days later, Washington learned that the Soviets planned to sign a mutual assistance pact with the Lublin Poles. Vyshinski argued that nothing in the Yalta accords precluded a treaty with the Warsaw regime; he refused to show the treaty, signed on April 21, to British and American officials. Truman now resolved to lay it on the line when Molotov visited Washington en route to San Francisco. Admiral William D. Leahy, the president's Chief of Staff, predicted that Molotov "would be in for some blunt talking from the American side."[27]

On April 20, Truman conferred with Harriman, Stettinius, Under Secretary Joseph C. Grew, and Soviet expert Charles E. Bohlen. Harriman dominated the meeting. He urged the president to frame an effective policy that would assure the inclusion of London Poles in the Warsaw government. Any lasting agreement, Harriman added, would require concessions on both sides. "I declared," Truman recalled in his memoirs, "[that] we intended to be firm with the Russians and make no concessions from American principles or traditions in order to win their favor.... I would not expect one hundred percent of what we proposed. But I felt we should be able to get eighty-five percent."

Before his departure for Moscow, Harriman engaged the president privately to acknowledge his relief that the new administration shared the Moscow legation's perception of the Soviet problem.[28]

Truman's meeting with Molotov on April 22 was cordial enough. The president reminded the Soviet minister that "in its larger aspects the Polish question has become for our people the symbol of the future development of our international relations." Molotov reassured the president that the two powers could reach the desired agreement on the Polish question. At the White House, on April 23, Stettinius revealed to Truman that the subsequent conversation with Molotov had gone badly. "In fact," he said, "a complete deadlock had been reached on the subject of carrying out the Yalta agreement on Poland." Truman, conforming to the State Department's hard line, observed "our agreements with the Soviet Union had so far been a one-way street and that this could not continue." Others present, especially Secretary of War Henry L. Stimson and General George C. Marshall, urged caution. The Soviets, they noted, had carried out their military engagements faithfully; therefore, the United States should avoid an open break with the Kremlin over Poland.[29]

At their meeting that afternoon, Truman informed Molotov that the American and British proposals on Poland were reasonable and embodied the maximum Western concessions. The U.S. government would accept no political arrangement that did not represent the will of all the Polish people. "The Soviet Government must realize," Truman advised Molotov, "that the failure to go forward at this time with the implementation of the Crimean decision on Poland would seriously shake confidence in the unity of the three [Allied] governments and their determination to continue the collaboration in the future as they have in the past." Molotov denied that the Yalta decisions demanded Soviet compliance with Western proposals. Truman informed Molotov that U.S. friendship with the U.S.S.R. could continue "only on the basis of mutual observation of agreements and not on the basis of a one-way street." To Molotov's complaint, "I have never been talked to like that in my life," the president retorted, "Carry out your agreements and you won't get talked to like that."[30] Truman boasted to the pro-Soviet Joseph E. Davies that he let Molotov have it straight. Stalin, unmoved, informed the president that the Warsaw regime had widespread public support and would remain the core of any new Polish Government of National Unity.[31]

Truman's anti-Soviet attitudes, which reassured official Washington, were based on the exceeding alluring assumption that "the Russians need us more than we need them." Arthur H. Vandenberg, Republican leader in the Senate, found enough solace in Truman's words to Molotov to confide to his diary, "FDR's appeasement of Russia is over." The United States and the U.S.S.R. could live together in the postwar world, he wrote, "if Russia is made to understand that we can't be pushed around." Admiral Leahy rejoiced at the president's new mood of confidence. "Truman's attitude ... was more than pleasing to me," he noted in his memoirs. "I believed it would have a beneficial effect on the Soviet outlook."[32] Secretary of the Navy James V. Forrestal asserted at the White House meeting on April 23 that the United States might as well meet the Soviet challenge in Eastern Europe "now as later on." Later Forrestal informed a member of the Senate that Soviet Communism was "as incompatible with democracy as was Nazism and Fascism."[33]

In the State Department, Under Secretary Joseph Grew had long harbored a deep distrust of the U.S.S.R. He found nothing reassuring in the elimination of German power on the Eastern Front. With its stranglehold on its western border states, the Soviet Union, he warned, "will steadily increase and she will in the not distant future be in a favorable position to expand her control, step by step, through Europe. ... A future war with Soviet Russia is as certain as anything in the world can be certain."[34] Such top State Department officials as James C. Dunn, Assistant Secretary for European, Asian, Near Eastern, and African Affairs, and such regional office directors as H. Freeman Matthews and Loy Henderson shared Grew's deep anxiety toward the Soviet Union. For them any compromise with the Kremlin would merely encourage Soviet expansionism.

Americans who sought salvation from power politics looked to San Francisco where, from April to June, spokesmen for the victorious nations framed the UN Charter. Some, such as Sumner Welles, expected the conference to underwrite a body of moral principles that would govern international life. Vandenberg, key member of the U.S. delegation, anticipated a peace organization that would uphold the Yalta accords. Yet columnist Walter Lippmann had long warned that the Dumbarton Oaks formula offered no more than a forum for consultation.[35] During May, the conference defined the roles of the General Assembly and Security Council; it agreed to the creation of regional alliances to function when the Security Council failed to act. To assure Big Three unanimity, Yalta had granted the three powers the right of veto. But again at San Francisco the Soviets denied the Security Council the right to even discuss an issue that involved the

U.S.S.R. That demand threatened to break up the conference. Finally, in early June, Stalin accepted the British-American interpretation of the veto power, thereby resolving the last question before the conference.[36] Despite the general euphoria, the United Nations, like the earlier League of Nations, wielded no real power; it could never be more than an agency for individual national policies. It could not terminate the ongoing big power rivalry or resolve the divisive issues before the world. It could not achieve any genuine concert in international affairs or force its decisions through collective action on any major power. The United Nations created an excellent piece of machinery to bring nations together for debate; it did not create a new international order. Nothing would destroy it more quickly than the expectation that it perform as if it had, indeed, established some new world order in international society.

* * *

Berlin's fall, in early May 1945, marked the end of Germany's long quest for world leadership. The joyous meeting of American and Soviet troops at Torgau on the Elbe symbolized as well the termination of five centuries of European dominance in world affairs. The burden of defeating Germany exhausted Europe beyond its capacity to sustain the global position it once commanded. More than ever Britain's imperial greatness rested on the will of its more powerful allies. London had long detected in Soviet expansionism a genuine danger to its historic position in Europe, the Middle East, and elsewhere, one rendered more acute by the elimination of the wartime constraints on Soviet behavior. On April 29, Churchill warned Stalin not to misuse his narrowly won command of vast stretches of the Eurasian continent with policies that would ultimately tear Europe to pieces. "[D]o not, my friend Stalin," he pleaded, "underrate the divergences which are opening about matters which you may think are small to us but which are symbolic of the way the English-speaking democracies look at life." Even as London celebrated VE Day, on May 8, Churchill feared that his country's break with the U.S.S.R. was almost complete. "It is no longer desired by us," he acknowledged, "to maintain detailed arguments with the Soviet Government about their views and actions." Beneath the triumphs, Churchill confided to his wife, lay deadly international rivalries.[37]

Churchill as well as the British Chiefs of Staff acknowledged that the United States alone could defend Britain's worldwide interests against Soviet aggression, and thereby extend its historic role into the postwar era. Unfortunately, British leaders could detect no genuine American concern for the perpetuation of the British Empire or even Britain's role in world affairs. That Churchill had failed to forge stronger ties with the United States during the war years reflected less a divergence of interests than Britain's marked decline in the global hierarchy of power. Richard Law of the Foreign Office advised Churchill in May 1945, "I see a great deal of evidence from the United States which suggests . . . that the Americans . . . are tending to regard us as a factor of little account in world affairs in the future. They are beginning to feel that it is Russia, not we, who are the only partners equal to them in strength."[38]

What Britain—no less than Washington hard-liners—faced was an American public, including many leading writers, who rejected the notion of a Soviet threat to any vital Western interests. General Marshall, like countless members of the armed forces, was not prepared to view the country that had carried the major burden of the recent war as a potential enemy. Many Americans—perhaps the vast majority—regarded Soviet behavior in Eastern Europe, if not desirable, at least understandable, and thus no excuse for the continuing quarrel over the meaning of Yalta. For them, Eastern Europe was perhaps the world's least important area. Military analyst Hanson W. Baldwin of the *New York Times*, with other critics, believed that the Soviet Union's direct security interests in Eastern Europe justified its behavior. For Lippmann, the Allied victory over Germany had divided Europe inescapably into two exclusive spheres of influence, one dominated by the United States, the other by the U.S.S.R. "No nation, however strong," Lippmann wrote, "has universal world power which reaches everywhere. The realm in which each state has the determining influence is limited by geography and circumstance. Beyond that realm it is possible to bargain and persuade but not to compel, and no foreign policy is well conducted which does not recognize these invincible realities."[39] For diplomat George Kennan, the United States should entertain no expectation of exerting influence in Eastern Europe; any behavior that suggested otherwise would merely mislead. Similarly, John Fischer noted in the August issue of *Harper's* that the Western powers, with no intention of enforcing their views of Yalta, had only the choice of recognizing the Soviet sphere or extending the wartime policy of postponement into some unknown future.[40]

Many writers and observers condemned the State Department's hardening attitude toward the U.S.S.R. as both unwarranted and dangerous. Too many Washington officials, the *New Republic* charged, refused to deal with the postwar world except "on impossible terms of American domination and dictation." The writer denied that the United States and the U.S.S.R. faced any problems that forthright diplomacy could not resolve. Noted news commentator Raymond Gram Swing declared, in a radio broadcast, that American diplomats who had lost faith in U.S.-Soviet relations were expendable. In May, Henry A. Wallace, secretary of commerce, advised the president to reject State Department representations on the U.S.S.R. until the White House had studied them carefully. Archibald MacLeish reminded Grew that three-fourths of the American people favored cooperation with the Soviet Union.[41]

Discovering no reason to confront the U.S.S.R., such Americans resented Britain's apparent willingness to do so. For them Britain, without legitimate cause, seemed determined to make itself the Kremlin's special antagonist and enlist the support of the United States in the process. Such convictions warred against the close U.S.-British ties that London desired. Americans generally discounted the importance of Britain's imperial interests from Malta to Hong Kong as matters of international concern. Lippmann observed in June that the United States, facing no challenges to its vital interests from any of the world's major countries, could well play the role "as mediator—that is, intercessor, reconciler, within the circle of the big powers." An Anglo-American alliance against the U.S.S.R., he warned, would render any world organization unworkable by aggravating the conflict of interests between London and Moscow and thus dividing the organization into blocs.[42]

Sharing the country's mood of confidence in the summer of 1945, Truman himself refused to confront the Kremlin with active policies of opposition. He had no interest in publicizing his private displeasure with Soviet policies and thereby suggest to the American people that their wartime exertions had achieved, at best, a doubtful victory. The continuing need to perpetuate the Grand Alliance in the interest of Europe's postwar reconstruction overrode, for Truman, the ongoing disagreements over the meaning of Yalta. With Germany's defeat, however, Churchill addressed the president on the need to confront the Soviets in their zone of occupation by refusing to withdraw U.S. and British forces before the Kremlin adopted a satisfactory arrangement in Poland, the Balkans, and Germany. Otherwise, he warned Truman on May 11, "the tide of Russian dominance [would sweep] forward 120 miles on a front of 300 to 400 miles, ... an event which, if it occurred, would be one of the most melancholy in history." Churchill wired the president again on the following day, urging a settlement with the Kremlin while Western forces still held their advanced positions:

I have always worked for friendship with Russia, but like you, I feel deep anxiety because of their misinterpretation of the Yalta decisions. . . . Surely it is vital now to come to an understanding with Russia, to see where we are with her, before weakening our armies mortally or retire to the zones of occupation.[43]

Truman accepted the advice of Joseph Davies, his special envoy to London, who argued that the prime minister was too concerned with British interests on the continent. With his advisers concurring, the president decided against the employment of the advanced positions for the purpose of bargaining. The deliberations over troop withdrawals did not include any formal Soviet guarantees on the question of Western access to Berlin. Following the Allied occupation of Berlin, the massive requirements for adequate transportation facilities into the city became obvious. On June 28, General Eisenhower requested several roads and rail lines, as well as unrestricted air travel, between the American and British zones and the Western sectors of Berlin. When one air lane proved to be inadequate, the Soviets offered three Western air corridors into West Berlin.

* * *

However limited the official U.S. perceptions of danger in Europe, Washington assured London that it would not recognize any legitimacy in the Kremlin's Polish and Balkan policies. The record of Soviet repression, reported in detail by U.S. diplomats, reinforced the conviction that any recognition of the existing Soviet hegemony, itself the creation of that repression, would be totally reprehensible. Unless the United States and Britain made the effort to establish self-determination in the occupied states, Harriman recalled, history would condemn them for willfully selling out these countries. In May, Truman addressed the question of Poland's future unilaterally when he accepted Harriman's advice to dispatch Harry Hopkins on a special mission to confer with Stalin in Moscow. The president presumed that Stalin would have the good political judgment to sustain the notion that he intended to keep his word.[44]

Hopkins reached Moscow in late May to reassure Stalin that the United States did not want a government in Poland unfriendly to the U.S.S.R., but he reminded the Soviet leader of the importance of the Polish question to the American people. He pressed Stalin to broaden the base of the Warsaw government in accordance with the Declaration on Poland and to release the leaders of the Polish underground. Stalin recalled that Germany, in the course of one long generation, had invaded Russia twice through Poland. This had been possible, he continued, "because Poland had been regarded as a part of the *cordon sanitaire* around the Soviet Union and that previous European policy had been that Polish Governments must be hostile to Russia."[45] On the question of Poland's government, Stalin remained adamant. Perhaps four or five London Poles, he said, could enter the Lublin cabinet. Harriman explained Hopkins's failure to move the Soviet leader:

I am afraid that Stalin does not and never will fully understand our interest in a free Poland as a matter of principle. The Russian Premier is a realist in all of his actions, and it is hard for him to appreciate our faith in abstract principle. It is difficult for him to understand why we should want to interfere with Soviet policy in a country like Poland which he considers so important to Russia's security unless we have some ulterior motive.[46]

To Stalin neither American opinions nor principles meant anything; there would be no American solution to the Polish question.

If Stalin refused to alter his purposes toward Warsaw, he did agree with Hopkins to name the Poles that the Allied commission in Moscow would consult in the reorganization of the Polish regime. Stalin accepted several representatives of the London Poles, including Stanislaw Mikolajczyk.[47] During June the Poles formed a Provisional Government of National Unity to fulfill the Yalta pledge. The new government included Boleslaw Bierut as Prime Minister, Mikolajczyk as Vice Prime Minister, and four members of the anti-Communist Peasant Party. Harriman assured Washington that the non-Lublin Poles had gained the best arrangement available.[48] London and Washington recognized the new Provisional Government of National Unity on July 5. Truman confirmed that its establishment was "an important and positive step in fulfilling the decisions regarding Poland reached at Yalta."[49] Bierut had avoided any promises regarding free elections, but that mattered little. Under Kremlin direction, the Lublin-dominated government in Warsaw gained complete control of Poland. Eventually some London Poles returned to Warsaw and received minor posts; their influence proved to be temporary and inconsequential.

* * *

Meeting at Potsdam, outside Berlin, from July 17 to August 2, Truman, Churchill, and Stalin were no longer wartime leaders seeking victory over Germany; they were now political leaders burdened with the task of blocking out the territorial, economic, and administrative arrangements for Europe's reconstruction. Truman and James Byrnes, secretary of state since July 3, understood that they would possess little bargaining power at Potsdam. Byrnes had long established a reputation as "a cautious mediator and conciliator in the most strained and tangled situations." His career before Potsdam, however, had been limited almost exclusively to domestic politics; in external affairs he possessed little expertise.[50] Following the Labor Party's victory in Britain's general election, Clement Attlee replaced Churchill at the conference. The Big Three achieved quick agreement on the creation of a Council of Foreign Ministers to negotiate treaties for Italy and the former Axis states—Rumania, Bulgaria, Hungary, and Finland. In May, Stalin had urged Washington to recognize the governments of Rumania, Bulgaria, and Finland. In accordance with State Department advice, Truman recognized the government of Finland, but not those of Rumania, Bulgaria, and Hungary.[51]

Figure 3.1
Premier Josef Stalin, President Truman, Prime Minister Churchill at Potsdam, July 1945 (Courtesy: National Archives)

At Potsdam, Stalin remained uncompromising in his defense of Soviet policy toward Eastern Europe. "A freely elected government in any of these Eastern European countries," he admitted, "would be anti-Soviet, and that we cannot allow." He denounced the U.S. demand for changes in the governments of Rumania, Bulgaria, and Hungary, reminding the Western leaders that the Soviets had not meddled in Greek affairs. Molotov suggested that the Western Allies simply recognize the Balkan states; Allied supervision of elections was unnecessary. The United States, Byrnes assured him, did not want to become involved in the elections of Italy, Greece, Rumania, Bulgaria, or Hungary; it merely wished to join others in observing them.[52] Eventually, under such prodding, the conference made a major concession to Yalta by agreeing that only those states of Eastern Europe with "recognized democratic governments" would be permitted to sign peace treaties or apply for membership in the United Nations. No decision at Potsdam guaranteed the implementation of this agreement. The procedural gains at Potsdam left all fundamental Eastern European issues essentially untouched. Admiral Leahy observed later that "the only possibility of agreement would have been to accept the Russian point of view on every issue." Stalin failed to gain recognition of the Kremlin's paramount position in Eastern Europe, but that failure in no way diminished its monopoly of power throughout the region.[53]

At Potsdam, the Western Allies faced the task of gaining Soviet collaboration in designing a fair and promising German settlement. The Yalta accords anticipated the creation of a reformed and peaceful Germany but left unresolved the precise nature of that country's postwar role. Stalin demanded heavy reparations to limit Germany's industrial capacity and compensate the U.S.S.R. for its wartime losses. Churchill, convinced that Germany's economic recovery was essential for European reconstruction, opposed reparations that would cripple Germany's economic revival. Roosevelt, committed to a united policy for Germany, agreed to large reparations provided that they were paid in capital goods and not from financial resources. At the July 13 meeting of the Allied Reparations Commission in Moscow, the U.S. delegation, led by Edwin Pauley, insisted that reparations not infringe on Germany's capacity to maintain a minimum level of subsistence without continued external relief.[54]

Ignoring the American formula, the Soviets, during the weeks preceding Potsdam, proceeded to remove from their zone what the war's demolition had missed—machines, trolleys, trains, blueprints, drawings, and all useful information from the files of ravaged companies.

At Potsdam, Byrnes suggested that the Soviets take industrial material and equipment from the Western zones, provided that they pay for it with shipments of food and fuel from the Soviet zone. In addition, he offered the Soviets 10 percent of all industrial capital equipment in the Western zones not required for Germany's peacetime economy. In accepting this arrangement, the Soviets gave up their claim for $20 billion in reparations.

At Potsdam the Big Three established the Allied Control Council, with headquarters in Berlin, to manage the occupation. Politically, the occupying powers were to denazify and democratize the country; unfortunately, they could never agree on the meaning of democracy. To the Soviets, the Communist-controlled government in their zone was democratic. Economically, the Allies, by previous agreement, were to disarm and demilitarize Germany while treating it as an economic unit. Instead, the Soviets continued to dismantle factories for shipment to the U.S.S.R. and appropriate much of the output of the factories still in production. Rather than attempt to influence Germany's total reconstruction, Stalin now chose to convert the Soviet zone into an exclusive sphere, binding Poland to the U.S.S.R. by assigning that country new western frontiers along the Oder-Neisse rivers at Germany's expense. This decision, opposed by both Churchill and Truman, tied Poland's security to Soviet control of Germany's eastern zone. Such divergent political and economic objectives lifted high the barriers between the Soviet and the three Western zones. There would be no unified control system for Germany.[55]

Truman chose to bury the failures of Potsdam from public view. In his report to the American people he declared that the Allies "are now more closely than ever bound together.... From Teheran, and the Crimea, and San Francisco, and Berlin—we shall continue to march together to our objective."[56] Privately, the president and his advisers were not reassured by their recent experience. Stalin impressed Truman as smart, personally likeable, but scarcely trustworthy. Later Truman recalled the deep and unpromising divisions among the three wartime Allies at Potsdam:

Potsdam brings to mind "what might have been." ... Russia had no program except to take over the free part of Europe, kill as many Germans as possible, and fool the Western Alliance. Britain only wanted to control the Eastern Mediterranean, keep India, oil in Persia, the Suez Canal, and whatever else was floating loose. There was an innocent idealist at one corner [of] that Round Table who wanted free waterways—Danube-Rhine-Kiel Canal, Suez, Black Sea Straits, Panama—a restoration of Germany, France, Italy, Poland,

Czechoslovakia, Rumania, and the Balkans, and a proper treatment of Latvia, Lithuania, Finland, free Philippines, Indonesia, Indo-China, a Chinese Republic, and a free Japan. What a show that was! But a large number of agreements were reached in spite of the set up—only to be broken as soon as the unconscionable Russian dictator returned to Moscow![57]

* * *

As late as Potsdam, Washington faced a continuing war in the Pacific against Japan. At the Quadrant Conference of August 1943, Allied leaders agreed that "operations should be framed to force the defeat of Japan as soon as possible after the defeat of Germany." With Germany's surrender in early May, U.S. officials were aware of this national goal as well as the burgeoning public impatience for peace in the Pacific. But Japan, long defeated by Western standards, seemed determined to defend its home islands against invasion, whatever the price in further death and destruction. American soldiers, who had escaped with their lives in North Africa, Italy, France, and Germany, dreaded the prospect of joining the Pacific forces for an invasion of Japan.[58] Even as the country anticipated additional fighting in the Pacific with declining enthusiasm, the official demonization of Japan and its Emperor held leaders and public alike to the popular goal of unconditional surrender.

Still, in the summer of 1945 the reliance on power to end the war seemed promising enough. By June 1944, the long American advance across the Pacific had reached the Marianas, bringing Japan within bombing range of the B-29s. After a month of heavy fighting, U.S. forces, on March 24, 1945, captured the Japanese outpost of Iwo Jima with its two airstrips 760 miles from Japan. General Curtis LeMay's successful low altitude raids on Tokyo that month demonstrated the vulnerability of Japanese cities to incendiary bombs. By early June, incendiary attacks had devastated Japan's six leading industrial centers—Tokyo, Nagoya, Kobe, Osaka, Yokohama, and Kawasaki, leaving 40 percent of their urban areas gutted and millions homeless. Thereafter LeMay's bomber force rained destruction at will on dozens of lesser cities and manufacturing centers.[59] By late June, the massive U.S. assault on Okinawa had cleared the island of Japanese resistance, providing the United States a huge base only 350 miles from Japan's southern island of Kyushu.[60] The U.S. Pacific Fleet had virtually cleared the Pacific of the Imperial Navy.

What troubled Washington, despite these advances, was the realization that the Japanese fought more fiercely as the war approached the home islands. Japan lost 110,000 in the Okinawa's defense; the American dead and wounded exceeded 30,000. "In size, scope, and ferocity," observed *New York Times* military analyst Hanson W. Baldwin, "[Okinawa] dwarfed the Battle of Britain. . . . Never before, in so short a space, had the Navy lost so many ships; never before in land fighting had so much American blood been shed in so short a time in so small an area."[61] After June, American intelligence reported Japan's meticulous preparation for the defense of Kyushu, transforming the island into a mighty stronghold with its thousands of suicide weapons.[62] High-ranking Japanese officials, almost without exception, agreed in retrospect that Japanese forces were prepared to die in defense of their homeland.[63]

U.S. naval officers presumed that additional months of blockading would starve the Japanese into submission. Admiral Leahy recalled in his memoirs: "I was unable to see any justification for an invasion of an already thoroughly defeated Japan." Other high-ranking naval officers, including Admiral Ernest J. King, agreed.[64] General Henry H. Arnold, chief spokesman for the Air Force, assured his fellow officers that, by October, the B-29s would flatten the country and break the Japanese will.[65] But most of Washington agreed with General Marshall and General Douglas MacArthur that nothing short of the two planned invasions of Japan—the assaults against Kyushu (OLYMPIC) on November 1, 1945, and against Honshu (CORONET) in the spring of 1946—would produce the desired Japanese surrender. In late June, the Joint Chiefs of Staff presented the alternatives to the president, who ordered the invasion of Kyushu, as planned. The Honshu invasion would await developments.[66] At the end, all branches approved the invasion, accepting the blockade, the bombing, and the invasion as elements of a single, overwhelming assault against Japan.

No less than Washington officials, Japanese moderates in Tokyo contemplated the price of war on Japanese soil with horror. During the battle of Okinawa, Emperor Hirohito instructed the Japanese cabinet to examine the means for ending the war. On June 3 the Japanese approached Jacob Malik, the Soviet ambassador in Tokyo, for Kremlin support. Malik offered no encouragement. Later that month Foreign Minister Togo Shigenori instructed Ambassador Sato Naotake in Moscow to seek Soviet mediation. The quest had no future; the Kremlin, after Yalta, had no interest in a shortened Pacific war. Unfortunately, the elusiveness of peace lay in the determination of Tokyo's controlling military faction, despite Japan's declining fortunes, to perpetuate its totalitarian political and social structure, based

on the army, the Emperor, and a long tradition of nationalistic indoctrination. Such purposes required the avoidance of surrender and an
American occupation. Japan's considerable peace faction anticipated
no less than Washington's postwar acceptance of the Emperor. What
that element was prepared to concede mattered little; War Minister
Anami Korechika and the army zealots were in command. On April 25,
Anami ordered the arrest of 400 suspected peace advocates.[67] Conscious
of the peace faction's minimum demand for the Emperor, Acting Secretary of State Grew urged the president, in May, to reassure the Japanese
government on the question of the Emperor.[68] But Truman, like
Roosevelt, regarded Japan's acceptance of total defeat—an objective that
required unconditional surrender—essential. Washington officials,
moreover, feared that any major concessions after Okinawa would
appear as an American effort to escape another costly encounter and
thereby play into the hands of Japanese extremists. Under Admiral
Suzuki Kantaro, premier after April 1945, the war of attrition continued.
In Moscow, Molotov was too busy to see Sato. As Stalin and Molotov
departed for Potsdam in mid-July, the Kremlin offered no response to
the Japanese plea for mediation.[69]

* * *

During the summer of 1945 the administration's range of options suddenly expanded when it learned that the secret Manhattan Project was on
the verge of producing its first atomic bomb. Throughout the war years
Roosevelt and Churchill refused to share the secrets of the Manhattan
Project with Stalin, especially against the advice of the famed Danish
physicist, Niels Bohr, who reminded them that the Western powers possessed no monopoly of atomic science. To prevent a dangerous competition between the United States and the U.S.S.R., he warned, they should
include the Soviet Union in the Manhattan program and thereby establish the requisite foundations for the international control of atomic
energy. Both Roosevelt and Churchill spurned Bohr and his appeals.[70]
Until his death, Roosevelt awaited the occasion when atomic diplomacy
might extract special concessions from the Soviet Union. Meanwhile,
Roosevelt and his advisers never questioned the legitimacy of the new
weapon. General Leslie Groves, director of the Manhattan Project, later
asserted that "we were developing a weapon to be employed against the
enemies of the United States."[71]

Truman inherited the atomic program, unwilling or powerless
to reassess its need or legitimacy. When, on April 25, Stimson and
Groves informed Truman of the project, none of the three questioned

its use against Japan. With the projected test of the first bomb only three months away, Stimson, with the president's approval, appointed a top-secret Interim Committee to consider the bomb's future. Stimson remained chairman. The other six members were James B. Conant, scientific adviser and president of Harvard University; Vannevar Bush, director of the Office of Scientific Research and Development; Karl Compton, physicist and president of the Massachusetts Institute of Technology; Ralph Bard, under secretary of the Navy; William Clayton, assistant secretary of state; and James F. Byrnes, soon to become secretary of state.[72]

In its report of June 1, the Interim Committee advised the president to use the bomb against a suitable Japanese military target as quickly as possible and without prior warning. Nothing less, Stimson argued, would extract a genuine surrender from the Emperor. To deny the use of the bomb as an alternative to an invasion seemed unconscionable. The Interim Committee attempted to define the proper target for the new weapon. Stimson, at Conant's suggestion, observed that "the most desirable target would be a vital war plant employing a large number of workers and closely surrounded by workers' houses." For Groves and others it was essential that the target be large enough— and sufficiently free of ruination from previous bombing—to reveal the full destructiveness of the weapon.[73]

Not all Manhattan Project insiders agreed. Early in June, scientists at the University of Chicago's Metallurgical Laboratory, under the chairmanship of the distinguished émigré scientist James Franck, prepared a report on the implications of the Interim Committee's decision. The loss of confidence as well as the horror and revulsion resulting from the ruthless use of the bomb, they warned, could outweigh the military advantages, even the saving of lives. They advocated a demonstration of the bomb before representatives of the United Nations on a barren island. They predicted, moreover, that the indiscriminate military use of the bomb would virtually eliminate any possibility for achieving international control of atomic energy.[74]

On June 11, Stimson referred these warnings to a panel of distinguished American nuclear scientists, consisting of Arthur H. Compton, Enrico Fermi, Ernest O. Lawrence, and J. Robert Oppenheimer. The panel opposed both a demonstration and a warning to Japan. It concluded, in its June 16 report to the Interim Committee, that only direct military use of the bomb would be effective in terminating the war. Furthermore, the panel rejected the notion that the use of the bomb would prejudice future negotiations on international control.[75]

Drawing an opposite conclusion, members of the Franck Committee retorted that the greater the impact of the bomb, the greater the danger of an arms race. Only by *not* using the bomb against Japan could the United States assure the Soviets that the atomic monopoly would not be turned against them. Hungarian physicist Leo Szilard made this point to Oppenheimer. "Don't you think," Oppenheimer opined, "if we tell the Russians what we intend to do and then use the bomb in Japan, the Russians will understand it?" "They'll understand it only too well," ran Szilard's reply.[76] In his July 2 memorandum to the president, Stimson still consigned the achievement of Japan's unconditional surrender to the Kyushu invasion, backed by air and sea power. The atomic bomb remained secret and untested.[77]

On July 16, one day before the Big Three conference opened at Potsdam, the first atomic device exploded successfully in a spectacular demonstration at Alamogordo, New Mexico. For a fraction of a second, the light produced by Trinity—the equivalent of 20,000 tons of TNT—was greater than any ever produced on earth, and could have been seen from another planet.[78] Stimson, reporting the news to Truman, noted that the president responded with a new mood of confidence. Truman conveyed the news to Churchill who now saw "the end of the whole war in one or two violent shocks." Truman's advisers at Potsdam agreed that the bomb should be launched against Japan without delay. The decision to preserve the bomb's secrecy ruled out any advance warning to Tokyo. Not until July 24 did the president inform Stalin of the bomb's existence. The Soviet leader, he recalled, "showed no special interest." Anthony Eden noted that Stalin merely said "thank you," without further comment.[79] Actually Stalin knew of the Manhattan Project and, through London, had followed its progress. Late in 1943, he established a small atomic project of his own. Perhaps Stalin's passive response to Truman's announcement simply measured his failure to comprehend the bomb's potential significance; if so, this would soon change. Stalin informed Truman of the Japanese overtures. Neither admitted any interest in negotiating an end to the Pacific war.[80]

Stalin assured Truman that the U.S.S.R. would enter the Pacific war soon after August 8. He still awaited China's acceptance of Roosevelt's Yalta concessions of the Kuriles and southern Sakhalin to the Soviet Union. Stalin had opened his discussions with T. V. Soong on June 30 only to face stiff Chinese resistance. Harriman urged Soong to remain firm. Byrnes cabled Soong from Potsdam to concede nothing to the Soviets.[81] To the Kremlin it became clear that Washington intended to end the war before a Soviet entry, both to prevent the U.S.S.R. from strengthening its position in the northern Pacific and to eliminate a potential Soviet role in the occupation of Japan. Nikita Khrushchev recalled that Stalin distrusted American intentions, fearing that a Japanese capitulation would produce a denial that the United States owed the Soviets anything.[82]

At Potsdam, U.S. officials moved to end the war quickly without Soviet involvement. In the Potsdam Declaration of July 26, the United States, Britain, and China demanded Japan's unconditional surrender without reference to the atomic bomb or the Emperor. The United States set the terms of surrender. Japanese diplomats observed immediately that the presentation of terms defined the reality of unconditional surrender. The terms demanded the unconditional surrender of the Japanese armed forces, the elimination of Japanese militarism, the concession of all conquered territories, and a peaceful occupation. But the Potsdam Declaration promised to continue Japanese sovereignty in the home islands; permit the military forces "to return to their homes with the opportunity to lead peaceful and productive lives"; guarantee freedom of speech, religion, and thought; and allow civilian industry and, eventually, the reestablishment of Japan's international trade. The occupation would end with the creation of a new government. Leaders of the Japanese peace faction readily accepted the Potsdam terms as preferable to a continuation of the war. Foreign Minister Togo observed that the Potsdam terms were not synonymous with unconditional surrender; they imposed neither economic sanctions nor reparations. Kase Toshikazu of the Foreign Office, in his *Journey to the Missouri*, noted that the American demand for unconditional surrender included only the armed forces, sparing the Emperor from such indignities. He recalled that many Japanese citizens came to the Foreign Office to urge the acceptance of the American terms. Baron Hiranuma Kiichiro, president of the Privy Council, consented to the declaration because it maintained the Imperial House. Premier Suzuki shared the approval. Reporter Kato Masuo, in *The Lost War*, concluded that the U.S. offer "left Japan no sane alternative but acceptance."[83]

Discounting the Potsdam Declaration's assurances of a free, democratic Japan under occupation authority, assurances that meant salvation for countless Japanese citizens who feared and loathed their country's totalitarian regime, writers condemned the declaration because of its emphasis on unconditional surrender. Martin Sherwin charged that the Potsdam Declaration, by calling for unconditional surrender, damaged the cause of peace with a policy that "bound together a fracturing war party in Japan." Historian Leon V. Sigal was even more contemptuous of the declaration. In *Fighting to the Finish*, he condemned it as adding "little to the threats and promises that might alter Japan's calculations to continue the war." In denying Japan time for rational choice, the declaration, he concluded, was no more than propaganda. More than other writers, Gar Alperovitz, in *The Decision to Use the Bomb*, focused on the pitfalls of unconditional surrender, condemned repeatedly by Americans whom he cites in accumulating evidence against Washington's refusal to grant Tokyo reassurance that the imperial throne would survive.[84] Alperovitz, like other critics, gave no credence to Washington's insistence that the Japanese acknowledge defeat. Beyond the avoidance of the phrase "unconditional surrender" and the outright acceptance of the Emperor, it is not clear what concessions the critics of the Potsdam Declaration believed permissible to advance the cause of peace and reform of the Japanese political order.

Such judgments on the meaning of the Potsdam Declaration were lost on those who controlled Japan's wartime cabinet. MAGIC intercepts of Japanese diplomatic communications revealed that "the advocates of continuing the war were winning over those prepared to surrender."[85] War Minister Anami and his supporters were determined to prevent a full American occupation, sustain the old order, and retain Manchuria and Korea. Powerless to challenge the adamant opponents of surrender, Suzuki, on July 28, announced to the press that Japan would ignore the declaration.[86] Thereupon Truman ordered General Carl A. Spaatz to drop the first bomb when the weather permitted—after August 3. On August 6 the American crew aboard the *Enola Gay* released the bomb over Hiroshima to formally open the atomic age. The death toll, largely the result of instant incineration, reached between 80,000 and 140,000 people and seriously injured 100,000 more. On August 9, Sato secured a meeting with Molotov to announce Konoye's forthcoming peace mission to Moscow. He learned that the U.S.S.R. had already entered the war that day with a well-prepared invasion of Manchuria. Later, on August 9, a second atomic bomb struck Nagasaki, instantly killing 24,000 and wounding 23,000.[87] Not until August 14 did Soviet and Chinese officials sign the Sino-Soviet Treaty of Friendship and Alliance. The treaty endorsed all elements of the Yalta agreements that related to China. Within a week, and with breathtaking ruthlessness, the Soviet Army in the Far East proceeded to occupy all northern China, northern Korea, southern Sakhalin, and the Kuriles, killing more than 80,000 Japanese troops. The writing was on the wall.

Still, Japan's capitulation remained elusive. Anami's power over Japan's Supreme Council for the Direction of the War—the Big Six—rested on Emperor Hirohito's continued acquiescence to the principle of unanimity. After long debate on August 9–10, the Supreme Council agreed unanimously only on the acceptance of the Potsdam Declaration, with the understanding that it not prejudice "the prerogatives of His Majesty as a Sovereign Ruler."[88] At Truman's White House meeting on August 10, State Department officials, led by Byrnes, feared that acceptance of the Japanese proviso would create a backlash from the Emperor's outspoken congressional and public enemies. Stimson countered that the Emperor alone could assure the surrender of Japanese forces throughout Asia and the Pacific. Byrnes's official reply of August 11 was intentionally ambiguous. It accepted the Emperor as long as his rule was subject to occupation authority; to the people it assigned the right to determine the ultimate form of the Japanese government. Truman, thoroughly attuned to American opinion, conceded only what was essential.[89] While Washington awaited the Japanese response, Truman permitted the aerial demolition of Japanese cities to continue. On August 14 the Air Force dropped twelve million pounds of bombs on six Japanese targets. Still determined to prolong the war, Japanese zealots in Tokyo attempted a final coup. The effort failed.[90] To the end both American and Japanese hawks held the psychological advantage, forcing the moderates to demonstrate that enemy terms were preferable to continued war. The Emperor, using his superior power, overruled the military. From Tokyo the Emperor's message reached the Japanese legation in neutral Bern, Switzerland, where Allied emissaries awaited the Japanese surrender. On August 15, he announced to the Japanese people the end of the Pacific war, acknowledging only that "the general trends of the world and the actual conditions obtaining in Europe" recommended a settlement of the present situation.[91] The formal surrender ceremony occurred on September 2 aboard the battleship *Missouri* in Tokyo bay.

* * *

President Truman took full responsibility for the bomb decision, believing he made the best decision he could, given the information he had. Oppenheimer averred that he and other scientists always assumed that the bomb, if needed, would be used. Stimson recalled that no responsible official ever believed otherwise. None regarded the Hiroshima decision a moral issue.[92] The basic justification was simple. The atomic explosion, the president explained after Hiroshima, ended the war without an invasion, and thereby saved countless American and Japanese lives. For Americans generally, and especially for members of the armed forces, that explanation appeared understandable and conclusive. Even the American public had long become inured to such ruination from the skies.[93]

Actually, among U.S. leaders there was no agreement on the role of the Hiroshima bomb. The U.S. Strategic Bombing Survey's *Summary Report* of mid-1946, against strong countering evidence, declared that Japan, in all probability, would have surrendered by November 1 "even if the atomic bomb had not been dropped, even if Russia had not entered the war, and even if no invasion had been planned or contemplated." Admiral Chester Nimitz attributed Japan's surrender to the pounding administered by the Pacific Fleet. General Arnold found victory in the destructive air bombardment of Japan. General Claire L. Chenault pointed to the Soviet declaration of war as the final blow that brought Japan's capitulation.[94] None of these explanations ruled out the validity of the others. Together, the atomic bomb, the Soviet entry, the continuing blockade, and the ruinous conventional bombing created a crisis that enabled those in Tokyo who favored peace to prevail.

Truman's dismissal of the moral issue, as well as the piecemeal disclosures of doubt regarding the Hiroshima bomb's necessity, soon unleashed a flood of criticism. From the left came Dwight Macdonald's immediate charge that the Hiroshima bomb placed the United States on a moral level with Nazi exterminators. The Catholic *Commonweal* declared that the bomb defiled America's victory, while the Protestant *Christian Century* termed Hiroshima "America's atomic atrocity." Editor David Lawrence of *U.S. News* believed that Americans, after examining their inner thoughts honestly, would be ashamed of the bomb decision. Samuel McCrea Cavert, general secretary of the Federal Council of Churches of Christ in America, reminded the president that his resort to the bomb "sets [an] extremely dangerous precedent for [the] future of mankind." The early criticism culminated in Baldwin's *Great Mistakes of the War* (1950). Baldwin lamented, "We are now branded with the mark of the beast."[95]

What concerned many critics was the unprecedented horror of atomic destruction, producing not only the instantaneous incineration of tens of thousands of civilians, but also the death and disfigurement of additional multitudes from radiation.[96] The conviction that the accumulating effectiveness of American air and naval power, not the atomic bombs, had probably terminated the war, merely aggravated the moral disquietude.[97] Others condemned the decision to drop the bombs three months before the November 1 deadline, thereby denying Tokyo the necessary time to respond realistically to its deteriorating strategic position. What troubled British Nobel Laureate P. M. S. Blackett was the U.S. reliance on speed to block Soviet expansion into the northern Pacific, whatever the cost in a "cold diplomatic war" with the Kremlin.[98] Finally, critics decried the pursuit of a quick, total victory at Hiroshima without concern for alternatives. If the bomb was not necessary for victory, as many claimed, why did the administration not provide a peaceful demonstration, offer a warning to Japan, or offer less ambiguous terms of surrender?[99]

Washington officials met the Hiroshima critics head on, defending the atomic bombs as legitimate weapons, used justifiably to break the interminable Japanese resistance to surrender, and possibly save tens of thousands of lives. Karl Compton opened the offensive with an essay in the *Atlantic Monthly* of December 1946, arguing that the Hiroshima decision was the best available. Under administration pressure, Stimson answered the critics in the February 1947 issue of *Harper's*. He reminded his readers that the administration, guided by the single objective of a quick victory, never sought to avoid use of the bomb. "The destruction of Hiroshima and Nagasaki," he wrote, "put an end to the Japanese war. It stopped the fire raids, and the strangling blockade; it ended the ghastly specter of a clash of great land armies." The alternatives, he declared, would have consumed time and perhaps encouraged Japan to believe that U.S. resolve was weakening.[100] Fundamentally, the defense of the Hiroshima bomb rested on two assumptions: that it saved lives, and that it created the necessary conditions for the Japanese surrender.

Japan resisted surrender far beyond the point where the marginal benefit exceeded the marginal cost. Whether it would have capitulated before the November deadline remained a matter of conjecture, without substantive evidence. Equally questionable was the widespread moral condemnation of Hiroshima decision. The moral issue in the Hiroshima bombing was the instant destruction of a large civilian population. But none of the Hiroshima critics condemned the targeting of cities. Not even scientist Leo Szilard's admonition of July 17, asking the president to consider the moral implications of the bomb, contained any condemnation of warfare against civilian targets. The systematic firebombing of Japanese cities had razed over two million homes and killed some 400,000 people.[101] America's real choice in August 1945 was not between an invasion and resort to the atomic bomb, but between the bomb and weeks or months of LeMay's firebombing of every conceivable Japanese target—which, in time, would have created more additional death and destruction than the atomic bombs. Starving the Japanese into submission was scarcely a humane option. The Truman administration faced the imperative of ending a victorious war quickly and under terms that embodied both the country's minimum objectives and the realities of the war itself. To end it, Washington confronted alternative modes of coercion, all increasingly drastic and effective. For such painful choices, the Japanese carried their own heavy burden of responsibility by refusing to deal, earlier and forthrightly, with the inescapable necessity of coming to terms with defeat.

* * *

If the Manhattan Project's primary objective in 1945 was victory in the Pacific, it carried a secondary, perhaps more pervading, purpose of assuring the United States a predominant postwar role in international affairs. In sole possession of the atomic bomb, the United States, through a clear demonstration of its destructive power, might eliminate the Soviet infringements on Yalta, if not the unfortunate consequences of the war itself. To that end, Truman, in June, postponed the Potsdam meeting of the Big Three until he had received some assurance of a successful test at Alamogordo. The bomb, Stimson informed the president, would be the "master card," bestowing enormous diplomatic advantage on the United States. If the bomb worked, Truman remarked in July, "I'll certainly have a hammer on those boys [the Soviets]." The bomb was needed, observed Byrnes, not to defeat Japan, but to "make Russia manageable in Europe." Byrnes boasted that the bomb "might well put us in a position to dictate our own terms at the end of the war."[102]

After Hiroshima, U.S. officials and members of Congress hoped to command the future of atomic power by protecting the country's alleged monopoly of atomic science and technology. Scientists reminded Washington that the knowledge that produced the bombs was scarcely secret. No less than the scientists, Stimson, troubled by the disintegration of U.S.-Soviet relations at Potsdam, recognized the importance of preventing an atomic arms race with the U.S.S.R. through the international control of atomic energy. He suggested to Truman on September 12 that the United States approach the Soviets with an offer "to enter an arrangement . . . to control and limit the use of the atomic bomb as an instrument of atomic power for peaceful and humanitarian purposes." Truman demurred. So continuous was the national opposition to the sharing of atomic secrets that he announced his intention to protect them all.[103]

Unfortunately, the Soviets, regarding the American atomic monopoly a threat to their security and international standing, accepted the atomic challenge. Within weeks after Hiroshima, Stalin expanded the Soviet atomic project, with orders to restore the power balance as quickly as possible. To the Kremlin the American atomic monopoly represented economic, technological, and military predominance that the Soviets hoped to equal, if not surpass. In rendering atomic power a key element in international predominance and prestige, rather than an issue to be put to rest, the bomb decision and the attitudes of superiority that it generated opened a Pandora's box of competing atomic strategies of unimaginable magnitude, danger, and cost.[104] Whether the American failure to advance the cause of international control exacerbated the burgeoning disagreements over Eastern Europe and Germany is doubtful. The issues in conflict had foundations sturdily formed during the war years. Any future competition over atomic power would reflect the accumulating fears and tensions, not create them.[105]

Byrnes, emboldened by the bomb, went to the London Foreign Ministers Conference in September more determined than ever to avoid any concessions to the Kremlin. Molotov, matching the secretary's toughness and intransigence, instructed Byrnes that the Soviets would not be intimidated. Byrnes' experience quickly demonstrated the profound limits of atomic power in the world of international diplomacy. Threats of atomic destruction could affect Soviet behavior only if the Kremlin chose to take them seriously. Washington would never persuade the Soviets that the United States had any interests in Eastern Europe worth the price of a war.

At London, the Foreign Ministers tackled their first assignment of drafting peace treaties for Italy, Rumania, Bulgaria, Hungary, and Finland. Byrnes repeated the American position that the Kremlin should establish governments in Eastern Europe both representative and friendly to the Soviet Union. Molotov was not impressed. He denied the possibility of forming governments both friendly and free. Moreover, he found gross inconsistency in American policy. The Radescu regime of Rumania, he reminded Byrnes, was hostile to the U.S.S.R. but received American and British support. The United States then refused to recognize the new governments of Rumania and Bulgaria although they were friendly to Moscow. The Rumanian government, ran Byrnes's retort, was the product of Soviet interventionism. Molotov observed that the Kremlin faced the obligation to root out German fascism. When Byrnes insisted that the United States desired governments based on free elections, Molotov asked him why the United States had no trouble with governments in Italy and Greece when they had never held free elections. Byrnes moved to break the deadlock by recognizing the government of Hungary, one friendly to the U.S.S.R., on the promise that it would hold free elections. On Rumania and Bulgaria, Byrnes and Molotov reached no agreement at all.[106]

At London, Germany again emerged as the central issue confronting the Allies. To the Western powers a reconstructed German economy remained the necessary prelude to Germany's political independence. The Soviet's persistent removal of German assets from their zone in the name of security against Germany not only crippled German production but also created an enormous drain of resources from the Western zones. The issue for Soviet policy, Molotov argued, was the ease of the German advance across Poland, Hungary, Rumania, and Bulgaria in 1941. Byrnes countered Molotov's continuing security demands by offered a pact binding the United States to Germany's demilitarization for 25 years. Molotov agreed only to report to Moscow. Soviet intransigence at London had the effect of driving the Western ministers into a solid, opposing bloc. When it became obvious that every disagreement produced a unified, anti-Soviet reaction among the American, British, French, and Chinese delegates, the Soviets demanded French and Chinese exclusion from the critical decisions. After staggering through a series of stormy sessions, marked by uncompromising Soviet maneuvers, the conference adjourned without reaching a single substantive agreement.[107]

Following London the Western powers faced the immediate challenge in the impending division of Europe into permanent spheres of influence. In early October the *London Observer* noted the accumulating price of disagreement. "[A] line drawn north and south across Europe, perhaps somewhere in the region of Stettin to Trieste," it warned, "is likely to become more and more of a barrier separating two very different conceptions of life." Washington redoubled its search for an Eastern European formula acceptable to all members of the Grand Alliance, one that would maintain Europe's essential unity. Byrnes responded to the ongoing conflict over Rumania and Bulgaria by dispatching Mark Ethridge, editor of the Louisville *Courier-Journal*, to provide an unbiased evaluation of the two Balkan governments. Ethridge discovered that both countries defied the principles of the Yalta Declaration on Liberated Europe. In his December report, Ethridge recommended the continuation of official nonrecognition.[108]

In Washington the search for an acceptable Eastern European settlement was unproductive. In a long memorandum of October 18,

Bohlen suggested greater East-West economic and diplomatic cooperation as an antidote to Soviet exclusiveness in Eastern Europe. One week later, Cloyce K. Huston, chief of the Division of Southern European Affairs, released a report that recognized legitimacy in the Soviet determination to prevent an anti-Soviet *cordon sanitaire* along that country's western periphery, but, like Bohlen, he rejected the exclusiveness of Kremlin policy. Huston recommended a forthright U.S. declaration of its desire to see governments in Eastern Europe friendly to the U.S.S.R.[109] Byrnes had already offered the Kremlin such assurances at Potsdam and London. In his noted Navy Day speech of October 27, the president advocated self-determination for Eastern Europe, nothing more. In his *New York Herald-Tribune* Forum address four days later, Byrnes again recognized the Soviet right to friendly governments in its western neighbors, but added the customary proviso: "It is our belief that all peoples should be free to choose their own form of government . . . based on the consent of the governed."[110] Byrnes's prescription that the Soviets accept democratic border regimes overlooked the fact that the region contained powerful anti-Soviet elements that Stalin and Molotov had repeatedly declared dangerous and unacceptable.

What national interest was served by this uncompromising pursuit of the unachievable was not obvious. Lippmann noted in late October that the appeal to principles was inspiring but gained nothing.[111] He, like countless Americans, saw little danger to U.S. security in Rumanian and Bulgarian political abuses. Bohlen observed, that month, that the United States and the U.S.S.R., with no concrete interests in conflict, need not experience diplomatic failure or war. "The geographical location of the two countries," he wrote, "do[es] not provide places where the friction arises automatically." Stimson noted in his diary that the Soviet and American orbits need not "clash geographically." Similarly General Eisenhower testified before the House Military Affairs Committee in November that "Russia has not the slightest thing to gain by a struggle with the United States."[112] But for some Washington officials the Soviet power base in Eastern Europe and the Balkans had become a measure, not of Soviet repression, but of Soviet expansionism. John D. Hickerson, Deputy Director of the Office of European Affairs, warned Byrnes that the Soviet concern for friendly bordering states clouded the larger ambition to extend the security zone through the Balkans into the eastern Mediterranean. The Joint Chiefs of Staff observed that Eastern Europe, if not strategically vital, added immeasurably to Soviet military potential.[113] The notion that Eastern Europe was merely a stepping stone to broader Soviet aggressions and occupations introduced a new, ultimately frightening, element into U.S.-Soviet relations.

Such suppositions that Western civilization faced new dangers exposed to troubling scrutiny the reality that the war had weakened or destroyed all the traditional sources of European and world stability. The historic international equilibrium had vanished. Western Europe was politically demoralized, economically prostrate, and militarily defenseless. Disease, famine, and anarchy created a revolutionary environment. Following the Soviet Union's heroic victory over Germany, Communist party membership soared in Italy, France, Belgium, Holland, Czechoslovakia, Hungary, and Finland. In France and Italy Communist parties, with suspected ties to Moscow, were members of coalition governments. The opportunities that political ferment and economic upheaval offered to Europe's Communist organizers seemed limitless. Britain, historically the protector of the Ottoman Empire, the eastern Mediterranean, and the Indian Ocean, could no longer defend those strategic regions against the forces for change. For American officials, Moscow's perceived ambitions in Iran, Turkey, and Greece suddenly became challenges that demanded attention. The futile and ultimately humiliating U.S. experience in Eastern Europe drove Washington to act resolutely elsewhere and thereby rendered a pervading conflict with the Soviet Union inevitable.

CHAPTER 4

End of the Grand Alliance

The Grand Alliance, in large measure, became history itself with its triumph over the Axis in the summer of 1945. As a military organization it had no further mission. Yet, as the predominant actors in the creation of the United Nations, the five major wartime allies, as permanent members of the Security Council, carried major responsibility for leading the world from its recent horrors to the final establishment of peace. A war-weary world, as late as December 1945, could still presume that the world's victorious powers, having performed well in war, would labor with equal effectiveness and success in facing the challenges of peace. It mattered to the world that the wartime coalition would continue to operate in essential unity. The persistent postwar disagreements over the future of Germany and East-Central Europe, as demonstrated at the Potsdam and London conferences of August and September, remained largely matters of principle, not security. Still, for the doubtful, the continuing Soviet occupation of the Balkans rendered bordering regions vulnerable to Soviet expansion. It required only the Kremlin's demands on Iran and Turkey to unleash visions of Soviet military advances into the Middle East.

Iran emerged in late 1945 as that region's major point of challenge. At the London Conference, the Allies had established March 2, 1946, as the final date for the evacuation of all foreign troops from Iran. Partially in retaliation for Teheran's refusal to negotiate mineral and oil rights, the Soviets supported the local Communist attempt to take control of autonomous Azerbaijan. In November 1945 a radical coup overthrew the Iranian regime. Soviet forces moved in, surrounded the Iranian headquarters at Tabriz, and expelled officers who refused to join the Azerbaijani army. In December the rebels proclaimed their independence. In Washington, the Iranian ambassador warned the

State Department that Azerbaijan was only the initial move "in a series which would include Turkey and other countries in the Near East." If the Soviets succeeded in holding Azerbaijan, he added, "the history of Manchuria, Abyssinia, and Munich would be repeated and Azerbaijan would prove to have been the first shot fired in [the] Third world war."[1]

In Greece, the British maintained some semblance of order against Communist infiltration from Yugoslavia, Albania, and Bulgaria. By late November the struggle for power had become so acute that London postponed elections until March 1946. Soviet ambitions in the Middle East appeared even more threatening when, in March 1945, the Kremlin announced that it would terminate its interwar treaty arrangements with Turkey. On June 7, the Soviets informed the Turkish ambassador in Moscow that they wanted the border districts in the Caucuses that the Russians had taken in 1878 but returned to the Turks after World War I, a revision of the Montreux Convention governing the Straits, and a lease of strategic bases in the Straits for joint defense. Turkey rejected the demands outright. Washington regarded Soviet pressure on Turkey as evidence enough of the Kremlin's revived ambitions in the Middle East. In December, Loy Henderson observed that the Soviets seemed determined to destroy Britain's historic position in the region "so that Russian power can sweep unimpeded across Turkey through the Dardanelles into the Mediterranean, and across Iran and through the Persian Gulf into the Indian Ocean."[2] Soviet demands on Turkey and Iran suggested that the Kremlin intended to dominate the eastern Mediterranean as well as the waterways, pipelines, and oil fields of the Middle East. With the danger of a Communist coup in Greece, Truman recalled, "this began to look like a giant pincers movement against the oil-rich areas of the Near East and the warm-water ports of the Mediterranean."[3]

To resolve the ongoing issues of Rumania and Bulgaria, Secretary Byrnes traveled to Moscow, in December, without much preparation or Republican advisers. He was on his own. Diplomats and columnists warned him against venturing into a conference with Stalin without a precise agenda, agreed to in advance. But Byrnes believed, as he wrote in his defense, "that if we met in Moscow, where I could have a chance to talk to Stalin, we might remove the barriers to the peace treaties."[4] Byrnes's advisers in Moscow, Harriman and Bohlen, agreed that continued nonrecognition of Rumania and Bulgaria would achieve nothing. When Byrnes raised the troublesome issue of these two countries, Stalin proposed that the Allies urge the Bulgarian parliament to include some opposition members and the Rumanian government to add leaders from two opposition parties. Byrnes suddenly found the way open to recognize the two governments. He asked only that the conference's final communiqué include a statement of Allied support for civil liberties and free elections. Unfortunately, such phraseology was no guarantee of self-determination.[5] George Kennan, then in the U.S. embassy, revealed only contempt for Byrnes's effort to rescue the Yalta Declaration by accepting an arrangement that would hide the reality of Soviet-controlled dictatorships across Eastern Europe. Never again did the Kremlin even pretend to compromise its dominance of the occupied regions.[6] If Byrnes's agreements represented a retreat from previous U.S. positions, they also recognized that Washington had few choices remaining. Byrnes eventually gained Stalin's support for a peace conference in 1946, but accepted Stalin's demand that France and China be eliminated from the treaty-drafting process.[7]

At Moscow, Byrnes's actions accentuated Britain's declining role in Allied decision-making. For London this was deeply disturbing. Britain's long quest for some U.S. commitment to its imperial interests had become critical as Britain faced the prospect of a direct Soviet challenge to the oil and sea lanes of the Middle East. Byrnes arranged the Moscow Conference with no effort to coordinate British and American policies; at Moscow, Byrnes largely ignored the British delegation, often meeting with Stalin alone. When Foreign Minister Ernest Bevin informed Byrnes that the Soviets threatened the British position in the Middle East, the American secretary of state agreed only to discuss the matter with Stalin privately. Kennan noted Bevin's profound disgust over Byrnes's lack of concern for British interests. Indeed, the Moscow Conference marked the nadir of U.S.-British relations.[8]

Washington concern for Britain's economic welfare was no greater than its care for Britain's role in world affairs. Truman announced at Potsdam that Lend-Lease would be limited to munitions, not capital investment, and would end with Japan's defeat. Churchill believed the decision unnecessarily harsh; Chancellor of the Exchequer Hugh Dalton complained that it came without warning or discussion. "We had expected," he wrote, "at least some tapering off of Lend-Lease over the first few months of peace." Prime Minister Attlee reminded Truman that Britain's war effort had ruined its finances. In desperation, the British, with little encouragement from Washington, pressed for a loan. Vandenberg argued that the United States should grant Britain a loan only if it was prepared to grant a similar one to the U.S.S.R. To do otherwise, he said, would terminate the Grand Alliance.[9]

Treasury Secretary Fred M. Vinson expressed no sympathy for the British request. Finally in December, a U.S.-British loan agreement extended a $3.75 billion line of credit at two percent interest, repayable in 50 years. The United States cancelled the $20 billion debt owed on Lend-Lease. What troubled the British, however, was the provision that sterling would become freely convertible one year after the effective date of the loan. Churchill regarded the arrangement so perilous that in practice it would become self-defeating. The *Economist* (London) declared that "our reward for losing a quarter of our total national wealth in the common cause is to pay tribute for half a century to those who have been enriched by the war."[10] The loan agreement had yet to pass the congressional gauntlet.

* * *

Truman received the Moscow communiqué on December 27. "I did not like what I read," he recalled. "There was not a word about Iran or any other place where the Soviets were on the march. We had gained only an empty promise of further talks." The president's contentiousness reflected the country's changing mood. The earlier frustration over Soviet defiance of Yalta was giving way to feelings of insecurity as Soviet ambitions appeared to reach beyond established limits. For some editors, Byrnes, in his determination to reach agreement, had given too much away.[11] When Byrnes returned to Washington, the president accused him of making concessions without any evidence that the Soviets intended to constrain their behavior. The secretary, he recorded, had attempted "to move the foreign policy of the United States in a direction to which I could not, and would not agree." On January 5, he prepared his bill of particulars:

There is no justification for [the Russian program in Iran]. It is a parallel to the program of Russia in Latvia, Estonia, and Lithuania. . . . There isn't a doubt in my mind that Russia intends an invasion of Turkey and the seizure of the Black Sea Straits to the Mediterranean. Unless Russia is faced with an iron fist and strong language another war is in the making. . . . I do not think we should play compromise any longer. We should refuse to recognize Rumania and Bulgaria until they comply with our requirements; we should let our position in Iran be known in no uncertain terms and we should continue to insist on the internationalization of the Kiel Canal, the Rhine-Danube waterway and the Black Sea Straits.

Truman later designated his memorandum to Byrnes as the point of departure in American policy.[12] Whether Truman's confrontation with Byrnes actually occurred is doubtful. At their first meeting, Byrnes briefed the president on the Moscow agreements. He termed the Rumanian formula satisfactory, the Bulgarian not. Byrnes acknowledged that he had inaugurated a program for the international control of atomic energy. The U.S. atomic monopoly, he feared, had become a dangerous source of Soviet-American controversy. All other agreements, Byrnes declared, had followed established policies. Iran's future remained in doubt, but Byrnes had reminded Stalin of the Soviet promise to evacuate by March 2. Stalin replied simply that he would not embarrass the United States. Leahy noted Truman's satisfaction with Byrnes's account and arranged for the secretary to address the nation on CBS radio.[13]

After January 1946, U.S. relations with the Soviet Union began to unravel while those with Britain began to improve. Stalin inaugurated the process with his Moscow address of February 9. Again he raised the old Bolshevik concept of "capitalist encirclement" and the continuing hostility between the Communist and capitalist worlds. Stalin attributed the recent war to the dialectical imperatives of capitalism; those same forces, he warned, again endangered the peace. His words were not reassuring: "Our Marxists declare that the capitalist system of world economy conceals elements of crisis and war. ... [W]orld capitalism does not follow a steady and even course forward, but proceeds through crises and catastrophes." Thus Stalin explained the need of a new five-year plan to prepare the country for any eventuality.[14] He did not intimate that the Soviet Union required a Communist world order to prevent war; nor did he threaten open conflict with the capitalist antagonist. To Soviet expert Elbridge Durbrow, the speech was designed to gird a reluctant populace for a program of industrial expansion that would further cripple its standard of living. But for many Americans, Stalin's references to capitalist iniquities seemed to inaugurate ideological warfare against the non-Communist world. *Time* viewed the speech as the most ominous statement of any world leader since the end of the war. Justice William O. Douglas termed it "The Declaration of World War III." At the suggestion of H. Freeman Matthews, Byrnes requested Kennan to produce an analysis of possible Soviet implementation of the Stalin speech.[15]

To counteract the trend toward a hardening, fear-ridden approach to the Soviet Union, Bohlen and Geroid T. Robinson, a noted pioneer in Russian studies at Columbia University, prepared a detailed evaluation of postwar Soviet capabilities and intentions, including their possible significance for American policy. Their ultimate proposals, evolving slowly between December and February, rested on the assumption of America's military dominance, rendering Soviet intentions irrelevant for the foreseeable future. They concluded that the Kremlin, despite Communism's waning appeal, would maintain its authority, but that its official dogma included no rigid blueprint for revolutionary expansion. Regarding a hard-line policy, backed by the pursuit of military preponderance, unnecessary and counterproductive, they advocated a moderate reassuring approach to the Soviet Union, the sharing of atomic energy, and the avoidance of public declarations designed to antagonize the Soviets. Should such policies fail to influence Soviet behavior, Washington could then adopt tougher, less accommodating approaches.[16]

Such appeals to moderation had no chance against Kennan's "Long Telegram" of February 22, which offered Washington officialdom a frightening, yet totally welcome, definition of the Soviet problem. By attributing Soviet behavior to internal rather than external causes, Kennan absolved the United States of all responsibility for the continuing breakdown of U.S.-Soviet relations. Soviet paranoia, demanding endless struggle against external enemies, assured unsatisfactory U.S. relations with the Kremlin. "We have here," Kennan advised, "a force committed fanatically to the belief that with the United States there can be no permanent modus vivendi, which it is desirable and necessary that the internal harmony of our society be disrupted, our traditional way of life destroyed, the international authority of our state broken, if Soviet power is to be secure." Never in modern history had any major power faced dangers from afar so total and pervading. Kennan's analysis established the foundation of a new foreign policy consensus that recognized the U.S.S.R. as a hostile power whose irreconcilable differences with the West, not the perpetuation of the wartime alliance, should govern U.S. policy.[17] Kennan's analysis created a sensation in official Washington. Matthews heralded the telegram as magnificent. In a note to the U.S. ambassador in Paris, he praised it as "about as fine a piece of writing and as clear an analysis of a highly complicated and vital situation as has ever come out of the Foreign Service." Henderson declared that the dispatch "hit the nail on the head." For Durbrow things were coming into proper perspective. Forrestal recorded that he had finally found the trenchant analysis of Soviet behavior that he had sought in vain. Bohlen accepted Kennan's analysis, making no further reference to the Bohlen-Robinson report. Assistant Secretary of State William Benton asked Kennan to accept an appointment to the State Department where he might educate the nation and the world on the dangers posed by the Soviet Union.[18]

It is not strange that those who shared such views discounted the telegram's inconsistencies and exaggerations. Kennan predicted endless struggle emanating from Soviet paranoia, yet nothing in the Soviet record ruled out coexistence. It was either that or war. In 1946 the United States and the U.S.S.R. had no direct interests in conflicts that were worth a morning of armed conflict. Kennan himself acknowledged the Soviet Union's financial and military inferiority, as well as its desire to avoid war. By insisting that the United States could meet the Soviet threat successfully without war, Kennan rendered the burgeoning attitude of "getting tough" with the Soviets reasonable and scarcely dangerous. Yet he never accepted that fundamental judgment as relevant to his analysis of the Soviet danger. Soviet notions of capitalist encirclement or addiction to dogmas, conspiracies, and propaganda could hardly undergird a body of rational and successful external policies. Kennan's solutions, moreover, had no relationship to the dangers he described. He advocated only that the West keep its house in order and its eyes on the Kremlin; there were no appeals for vigorous, power-based responses to the Soviet Union's alleged designs on the United States, suggesting that there was, after all, nothing vital at stake.[19]

Republican pressures for a tougher U.S. response to Soviet actions, complemented by editorials in leading Catholic journals such as *The Commonweal* and the *Catholic World*, reinforced the new anti-Soviet consensus.[20] Vandenberg took up the Soviet challenge with a telling speech in the Senate on February 27. On the following day Byrnes continued the verbal assault on the Kremlin before the Overseas Press Club in New York (one wit termed it the Second Vandenberg Concerto).[21] Still, in the realm of policy the new "get tough" rhetoric, condemning Soviet behavior as reprehensible and dangerous, offered no genuine response. Whatever the needs of the hour, demobilization was in the air. Columnist Anne O'Hare McCormick rebuked the nation for expecting action abroad where Soviet behavior did not demand it and U.S. capabilities did not permit it. "When Americans demand in one breath that their Government take a firm stand on principle and in the next that the bulk of our forces be withdrawn from Europe," she wrote, "they should not complain of unsatisfactory compromises." The *New Republic* acknowledged that Vandenberg's speech "was undoubtedly popular; the only trouble was that he did not indicate any means of carrying it out or, indeed, seem to recognize the implications involved." The writer observed that the senators who applauded Vandenberg's proposed "manifestation of America's strength and 'moral leadership' have been the most vociferous in demanding that the boys come home."[22] Byrnes ignored the question of means completely.

* * *

Winston Churchill, on March 5, battled this national unconcern for preparedness by raising the issue of Soviet expansionism and the American responsibility in meeting it. "With primacy in power," he asserted at Fulton, Missouri, "is also joined an awe-inspiring accountability for the future." Churchill drew a somber picture of the strength and outreach of the U.S.S.R. and the need for another alliance of the English-speaking peoples to meet the danger. The Soviets, Churchill believed, did not desire war, but, he added, "I am convinced that there is nothing they admire so much as strength and there is nothing for which they have less respect than for military weakness."[23] London responded with unstinting approval, Moscow with a burst of hysteria. For Stalin, as Nikita Khrushchev recalled, Churchill's speech signaled the end of the Grand Alliance: "Our relations with England, France, [and] the USA . . . were, for all intents and purposes, ruined."[24] Members of Congress and the public were still reluctant to commit U.S. power to Europe's defense, or even acknowledge that Soviet expansionism had reached the dangerous state that Churchill described.

Despite the unfavorable American response to Churchill's plea, successive events in 1946 were forming ever-closer British-American cooperation. The first was the coming Iranian crisis of March 1946. The March 2 deadline for Soviet withdrawal from Azerbaijan passed without any Soviet response. On March 5, Byrnes sent a protest to Moscow and prepared for a showdown. Iran appealed to the UN Security Council; Byrnes and Britain's Bevin called for an early meeting. When the Council met on March 25, the Kremlin announced an agreement with Iran that included oil concessions and a Soviet withdrawal in five to six weeks. On April 15, the Iranian government withdrew its complaint as Soviet troops began their withdrawal. The Iranian crisis, while it lasted, created an unprecedented occasion for British-American collaboration. Byrnes informed the country that the administration did not contemplate an alliance with Britain, yet the Iranian experience suggested strongly that Britain's historic concerns in the Middle East were becoming those of the United States as well.

Meanwhile, in March, Byrnes requested the Joint Chiefs of Staff to consider the significance of Soviet pressures on Turkey. The Joint

Figure 4.1
Truman applauding Churchill at Fulton College (Terry Savage, Courtesy: Harry S. Truman Library)

Chiefs' response focused on Britain's role in sustaining America's world position: "The defeat or disintegration of the British Empire would eliminate from Eurasia the last bulwark of resistance between the United States and Soviet expansion. . . . Militarily, our present position in the world is of necessity closely interwoven with that of Great Britain." During the spring of 1946, the Joint Chiefs concluded reluctantly that the U.S.S.R. would be the likely adversary in another war. It was essential, therefore, that the United States buttress the British Empire against possible Soviet aggression. In early April, Matthews advised the nation's military planners: "If Soviet Russia is to be denied the hegemony of Europe, the United Kingdom must continue in existence as the principle power in Western Europe economically and militarily."[25]

This compatibility between American and British concerns sealed the fate of the British loan. Hearings on the loan opened on March 13 before the Senate Banking and Currency Committee. Under Secretary Dean Acheson assumed major responsibility for the loan's passage. Either the United States would accept its economic responsibilities, he warned, or it would witness the collapse of Europe. Acheson and the bankers he hailed before the committee justified the loan purely on economic grounds. When the hearings ended in April, the opposition remained strong. Vandenberg's decision to support the loan turned on his anti-Soviet bias, but it secured enough Republican votes to assure Senate passage on May 10, by a vote of 46 to 32. The House did not approve the measure until mid-July. What mattered, observed Congressman Christian Herter, was the need of a British friend to meet the impending Soviet challenge. There was no future, James Reston of the *New York Times* noted in late May, "in trying to break up the Anglo-American bloc or denying that it exists."[26] The propensity of congressmen to laud the British loan as a bulwark against Communist expansion doomed the passage of a similar Soviet loan. Still the conditions set down in the proposed Soviet agreement were so demanding on the question of Eastern Europe that informed officials saw no possibility of a Soviet acceptance.[27] Convinced that Congress would not approve a Soviet loan, the administration dropped the issue.

Anglo-American cooperation received an immense impetus from the often tumultuous Foreign Ministers Conference that opened in Paris's beautiful Luxembourg Palace on April 25. Byrnes invited Vandenberg and Tom Connally, Democratic leader in the Senate, to accompany him to Paris. At issue was a peace treaty for Italy and treaties with Hungary, Rumania, Bulgaria, and Finland—the former Nazi satellites. Byrnes insisted that the conference seek first an agreement on general principles; Molotov denied that generalities had any relevance. Trieste emerged as a special problem. This Adriatic city, with its predominantly Italian population, was surrounded by Yugoslav territory. Both the Italians and the Yugoslavs, the latter backed by the Soviet Union, claimed the city. Byrnes supported the Italian claim under the principle of self-determination.[28] For the Soviets, Byrnes's persistent reliance on principle rather than bargaining was incomprehensible. At Paris almost every session ended in deadlock. After one heated session, Bohlen, adviser to the American delegation, remained behind to converse with a member of the Soviet delegation. "The Soviet representative," Bohlen reported, "said it was impossible for him to understand the Americans. They had a reputation for being good traders and yet Secretary Byrnes for two days had been making speeches about principles." With all sincerity, the Soviet delegate added, "Why doesn't he stop his talking about principles, and get down to business and start trading?"[29] The conference recessed on May 16 with little accomplished. The *Manchester Guardian* passed judgment on its failures: "What is clear is that relations between the Big Three have now reached a perilous stage and only a great effort of statesmanship can avoid a fatal breach."[30]

Meanwhile, the Allied disagreements over Germany's future had become profound. At Potsdam, the Allies agreed that reparations should leave sufficient industrial resources in Germany to enable the German people to subsist without external assistance. To that end, Germany required exports to cover the cost of its imports. But Soviet confiscations from non-war industries sustained a serious imbalance between exports and imports in the Soviet zone, leading to the continued demand for reparations from the other zones. Unfortunately, the Anglo-American preference for a highly productive Germany troubled Paris no less than Moscow. The French objected especially to the integration of Germany's economic and financial structure. Such integration, they feared, would eliminate French claims to the Ruhr, Rhineland, and Saar.[31] On May 3, General Lucius D. Clay, the U.S. deputy military governor of Germany, ordered a halt of further reparations shipments from the American zone. The ultimate solution of the German problem was already apparent. If a united, economically powerful Germany would again threaten European security, the Allies had no choice but to restrain Germany's economic growth or divide it. To avoid that choice, Byrnes invited the powers to create a single German economy by joining their zones to the American zone. Speaking at Stuttgart, Germany, on September 6, Byrnes repeated the need for centralized administration. Byrnes's advocacy of a unified German economy received scant approval in Moscow and Paris. The British now called for the formation of an

Anglo-American bizonia as the only program remaining for a self-sufficient Germany.[32]

Byrnes came to the second session of the Paris conference in mid-June, determined to push for an early showdown with Molotov; no longer would he permit the U.S.S.R. to capitalize on Europe's prolonged economic chaos. By the first week of July, Molotov had made significant concessions that permitted marked advances on the Balkan treaties.[33] The foreign ministers now agreed to call a general peace conference, to open in Paris in late July. The sudden summoning of the peace conference gave the lesser nations little time to consider the partially completed treaty drafts. During August the peace conference took up the task of finishing the treaties. What blocked the Italian treaty was the continuing disagreement over reparations and the future of Trieste. The peace conference adjourned in October without a formal settlement.[34] The foreign ministers moved to the Waldorf-Astoria Hotel in New York. There they completed the treaties and resolved the troublesome Trieste issue. Byrnes secured the Trieste agreement by convincing Molotov that Yugoslavia did not merit his long and arduous efforts in its behalf.[35]

Byrnes, at Paris, gave nothing away, but some critics wondered why he did not readily accept some accommodation with the U.S.S.R., based on the reality of divided Europe. Clyde Eagleton of New York University accused Washington in *Harper's* of denying the Soviets the right to a sphere of influence when the United States had built one across much of the Western Hemisphere. Contrasted to American success, he averred, "the efforts of the Russians in their part of the world look positively puny!" Throughout the Paris meetings, critics reminded Byrnes that his principles would always remain inoperative because they transcended U.S. economic and security interests. At Madison Square Garden, on September 12, Secretary of Commerce Henry A. Wallace advocated forthright U.S. recognition of the reality of two spheres of influence, the Soviet sphere in Eastern Europe and the Western sphere stretching from Europe to Latin America. Wallace's speech so antagonized Byrnes and others that the president called for his resignation.[36] Again that month Rheinhold Niebuhr suggested, in the *Nation*, that the United States "stop the futile efforts to change what cannot be changed in Eastern Europe." In December, Lippmann criticized Byrnes for relying on British-American power to outvote the Soviets. "Within a democratic state," he wrote, "conflicts are decided by an actual or a potential count of votes. . . . But in a world of sovereign states conflicts are decided by power, actual or potential, for the ultimate arbiter is not an election but war."[37]

Still, the peace treaties with Italy, Rumania, Bulgaria, Hungary, and Finland effectively eliminated Eastern Europe and the Balkans from the main currents of the East-West conflict. Byrnes had scarcely touched the Soviet hegemony, but that no longer mattered. His argument that the treaties were the best available acknowledged the realities of a divided Europe and the limits it placed on American will. No one, not even Vandenberg, suggested that another secretary would have negotiated more effectively. The treaties, moreover, included guarantees of fundamental freedoms and human rights, permitting Byrnes and Truman to assure the American people that the United States had upheld the country's principles. "During the long debate on these treaties," the president boasted, "we have made it clear to all nations that the United States will not consent to settlements at the expense of principles we regard as vital to a just and enduring peace."[38] Unfortunately, Washington had gained no authority to enforce its principles.

* * *

Two trends, slowly destroying the illusion of one world, converged during the summer and autumn of 1946 to destroy the Grand Alliance. The first was the structuring of a bipolar world. Noting the early confrontations between Byrnes and Molotov in Paris, *U.S. News* declared on May 24: "A pronounced trend is developing toward two big blocs in the world." The United States had deserted totally the role of mediator between Britain and the U.S.S.R. and ventured fully into the arena of world politics as leader of the English-speaking bloc. For Britain, the acceptance of that leadership came as a willing if bittersweet retreat from its traditional status. The United States alone could protect Britain's historic interests and thereby preserve what remained of its historic role. The astute *London Observer* commented on October 27: "Our relations with America and Russia are not the same. Those with America, though our views and interests are far from identical, are easy and friendly. . . . The same cannot, unfortunately, be said of Russia." During the autumn of 1946, meetings of American and British military leaders became increasingly frequent, suggesting that the United States and the British Commonwealth would stand together should war reappear.[39] The Kremlin, conscious of the strengthening Anglo-American coalition it faced, tightened its stands in solitary defiance.

What underwrote the new bipolarism was the adoption by both the United States and the U.S.S.R. of an intensely antagonist diplomacy, reflecting the conviction of both that the other was its special adversary. Conflicting East-West issues across Europe and the Middle East demonstrated that not all international problems were amenable to negotiation and compromise. They did not deny the possibilities of coexistence or eventual arrangements on questions that mattered. Still, much of American officialdom had long become disillusioned with Soviet behavior and had begun to question the Kremlin's ultimate intentions.[40] The information that flowed into Washington during 1946 focused increasingly on the Soviet Union as a dangerous international phenomenon, not on the acceptability or unacceptability of its immediate objectives. For many officials and analysts, Soviet ruthlessness revealed qualities of nationhood that rendered the U.S.S.R. a danger to the entire postwar international order.

Already, in 1946, the always threatening misuse of Soviet military power was troubling enough. It was military power that kept occupied Europe in leash. That Soviet power rendered vulnerable the bordering regions of Turkey, Iran, and beyond. The vision of Soviet armies marching, largely unopposed, recalled the movement of Italian, German, and Japanese forces through Abyssinia, Austria, Czechoslovakia, and Manchuria that brought war to the world. Soviet aggression would be an equal disaster. Joseph and Stewart Alsop, writing in the May 20 issue of *Life*, defined the Soviet threat in Hitlerian terms:

Already Poland, the Baltic States, Rumania, Bulgaria, Yugoslavia and Albania are behind the Iron Curtain. Huge armies hold Hungary and half of Germany and Austria. Czechoslovakia and Greece are encircled. . . . In the Middle East the Soviets are driving southward. Iran is in danger of being reduced to puppethood; Turkey and Iraq are threatened. Finally, in the Far East, the Kuriles and half of Korea are occupied and Manchuria has been stripped and left in condition to be transformed at will into another Azerbaijan. The process still goes on. One . . . must also wonder whether they will ultimately be satisfied with less than dominion over Europe and Asia.[41]

Iran remained a disturbing issue because the Azerbaijani settlement in April did not free that country from Soviet influence. In July, widespread rioting, led by the Communist-controlled Tudeh Party, threatened the oil region of southwest Iran, dominated by the Anglo-Iranian Oil Company. To end the violence, Prime Minister Qavam appointed three Tudeh members to his cabinet. Responding to Teheran's internal troubles, the Joint Chiefs, on October 12, declared that American military strategy required Iranian oil and bases from which to launch strikes against the U.S.S.R. in case of war. To underwrite those U.S. strategic requirements, the State Department offered loans and weapons to the Iranian government.[42] With strong U.S. support, Qavam settled a tribal revolt in the south and drove the Tudeh leaders from the cabinet. Then in November, the Iranian government dispatched the Imperial Army into northern Iran to regain control of the entire country. The American program of containment through arms sales and strong interference in Iranian politics had triumphed.[43]

In August 1946, the Soviets reignited the Turkish issue by massing forces along the border and addressing notes to Turkey, the United States, and Britain demanding a new Straits settlement. Reminded by the Joint Chiefs of Turkey's strategic importance, the administration responded to the Soviet note by dispatching a large naval vessel to the eastern Mediterranean. Acting Secretary of State Acheson and the Chiefs of Staff, with the advice of State Department experts, prepared a memorandum on Turkey that they presented to the president on August 15. This memorandum, signed by Acheson, Forrestal, and Secretary of War Robert Patterson, warned:

If the Soviet Union succeeds in its objective of obtaining control over Turkey, it will be extremely difficult, if not impossible, to prevent the Soviet Union from obtaining control over Greece and over the whole Near and Middle East . . . [including] the territory lying between the Mediterranean and India. When the Soviet Union has once obtained full mastery of this territory . . . it will be in a much stronger position to obtain its objectives in India and China.[44]

Only the threat of force, the three signers agreed, would preserve Middle Eastern peace against Soviet aggression. If the U.S.S.R. was bent on world conquest, the president added, the United States might as well fight in 1946 as later. Recognizing Turkey's strategic importance, he accepted the recommended course of action.[45] Acheson handed the Soviet chargé d'affaires in Washington a note that accepted three of the five Soviet requests, including a revision of the Montreux Convention but not bilateral control of the Straits. In September, the Soviets circulated another round of notes; again the Turks rejected any infringements on their control of the Straits. The Soviet now dropped their demands for a stronger role in Turkey—and the crisis passed.[46]

Greece, like Turkey, had become an American concern. The promised elections had conveyed a mandate to an essentially right-wing government; a plebiscite restored the British-backed monarchy. By the autumn of 1946, antigovernment forces, under Communist leadership, had reopened the civil war. This assault on Greece's faltering government continued with aid from Albania and Yugoslavia, but hardly from Bulgaria or the U.S.S.R. To Washington, however, the Kremlin underwrote the insurgency to guarantee a regime in Athens ultimately subservient to Soviet control. Acheson recognized Britain's primary responsibility in the region, but early in October he requested Henderson to examine U.S. strategic interests in Greece. Henderson responded on October 21, "Greece and Turkey form the sole obstacle to Soviet domination of the Eastern Mediterranean which is an economic and strategic area of vital importance. . . . We cannot afford to stand idly by in the face of maneuvers and machinations which evidence an intention on the part of the Soviet Union to expand its power."[47]

By November, the Greek economy was disintegrating so rapidly and the guerrilla forces becoming so threatening that Acheson moved to supplement the British role with an American aid program for Greece.[48] What remained uncertain was the occasion when Washington would assume responsibility for saving the Greek government from its Communist enemies.

* * *

However grave the Soviet military threat to the Middle East, it paled in contrast to the perceived dangers of Soviet ideological expansionism, a threat that embraced the entire world. What rendered the Kremlin uniquely dangerous was its alleged command of all Communist movements. Such powers to control the behavior of other states over vast spaces, without the necessity of military conquest, had no precedent in history. As early as January 1946, James Forrestal wondered whether Lippmann, in his moderation, was assuming that Communism and democracy could coexist satisfactorily. "[T]o me," he wrote, "the fundamental question in respect to our relations with Russia is whether we are dealing with a nation or a religion." Taking his cue from Kennan's long telegram, Matthews observed in April that, to the Kremlin, "the Soviet and non-Soviet systems cannot exist in this world side by side. This basic belief amounts to a religion to the true Communist and its implications make it impossible to visualize real peace in the world."[49]

John Foster Dulles added his own analysis of the Soviet danger in a long article that appeared in *Life* magazine, June 1946. Dulles asserted that Soviet foreign policy was "worldwide in scope. Its goal is to have governments everywhere which accept the basic doctrine of the Soviet Communist Party. . . . Thereby the Soviet Union would achieve worldwide hegemony—a *Pax Sovietica*." William C. Bullitt, in *The Great Globe Itself* (1946), again described the illimitable aims of Soviet ideology: "As conquest of the earth for Communism is the objective of the Soviet Government, no nation lies outside the scope of its ambitions." The Kremlin, pursuing world domination, would turn any agreement to its advantage.[50] For such observers, the reach of Soviet ideological conquest was apparently without limit.

In mid-July, Truman instructed Clark Clifford, White House counsel, and George Elsey, Clifford's assistant, to prepare an appraisal of the state of U.S.-Soviet relations. The Clifford-Elsey report, submitted in September, reflected the convictions of Washington insiders. The report opened with an ominous portrait of the Soviet challenge:

The fundamental tenet of the communist philosophy embraced by Soviet leaders is that the peaceful coexistence of communist and capitalist nations is impossible. The defenders of the communist faith, as the present Soviet rulers regard themselves, assume that conflict between the Soviet Union and the leading capitalist powers of the western world is inevitable and the party leaders believe that it is their duty to prepare the Soviet Union for the inevitable conflict which their doctrine predicts.

Clifford and Elsey, quoting Kennan's long telegram, argued that Soviet paranoia and global ambition eliminated any possibility of moderating the Kremlin's implacable animosity toward the Western world. "The key to an understanding of current Soviet foreign policy," the authors explained, "is the realization that Soviet leaders adhere to the Marxian theory of ultimate destruction of capitalist states by communist states."

For Clifford and Elsey, the global Soviet threat did not rest on the expansive power of ideology alone. They accused the Kremlin of developing atomic and biological weapons, guided missiles, strategic air power, and submarines to extend "the effective range of Soviet military power well into areas which the United States regards vital to its security." The report recommended that the United States rebuild its military capabilities and "be prepared to wage atomic and biological warfare." So frightening was the Clifford-Elsey case against the Soviet Union that Truman impounded all copies of their report.[51] Such growing fears and distrust of Soviet power eliminated what remained of the Grand Alliance and the chances of its revival.

For many U.S. officials, the Soviet-American conflict had transcended the quest for agreement to become one of the great confrontations of history, reminiscent of the deadly struggles between Rome and

Carthage, Europe and the Moslems, Napoleon and Europe, Hitler and the world. For such momentous contests, driven by the pursuit of absolute dominion, the solution lay not in diplomacy, but in victory or defeat. Still, as a purely military threat, the Soviet Union, confronting the combined and determined resistance of the entire external world, was scarcely commensurate with those of Napoleon or Hitler. The Soviet Union seemed reluctant to confront the West militarily even along its Iranian and Turkish borders where its strategic advantage was profound. Indeed, American officials seldom defined the Soviet danger in specific, military terms. It was Soviet ideological expansionism, transcending the limited possibilities and high costs of military adventurism, which defined the core threat to Western civilization. For this transcendent ideological danger there was no answer except in the determination of people everywhere to resist unpromising Communist solutions to their economic and societal disabilities. But even where they succumbed, there was no commanding Soviet presence. Without external military support, always elusive, Communist struggles for power, invariably indigenous, would succeed or fail on their own. Their danger to global security would always fall well below the threshold of an American military response.

CHAPTER 5

The Stabilization of Europe

Britain's decision to relinquish its historic role in the eastern Mediterranean assigned the chief burden of European stabilization to the United States. The process began when London, on February 21, 1947, informed Washington of its impending retrenchment in Greece, demanded by a collapsing British economy. In December 1946, the British government, in conformity with its loan agreement, permitted the pound to become freely convertible. The rapid flight of dollars and gold quickly destabilized the British economy, forcing the country to freeze its dollar assets, restrict its imports, institute an austerity program, and reduce its overseas commitments—including the termination of all financial assistance to Greece on March 31. U.S. officials, led by Under Secretary Dean Acheson, were primed for the crisis. By late February, President Truman had accepted the judgment of senior State Department officials, backed by the secretaries of State, War, and Navy, that the United States must assume Britain's traditional commitment to Greece.[1]

Turkey seemed no less vulnerable than Greece to Communist encroachment. That country faced neither civil war nor Kremlin pressure, but it bordered Soviet territory and was a region of unquestioned strategic importance. Turkey's transportation routes linked the Black Sea to the eastern Mediterranean; under Soviet control they would deny the West access to Middle Eastern airfields and military bases. Chief of Staff Dwight D. Eisenhower, no less than other members of the Joint Chiefs of Staff and top officials of the State Department, recognized Turkey's role in Western strategic planning. When officials of the State, War, and Navy departments gathered on February 28 to design an aid program for the president's presentation to the nation, they included Turkey.[2]

Troubled by the unknown in the Soviet Union's presumed expansionism, Loy Henderson, chairman of the State Department's Special Committee on Greece and Turkey, advocated an American strategy to confront Soviet expansionism everywhere. Acheson quickly embellished the theme, averring that the Kremlin threatened individual liberty and democracy throughout the world; aid to Greece and Turkey, he said, was "a matter of protecting our whole way of life." The emerging consensus embraced the proposition that the United States sought "a world in which nations shall be able to work out their own way of life free of coercion by other nations." To that end, the draft concluded, "[I]t must be the policy of the United States to support free peoples who are resisting attempted subjugation by armed minorities or by outside pressures." These passages, qualifying any country for U.S. assistance that could claim the presence of a Communist threat, entered the president's speech verbatim.[3] Such expansive obligations rested essentially on the burgeoning policy-related belief system that exaggerated the dangers embodied in the Soviet-American competition.[4]

To prepare the country to meet its expanding perils, Truman, General George C. Marshall, secretary of state since January, and Acheson conferred with congressional leaders on February 27. Marshall opened with the warning: "It is not alarmist to say that we are faced with the first of a series [of events] which might extend Soviet domination to Europe, the Middle East and Asia."[5] When Marshall's dire warning failed to move his listeners, Acheson asked permission to speak. He informed the congressmen that "not since the period of Athens and Sparta and of Rome and Carthage has there been such a polarization of power." Again a democracy faced "a police state exerting rigid control over the individual." Acheson warned that "a highly possible Soviet breakthrough might open three continents to Soviet penetration. Like apples in a barrel infected by a rotten one, the corruption of Greece would infect Iran and all to the east . . . Africa . . . Asia Minor and Egypt . . . Italy and France."[6] Senator Vandenberg assured the president that if he, using similar language, informed Congress of the implications of a Communist victory in Greece, he would have its support. The State Department's Will Clayton, under secretary for economic affairs, repeated Acheson's warnings in a memorandum of March 5, "If Greece and then Turkey succumb, the whole Middle East will be lost. France may then capitulate to the communists. As France goes, so Western Europe and North Africa will go."[7] Meanwhile the Greek government formally requested financial and military assistance from the United States.

With no evidence of Soviet designs on Greece, Truman, on March 12, presented his case to Congress and the nation:

It is necessary only to glance at a map to realize that the survival and integrity of the Greek nation are of grave importance in a much wider situation. If Greece should fall under the control of an armed minority, the effect upon its neighbor, Turkey, would be immediate and serious. Confusion and disorder might well spread throughout the entire Middle East. Moreover, the disappearance of Greece as an independent state would have a profound effect upon those countries in Europe whose peoples are struggling against great difficulties to maintain their freedom and their independence while they repair the damage of war.[8]

This widely repeated rationale for the defense of Greece and Turkey established the Munich syndrome as the guiding principle in meeting the Soviet challenge. Greece and Turkey had become symbols of the *status quo*; their fall, like that of Austria, the Sudetenland, and

Figure 5.1
Truman's March 12, 1947, speech announcing the "Truman Doctrine" (Courtesy: Harry S. Truman Library)

Czechoslovakia after 1938, would "undermine the foundations of international peace and hence the security of the United States." To meet the immediate threat the president asked Congress to appropriate $400 million in aid to Greece and Turkey and to authorize the dispatch of American personnel and equipment to the two endangered countries. Fundamentally, the Truman Doctrine sought to introduce U.S. power into the European theater to replace Britain as the key defender of Europe and the eastern Mediterranean.[9]

* * *

Acheson understood that Congress and the public responded to symbols, not facts. To legitimize the policy for Greece and Turkey, he believed it essential that the administration create an image of danger compatible with the recommended action. Nothing less would create the required national, cohesive anti-Soviet foreign policy elite. When Marshall objected to the "flamboyant anticommunism" in the president's speech, the State Department informed him that only an exaggeration of the Communist danger would compel the Senate to approve the new Truman Doctrine.[10] Vandenberg accepted the administration's prescription uncritically. He warned in a letter of March 12, "Greece must be helped or Greece sinks permanently into the communist order. Turkey inevitably follows. Then comes the chain reaction which might sweep from the Dardanelles to the China Sea.... I can only say that I think [our new American policy] ... is worth trying as an alternative to another 'Munich' and perhaps another war."[11] Senator Walter George of Georgia, after a briefing from the American ambassador to Turkey, declared that the aid bill was essential to stop Soviet expansion. "If unchecked," he said, "Russia will inevitably overrun Europe, extend herself into Asia and perhaps South America.... [T]his process may go on for a full century."[12] For countless Americans the domino theory became a self-evident truth. Yet the concept had no precedent in history. Aggression had always relied on instruments of force, but official dangers included no reference to Soviet armies, poised to enter Western Europe, Africa, or the Middle East. The threats remained rhetorical.

Whatever their level of accuracy, the unfolding perceptions of danger inaugurated a profound reorientation in the official American outlook. William Leahy observed that the Truman program comprised "a complete reversal of a traditional American policy to avoid involvement in the political difficulties of European states." Those engaged in the program for Greece and Turkey recalled the decisions with feelings of exhilaration, produced not only by the program's perceived necessity but also by the speed, enthusiasm, and unanimity with which they framed it. Acheson, Forrestal, and Clayton, no less than the State Department's top hierarchy, believed what they said and wrote, accepting the obligation to educate the public. Truman deserted the doubts that led him to bury the Clifford report of September 1946. In November he informed C. L. Sulzberger of the *New York Times* privately that "if Russia gets Greece and Turkey, then they would get Italy and France and the iron curtain would extend all the way to Western Ireland."[13] Truman's conversion was complete.

Never before had U.S. officials described external dangers in such varied and imprecise terms. The Truman Doctrine did not set forth a comprehensive definition of Soviet policy; rather it rationalized a program of containment without defining concretely what the country was committed to defend. Every national spokesman, free to offer his own version of the Soviet threat, invariably extended it far beyond Greece and Turkey. Kennan agreed that the perpetuation of the European balance of power was essential, but objected to the Truman Doctrine's open-ended promise to aid free peoples everywhere. He wondered why the president included Turkey in the program when that country was under no Communist threat. Others argued that the U.S.S.R. had every right to demand a revision of the Montreux agreement with Turkey.[14] Walter Lippmann favored a policy to keep Greece and Turkey out of the Soviet orbit, but he, like Kennan, objected to the Truman Doctrine's pledge to rescue any government that proclaimed itself a potential victim of Communist aggression. He accused the administration of launching a crusade, explaining that "a policy, as distinguished from a crusade, may be said to have definite aims, which can be stated concretely, and achieved if the estimate of the situation is correct. A crusade, on the other hand, ... has no limits because there is no concrete program."[15]

Acheson carried the administration's case before Congress during the hearings on the aid program. He predicted that the fall of Turkey would expose Iran to Soviet encroachments. Then he continued, "Iran borders on Afghanistan and India. ... India carries us on to Burma and Indonesia, and Malaya, areas in French Indochina ... and that carries you to China. ... And what we are trying to point out is that a failure in these key countries would echo throughout that vast territory." Such top Washington officials as George McGhee, Clark Clifford, Loy Henderson, and Dean Rusk defended the Truman program as a necessary measure to confront, in Rusk's words, "the phenomenon of aggression—an insatiable political doctrine backed by force ... insatiable because there were no world boundaries." One official warned that a Communist triumph in Greece would create instability, perhaps even war, throughout the entire Near and Middle East.[16]

Before March 1947, such official fears of the U.S.S.R. had, in large measure, remained confidential. Truman's speech provided the occasion for conveying those fears to the public; Clark Clifford termed it "the opening gun in a campaign to bring people up to [the] realization that the war isn't over by any means." Yet Acheson, under questioning, assured the Senate Foreign Relations Committee that aid for Greece and Turkey in no way set a precedent for subsequent policy. Future decisions would rest on the need and possible effectiveness of the aid program.[17]

Vandenberg opened the Senate debate with a ringing endorsement of the Truman program as "a plan to forestall aggression which, once rolling, could snowball into global danger of vast designs." Tom Connally, ranking Democrat on the Foreign Relations Committee, added that the Soviet Union's "mad march toward world domination must be arrested." James O. Eastland of Mississippi declared that the Soviet threat to the Middle East posed the greatest threat to Christian civilization since Genghis Khan was stopped in Poland.[18] Truman's opponents, Republican and Democratic, adhered to the isolationist doctrine that the United States should not waste its resources and energies in futile, unnecessary foreign involvements. No nation, declared Senator Kenneth McKellar of Tennessee, could challenge the United States in the Western Hemisphere. Senator Lee O'Daniel of Texas opposed taxes to underwrite a foreign dole; bankrupting the United States, he charged, would do little for the world. Four hundred million, O'Daniel predicted, would become four hundred billion. Recalling the isolationist warning of prewar days, Senator James P. Kem of Montana complained: "The American people are being asked to supply the venture capital now, and the manpower later, where and as required." Some Senators professed amazement that the administration would seek peace outside the United Nations.[19] Claude Pepper of Florida, reflecting the views of Henry Wallace, now editor of the *New Republic*, denounced the administration for exaggerating the Soviet danger:

In an honest but misguided zeal to strike out against what they call communism, as one does against horrible shapes and forms which accost one in a nightmare, they would sabotage the United Nations, destroy any hope of reconciliation with Russia, launch the United States upon an unprecedented policy of intervention in remote nations and areas of the world unilaterally, ally us with the reactionary and corrupt regimes of the world, subject this nation to the serious accusation of aspiring to become the new Rome or the old Britain, and ask for the American people a war which may destroy civilization.[20]

The predictions of disaster from Communist expansion overrode the still-powerful isolationist sentiment in Congress. In May, the Senate approved the aid bill, 67 to 23; the House, 287 to 107. A large majority of Republicans supported the measure in both houses.

* * *

Western Europe appeared safe from Soviet armed attack but not from Communist subversion. For U.S. officials the French Communist Party (PCF) had long posed a special danger. Charles de Gaulle's resignation, in January 1946, consigned the French government to a coalition of Communists, Socialists, and members of the Mouvement Republicain Populaire. Although the Communists held only six of nineteen seats in the cabinet, Britain's Ernest Bevin warned of "the imminent Sovietization of France and the extension of Russian power to the channel." Despite French Communist cooperation in France's reconstruction, U.S. Ambassador Jefferson Caffery proclaimed them agents of the Soviet Union.[21] Washington opposed the Communist presence in the French government, but hesitated to curtail financial assistance, fearful that French Communists would exploit the decision.[22] The Communists did well in the 1946 fall elections, prompting Leon Blum's faltering government to resign in January 1947.

At this point France's vulnerability to perceived Soviet encroachments became ominous. The State Department's John Hickerson, in February, observed that the Kremlin could now bore from within through the French Communist party. Benjamin V. Cohen, counselor of the State Department, warned Marshall that if the French government fell, the Communists would deny France an independent foreign policy and perhaps terminate the entire program of European reconstruction. What aggravated Cohen's fears was the realization that the United States could do little to stall "the invisible penetration and eventual capture of a modern democratic state by a resolute and well organized minority." Caffery informed the State Department, on May 12, that a Communist victory in France would facilitate "Soviet penetration of Western Europe, Africa, the Mediterranean, and the Middle East."[23] The new prime minister, Paul Ramadier, was Washington's remaining hope.

State Department officials had long believed that Europe's economic recovery was no less essential than the defense of Greece and

Turkey for achieving regional stability. Washington understood that Western Europe was vital to the establishment of a stable equilibrium between the United States and the U.S.S.R. The United States had spent $9 billion for European relief without preventing a repetition of the disastrous winter of 1946–1947. On March 5, 1947, Acheson directed Assistant Secretary of State John Hilldring, chairman of the State-War-Navy Coordinating Committee (SWNCC), to study conditions in Europe that might require U.S. financial and military support.[24] Its Ad Hoc Committee completed its report on April 21. The preamble defined the European security interests of the United States: the maintenance in friendly hands of all continental areas rendered strategically important by vital resources, substantial industrial potential, manpower and effective military forces, "or which for political or psychological reasons enable the U.S. to exert a greater influence for world stability, security, and peace." The report concluded that the United States alone was "capable of tiding Europe and other deficient areas over the period of reconstruction." Because of the dollar drain the world would be able to buy American exports for only 12–18 months. The report concluded by noting the relationship between international stability and national security:

The United States has need of friends in the world today and particularly needs to take care that other nations do not pass under the influence of any potentially hostile nation. . . . [I]t is to our advantage to strengthen their resolution to remain independent. . . . Broad purpose of U.S. aid is to support economic stability, orderly political process, oppose the spread of chaos and extremism, prevent spread of communist influence, [and] orient foreign nations toward the U.S.[25]

European recovery required above all a powerful German economy. But the United States could pursue an aid program for Germany only under conditions acceptable to Germany's neighbors, especially France. Washington had attempted to allay European fears of a reconstituted Germany with the offer of a Four Power Pact to enforce German adherence to the Potsdam agreement on permanent demilitarization. Unfortunately, the Soviets had rejected that proposal.[26] Again at the Moscow Foreign Ministers Conference of March–April 1947, Molotov rejected the Four Power Pact. Nor did the meeting reach agreement on the central issues of German unification and industrialization, or the international control of the Saar and the Ruhr. In the absence of an earlier agreement on Germany's future, the British and American governments, in December 1946, had merged their zones economically and assigned increasing numbers of Germans to important administrative posts. At Moscow, Marshall and Bevin agreed privately to reorganize the British and American zones to make them more productive and self-sustaining. Both France and the U.S.S.R. opposed the bizonal policy because it eliminated their influence over Germany's economic revival. France wanted no agreement on German steel production until Britain and the United States guaranteed adequate coal deliveries. Marshall and Bevin made the necessary concessions to France on coal.[27] The Treaty of Dunkirk, signed on March 4, 1947, was Bevin's effort to reassure the new French government that the British-American bizonal policy for Germany would not infringe on French security.

Despite France's uncompromising demands on Germany, Marshall blamed Molotov for the lack of progress at Moscow in reaching a German settlement. The secretary's private meeting with Stalin on April 19 merely aggravated his frustration. Charles Bohlen, acting as interpreter, recalled, "Stalin's seeming indifference to what was happening in Germany made a deep impression on Marshall. He came to the conclusion that Stalin . . . saw that the best way to advance Soviet interests was to let matters drift."[28] Walter Bedell Smith, U.S. ambassador in Moscow, noted that the Moscow Conference "resulted in clarifying beyond any possibility of misinterpretation the Soviet attitude toward Germany and Austria, and this in turn resulted in unifying the policies of France, Britain and the United States." On his return trip to Washington, Marshall ordered General Clay to further integrate the British and American zones. On April 28, Marshall, addressing a national radio audience, placed responsibility for the Moscow Conference's failure to advance Germany's rehabilitation on the Soviets. "We cannot ignore the factor of time . . . ," he declared. "The patient is sinking while the doctors deliberate. . . . New issues arise daily. Whatever action is possible to meet these pressing problems must take place without delay."[29]

Marshall instructed George Kennan to organize the Policy Planning Staff (PPS) and prepare a careful study of the problem of European reconstruction.[30] When Acheson agreed to speak on May 8 to the Delta Council in Cleveland, Mississippi, Joseph M. Jones, head of the State Department's public relations office, suggested that he use the Ad Hoc Committee report of April 21. In his speech Acheson dwelled on Europe's damaged economy and the hardships of the previous winter. The continuing dollar drain from Europe to the United States, he warned, threatened the economic welfare of both continents. Acheson assigned to the American people the duty and privilege of using their resources to improve both Europe's economic conditions and their own national security. He clarified the nation's priorities: "Free people who are seeking to preserve their independence and democratic institutions and human freedoms against totalitarian pressures, either internal or external, will receive top priority for American reconstruction aid." Vandenberg cautioned Marshall and the president against planning new, ever-larger appropriations for foreign aid without consulting congressional leaders.[31]

On May 23, Kennan's Policy Planning Staff submitted its recommendations. The report reaffirmed Europe's economic crisis, especially the shortages of coal. It introduced the principle that Europeans should take the initiative in determining their needs. The United States, the report added, should offer aid to all Europeans so that, if the Soviets refused to cooperate, the responsibility for a divided Europe would fall on them.[32] On May 19, Clayton returned from an inspection of the European economy. A Texas millionaire who had built his fortune on cotton trading, Clayton believed fervently in "the recuperative and peace-producing potentialities of international trade." After attending several European economic conferences, he concluded that Europe's immediate problem was France's growing desperation. In Geneva, French leader Jean Monnet complained that the United States had failed to deliver promised grain to France. "The present situation is so critical," Clayton informed Marshall on April 23, "[that] grave social, economic, and political consequences ... will almost certainly flow from our failure to provide this aid to France."[33] On May 27, Clayton presented to Acheson a memorandum covering his foreign observations. "Europe is steadily deteriorating ... ," he wrote. "One political crisis after another merely denotes the existence of grave economic distress." Such conditions, he continued, carried awful implications for the world's future peace and security. The collapse of Europe's buying power, he predicted, would affect drastically "our domestic economy: market for our surplus production gone, unemployment, depression."[34]

* * *

On the morning of May 28, the senior officials of the State Department gathered in Marshall's office to consider a massive aid program for European reconstruction. Present were Marshall, Acheson, Clayton, Kennan, Cohen, Bohlen, and Dean Rusk, assistant secretary for UN Affairs. No longer, declared Marshall, could the government sit back and do nothing. Three documents set the course of the discussion: The SWNCC report of April 21, the PPS report of May 23, and

Clayton's memorandum of May 27. Clayton pointed to the dollar drain and Europe's threatening incapacity to purchase American goods. He advocated U.S. expenditures of $6–$7 billion a year for three years for European reconstruction, as well as the reduction of all barriers to Europe's economic cooperation. Clayton hoped that the countries of Eastern Europe would abandon their economic ties to the U.S.S.R. and participate in an American plan. Kennan and Bohlen argued for European initiative in designing the recovery program. Acheson suggested that Marshall, within two or three weeks, make a speech, not to offer a solution, but to present the problem. Marshall instructed Bohlen to prepare the address.[35]

Marshall delivered his brief, undramatic speech to the Harvard alumni after the university's commencement exercises on June 5. The Marshall Plan, as the secretary's proposals came to be known, offered no blueprint for action. Marshall acknowledged Europe's economic chaos and its need for help. Leaving behind all ideological implications, he followed the outline prepared by the Policy Planning Staff. "Our policy," he declared, "is directed not against country or doctrine, but against hunger, poverty, desperation, and chaos. Its purpose shall be the revival of a working economy in the world so as to permit the emergence of political and social conditions in which free institutions can exist." Marshall took up Kennan's theme of European responsibility: "The initiative, I think, must come from Europe. The role of this country should consist of friendly aid in the drafting of a European program and of later support of such a program so far as it may be practical for us to do so." The secretary appealed to the American people to accept the responsibility that history had placed upon them. Then came his ringing conclusion: "We are too remote from all these countries to grasp at all the real significance of the situation. . . . [Y]et the whole world's future hangs on a proper judgment, hangs on the realization by the American people of what can best be done, of what must be done."[36]

Bevin lauded the speech and immediately asked French Foreign Minister Georges Bidault to join him in calling a conference to outline a constructive program for Europe. Molotov accepted their invitation to meet them in Paris on June 27.[37] The large number of advisers who accompanied Molotov suggested that the Soviets were serious. From the outset, however, it was doubtful that the U.S.S.R. would join a program dictated and financed by the United States. Many in Washington feared the loss of congressional support if the Soviets agreed to participate, yet believed that the Soviets alone should make the choice.

One U.S. provision seemed to assure an ultimate Soviet rejection of the Marshall Plan: the requirement that the European states coordinate their plans for economic reconstruction and submit their joint calculations to the United States. At the second meeting in Paris, Molotov accepted collaboration in principle, but only to the extent that each country would make its needs known to Washington directly. The Soviets had no interest in furnishing economic data to the other European countries. Molotov insisted, moreover, that former enemy states, including Germany, should be barred from the program. The third meeting, on June 30, was even more divisive. Western observers suspected that Moscow was planning to sabotage the Marshall Plan. The fifth session was Molotov's last. He accused the United States of attempting to dominate Europe and penetrate the Soviet sphere by insisting that future economic decisions serve the interest of all-European recovery, including that of Germany, to the detriment of the Soviet bloc.[38]

Ten days after Molotov's departure, on July 12, the 16-nation European Reconstruction Conference opened in Paris. Eight Iron Curtain countries surrendered to Soviet pressure and refused to attend. The hope for an all-European federation was now dead. What remained was the task of building Western Europe into a powerful economic bloc. Ambassador Lewis Douglas, in London, informed Bevin that the United States would negotiate no economic agreements with Britain apart from the Marshall program. For Washington, Germany's role in Europe's recovery was still the central issue. U.S. officials assumed that the Marshall Plan, in assisting all Western European countries to rebuild their economies, would make Germany's reconstruction acceptable to France and other wartime victims. During July, U.S. and British officials agreed on a program of increased steel production and reduced coal exports to make their zones self-supporting. Matthews expressed the State Department's concern that French opinion would prove troublesome if France failed to derive compensating advantage from the reorganization of the German economy.[39]

French leaders rejected the Anglo-American proposal. Bidault warned Clayton that any pressure on France to accept policies that gave priority to German industrial production would reopen the gates to the French Communists. French leaders opposed any agreement on the Ruhr that denied France total access. Bidault warned American officials that if the United States and Britain refused to accommodate France, there would be no Marshall Plan. Confronted by the near-panic in the French government and Bidault's threat to resign, the

State Department, with Bevin's approval, promised to postpone any bizonal level-of-industry decision until the French could present their views for full consideration. Jean Monnet emerged as France's chief spokesman for a program on coal and steel that would protect French interests.[40] Meanwhile, the 16-nation conference in Paris prepared national estimates and goals without interference from Washington. The final conference report of September 22 pledged the participants to mutual cooperation on increased production, currency stabilization, and the free movement of goods. The conference set targets for agricultural, coal, steel, and electrical production, but failed to resolve the German level-of-industry controversy.[41]

Moscow responded to the Western acceptance of the Marshall Plan and the creation of a Western European economic bloc by perfecting the Stalinization of Eastern Europe. The political and economic subjugation of the region had advanced throughout the occupation, but only after July 1947 did the Kremlin convert the countries under Soviet control into a Communist monolith. The Kremlin now eliminated non-Communist leadership where it existed and terminated all coalition governments, eliminating those who resisted with show trials and executions. No longer could the countries of Eastern Europe have relations among themselves without Kremlin approval. To tighten its grip on Eastern Europe, the Kremlin, in September, established the Communist Information Bureau, or Cominform, with headquarters in Belgrade, to coordinate the policies of the Soviet Union, Poland, Hungary, Rumania, Bulgaria, Albania, Czechoslovakia, and Yugoslavia. The Cominform's small staff produced a semimonthly newspaper; there was no administrative apparatus.[42] This final emergence of a consolidated Communist bloc reinforced the impenetrability of the Iron Curtain.

* * *

Amid the launching of the Marshall Plan, in July 1947, Congress passed the National Security Act. This massive reorganization of the nation's defense establishment resulted less from any immediate sense of crisis than from long, accumulating organizational problems that reflected the country's changing world role. The act established the National Security Council (NSC) to advise the president on questions of national defense, and a new National Military Establishment, headed by a Secretary of Defense, to supervise the military departments, including an independent Department of Air Force. The NSC carried the special obligation to integrate foreign and defense policy, reconcile military expenditures with domestic needs, and balance domestic capabilities with foreign commitments. The act established as well the National Security Resources Board, the Central Intelligence Agency (CIA), and the Joint Chiefs of Staff.

The CIA, presumed essential but operating secretly, received huge, but concealed, appropriations. Not even the General Accounting Office dared question its performance or expenditures. The CIA's power to operate covertly would protect many of its lapses and misjudgments from public scrutiny. That secrecy would veil its successes even more effectively, raising endless doubts that the agency was worth the cost. The National Security Act was designed to strengthen civilian control of the military, but the elaborate defense structure failed to eliminate the inter-service rivalries that, in large measure, had prompted the reorganization. The secretaries of War, Navy, and Air Force had cabinet stature and thus could carry their specific demands directly to the president. Truman appointed James V. Forrestal to the new position of Secretary of Defense; thereafter he revealed little interest in the NSC and seldom attended its meetings.[43]

Whatever their disagreements over the design of U.S. policy toward Europe, American officials, by mid-1947, shared notions regarding the world that were remarkably similar. These reflected the conviction that the U.S.S.R. carried the major responsibility for Europe's division, that the dangers posed by the Kremlin rendered the expanding containment policies both necessary and feasible, and that Soviet weakness assured the final triumph of the whole containment enterprise. George Kennan crystallized these three fundamental assumptions in his noted essay, signed "X," which appeared in the July 1947 issue of *Foreign Affairs*.[44] What rendered the Soviet Union dangerous and impenetrable, Kennan began, was its inherent insecurities. Representing only a small minority at home and facing powerful enemies abroad, Kremlin leaders sustained their authority by warring on all competing power, both internal and external. Internally, the proclaimed dangers of "capitalist encirclement" reflected the necessity of justifying totalitarian rule. Externally, Kremlin policies embodied "a cautious, persistent pressure toward the disruption and weakening of all rival influence and rival power." Soviet action abroad, wrote Kennan, moved forward in a fluid stream, but if it found "unassailable barriers" in its path, it would accommodate itself to them.

Kennan, secondly, advocated the containment of the Kremlin's expansionist tendencies through the "adroit and vigilant application of counterforce at a series of constantly shifting geographical and political points, corresponding to the shifts and maneuvers of Soviet policy." Containment would triumph, Kennan predicted finally, because "Soviet power, like the capitalist world of its conception, bears within it the seeds of its own decay." In time, Kennan concluded, containment would erode the whole Soviet structure, changing Soviet Russia overnight "from one of the strongest to one of the weakest and most pitiable of national societies."[45] However grave the danger, its demise seemed assured without war or even major risks or conflict.

Walter Lippmann, in a succession of 14 daily columns published in the New York *Herald-Tribune* during September 1947, characterized Kennan's "X" analysis of the Soviet danger as irrational and ideology-driven.[46] Kennan, he charged, distorted Soviet policy by failing to relate it to historic Russian ambitions. The Soviets were in Eastern Europe, he wrote, not because of Communist dogma or national paranoia, but because Hitler's defeat offered them the opportunity to be there. Whatever the Kremlin's ambitions outside Eastern Europe, Lippmann predicted, limited interests would compel it to stop wherever the West prevented further advance at reasonable cost.[47] Responding to a *Life* editorial which contended that the U.S.S.R. was working to bring about "the communization of the European continent," Lippmann assured publisher Henry R. Luce that Communism would achieve power in no Western country without the support of the Red Army. The Communist record in Europe had demonstrated that.[48]

To Lippmann, Kennan's program of containment was a "strategic monstrosity," doomed to failure. It challenged the U.S.S.R. not only along that country's remote periphery but also wherever arms, aid, or military missions established a Soviet presence. In seeking allies against Soviet-supported revolutionary movements, the United States would, of necessity, bind itself to corrupt, reactionary regimes with little popular support. Such an effort at containment, Lippmann warned, would require the United States to stake its policies:

upon satellites, puppets, clients, agents about whom we know very little. Frequently they will act . . . on their own judgments, presenting us with accomplished facts that we did not intend, and with crises for which we are unready. The "unassailable barriers" will present us with an unending series of insoluble dilemmas. We shall have either to disown our puppets, which would be tantamount to appeasement and defeat and loss of face, or must support them at an incalculable cost on an unintended, unforeseen and perhaps undesirable issue. . . . By forcing us to expend our energies and our substance upon these dubious and unnatural allies . . . , the effect of the policy is to neglect our natural allies in the Atlantic Community, and to alienate them.[49]

Lippmann regarded Europe the key to containment. There, he hoped, the United States and the Western powers, by reestablishing an effective balance of power, might reach a political settlement that reunified Germany and permitted the withdrawal of Soviet and Western forces from the regions of occupation. Successful diplomacy, Lippmann reminded Kennan, did not require intimate or cordial relations; it demanded the proposal of reasonable terms.[50]

* * *

At the London Foreign Ministers Conference of November–December 1947, the long effort to resolve the German question with a four-power settlement ground to a halt. The Soviets still demanded the formation of an independent, united Germany, giving them some influence over Germany's continuing evolution and access to additional reparations from the industrial production of the Ruhr. In pre-conference discussions, British and American diplomats agreed that they would reject any Soviet proposal that would challenge the Marshall Plan for Germany. That plan anticipated the full industrial development of its western zones, oriented toward the West, and contributing to the revitalization of Western Europe. For Marshall, nothing less than the anticipated restoration of the Western European economies would terminate the Soviet-American tug across Europe.[51] Kennan assured Marshall in early November that the Kremlin would accept an adverse decision on Germany, but would clamp down on Czechoslovakia as a dangerous salient in Moscow's tightening East European hegemony.[52] At London, Molotov revealed some flexibility on reparations, but such concessions no longer mattered; the Western powers were no longer interested in compromise. When the conference ended amid the usual recriminations, the Western powers were free to execute their plans for Germany without Soviet interference.[53] The conference disbanded on December 15 without setting a date or place for another meeting of the foreign ministers.

Before Marshall returned from London, President Truman, on December 19, submitted the European Recovery Program (ERP) to Congress. Continuing the long process of seeking the necessary congressional support, Truman emphasized the importance of Europe's economic recovery to Western civilization and the American way of life. "If Europe failed to recover," he said, "the peoples of these countries might be driven to a philosophy of despair. Such a turn of events would constitute a shattering blow to peace and stability in the world."[54] Despite the Marshall Plan's central purpose of furthering Europe's economic recovery, Washington officials dwelled as well on the issue of national security. Should Western Europe, including Germany, Forrestal declared, "be integrated with all its industrial and military potential . . . into a coalition of totalitarian states, it is possible that we in time would find ourselves isolated in a hostile world."[55] Similarly Vandenberg wondered what it would mean if the United States "should find itself substantially isolated in a communist world where the competition would force us into complete regimentation of ourselves beyond anything we have ever experienced."[56] Despite warnings that the United States would either rebuild Europe or face the Soviets alone, Congress refused to act.

For British leaders, the failure of the London Conference exposed Europe to ever-increasing dangers. On December 17, Bevin suggested to Marshall and Bidault the outlines of a new approach to European security. "We must devise," he said, "some democratic system comprising the Americans, ourselves, France, Italy, etc., and of course the Dominions. This would not be a formal alliance, but an understanding backed by power, money, and resolute action. It would be a sort of spiritual federation of the west." Kennan responded to Bevin's overture with unstinted enthusiasm; he insisted only that the union remain economic and political, not military. Marshall weighed the proposal briefly, but demurred when he realized that Bevin contemplated a defensive alliance that included the United States.[57] France remained sensitive to Germany's potential power and insisted that any defense system recognize the possibility of German aggression in accordance with the Anglo-French Treaty of Dunkirk. Only the Benelux countries welcomed Germany's membership in any Western European alignment. Despite such confusion on matters of European security, Bevin, with cabinet approval, raised the issue formally in a major speech before the House of Commons on January 22. "I believe," he told his audience, "the time is ripe for a consolidation of Western Europe." The United Kingdom, he declared, could no longer isolate its security from that of the continent.[58] Under Secretary Robert Lovett responded to Bevin's appeal with an assurance that the United States would support Britain and the Europeans if they revealed any firm determination to act together in their defense. Vandenberg and Marshall approved the burgeoning movement for European security, while Britain, France, and the Benelux countries entered into direct treaty negotiations.[59]

* * *

Suddenly in late February 1948 a Communist coup d'état in Czechoslovakia again threatened the Western position along the periphery of Soviet domination. After 1945, Czechoslovakia had held an anomalous position in European affairs. It was, like West Berlin, an area of free government behind the Iron Curtain. For some observers, including Kennan, the fall of the Czech government was expected, especially since the Communist Party commanded a large plurality in the national parliament. President Eduard Benes led the largest of the non-Communist parties, but the Czech premier and other members of the cabinet were Communists, including the minister of the interior who controlled the police. Non-Communist leaders threatened to break up the ruling coalition if Communists continued to dominate the police establishment. When the premier refused to comply with these demands, the non-Communist members of the government resigned. The Communist Party prevailed on the Social Democrats to join them in forming a new government. On March 10, the body of Foreign Minister Jan Masaryk was found outside his office window. Benes now capitulated to the Communist leader, Klement Gottwald, to complete the bloodless coup. Despite its democratic tradition, Czechoslovakia now became one of the most conformist of all the Soviet satellites in Eastern Europe.[60] Soviet control of Czech industries and lines of communication compensated the Kremlin in some measure for its potential losses to the Marshall Plan.[61]

So violent was the American reaction to Czechoslovakia's fall into the Soviet orbit that it created a war scare. Hitler, using similar tactics, had seized that nation 10 years earlier to inaugurate a general assault on the Versailles settlement. The *Chicago Tribune* observed in late February, "The American people can very well reflect that this is where they came in. It was 10 years ago this fall that the independence of Czechoslovakia was sacrificed at Munich." Harriman predicted trouble: "There are aggressive forces in the world coming from the Soviet Union which are just as destructive in their effect on the world and our own way of life as Hitler was."[62] If the Kremlin could so easily undermine the anti-Communist regime of Czechoslovakia, why not others? For State Department expert Hickerson the Soviets, employing fifth column activities, could topple other governments as readily as they did in Czechoslovakia. "There is no reason to expect," added the *New York Times* on February 26, "that Czechoslovakia will be the last target of Russo-Communist expansion." Truman reminded the nation that the Soviet Union and its agents had "destroyed the independence and democratic character of a whole series of nations in eastern and Central Europe." They now threatened to extend their ruthless course of action "to the remaining free nations of Europe."

In that growing crisis mood, Congress reconsidered the Marshall Plan and adopted it promptly with scant opposition. So enormous was the task of coordinating the demands of Marshall Plan administrators, the Treasury Department, and the Council of Economic Advisers that the president created the Economic Cooperation Administration (ECA) that brought together representatives of business and government. Truman chose Paul G. Hoffman, former president of Studebaker, to head the ECA, with Harriman as his assistant. Hoffman and Harriman characterized the public and private elements that formulated and executed the Marshall Plan. Historian Michael J. Hogan described and analyzed them in detail within the framework of "corporatism," a term that defined the cooperation between business leaders and government officials in the creation of national economic policies. Hogan found the origins of the Marshall Plan, as an extension of American organizational principles, in Herbert Hoover's design for business-government cooperation in the 1920s, as well as in the New Deal, itself the product of such cooperation. In the realm of external affairs, the corporative structure never embraced all interest groups in corporate America. Rather, it attracted the support largely of banking, investment, trading, and internationalist elements in American life. From such financial leaders and their lawyer allies, represented above all in the New York Council on Foreign Relations, came the business support and leadership in the creation and execution of the Marshall Plan and the Truman foreign policies generally.

With the fall of free Czechoslovakia went Europe's confident mood; for Bevin the Czech coup threatened the continent's future. A British cabinet paper declared that the "physical control of the whole World Island is what the Politburo is aiming at—no less a thing than that."[63] Bevin approached U.S. Ambassador Lewis Douglas, on February 25, for conversations, either in Washington or in Europe, aimed at the formation of an effective European security system. Douglas informed Washington that Bevin intended to involve the United States in a European alliance. Marshall informed the British ambassador that he was prepared to open conversations in Washington as soon as possible.[64] Meanwhile the British discussions with France and the Benelux countries culminated, on March 17, in the five-nation Brussels Pact.[65] The new alliance invited the support of the United States.

Washington was not prepared to commit the country to Europe's defense, especially in an election year. Still the Czech coup had weakened the old isolationist constraints against entangling alliances with Europe. Within days two competing groups emerged in Washington determined to establish a U.S. defense policy toward Europe. One group, led by the State Department's John Hickerson and Theodore Achilles, favored an Atlantic security pact that would include the Brussels Pact members as well as Canada, Italy, and the Scandinavian countries. Kennan's Policy Planning Staff, on March 23, presented a counter proposal that opposed membership in a Western Union, but held out the possibility for later association. Kennan advocated informal guarantees of armed support to the countries of Western Europe, but no alliance. Marshall, from the outset, preferred the Hickerson program, with its formal arrangements. To obtain congressional support, Under Secretary Robert Lovett took up the issue with Vandenberg. From the Lovett-Vandenberg conversations emerged the Vandenberg Resolution, adopted by the Senate on June 11, 64 to 4. That resolution, approved by Truman, established bipartisan support for American participation in a European system of collective defense.[66]

Accepting the views of the State Department, Vandenberg and Lovett anticipated the creation of a peacetime multilateral military obligation to Europe's defense unprecedented in American history. Again Kennan agreed to unilateral U.S. guarantees of Western European security, but a close partnership only with Canada. This proposal of two units, one in Europe and one in North America, ruled out close American association with the Brussels Union. Kennan doubted that the Soviet Union contemplated any use of force against Western Europe. Should it do so, and thereby threaten American security, the country could act in accordance with its own interests without any legal obligations. To avoid a decision that might appear aggressive to the Kremlin, Kennan argued that any Western military organization should be limited to the littoral countries of the North Atlantic, eliminating Germany, Italy, Greece, and Turkey. The absence of formal obligations would not prevent an Atlantic alliance, in the event of a Soviet threat, from acting in defense of countries bordering the Communist bloc. Kennan acknowledged, in his memoirs, that there was little that he could do to affect the course of events.[67] Behind the commanding movement for a formal Atlantic security pact was the critical conviction that an open U.S. commitment to Europe's defense would give Europeans a needed psychological lift and enhance their confidence in facing the future.[68]

Not until Truman's election in November 1948—and the reestablishment of Democratic control of both houses of Congress—was the administration free to embark on formal treaty negotiations. France, still fearing German as well as Soviet expansionism, demanded U.S. guarantees of automatic participation in any European war, whether the responsibility lay with Germany or the U.S.S.R. Washington refused to acknowledge any threat except that emanating from the Soviet Union. American negotiators reminded the French that the Western occupation of Germany assured France's security against another German aggression. Moreover, to cite Germany as a potential enemy would eliminate that country from eventual membership in any Western pact. At the end, the United States yielded to European, especially French, pressure for a far-reaching commitment to Europe's defense, but only against Soviet encroachment. That commitment reflected American insecurities and the concomitant need to join Western Europe in creating a new balance of power. It reflected as well the French threat that, without American security guarantees, there would be no French cooperation in the creation of a trizonal solution of the German problem.[69]

In April 1949, the five members of the Brussels Pact, along with the United States, Canada, Denmark, Iceland, Italy, Portugal, and Norway, signed the North Atlantic Treaty with appropriate ceremonies in Washington. Article 5 defined the primary responsibilities of the signatories:

The Parties agree that an armed attack against one or more of them in Europe or North America shall be considered an attack against them all; and consequently they agree that, if such an armed attack occurs, each of them, in exercise of the right of individual or collective self-defense recognized by Article 51 of the Charter of the United Nations, will assist the Party or Parties so attacked by taking forthwith, individually and in concert with the other Parties, such action as it deems necessary, including the use of armed force, to restore and maintain the security of the North Atlantic area.[70]

Acheson, who succeeded Marshall as secretary of state in January 1949, seized the burgeoning security policies of the administration and proceeded to mold them into one immovable defense against the U.S.S.R. What mattered to him was essentially the power and unity of the Atlantic community. If the Kremlin, he warned, ever succeeded in breaking up the Western coalition, it would have a free hand in dealing with all the countries of the world. In April, Acheson appeared before the Senate Foreign Relations Committee to defend the new Atlantic pact. NATO, he said, was a defensive alliance, designed primarily to fulfill the intentions of the UN Charter. He refused to dodge the issue of commitment. "If you ratify the Pact," he told the senators, "it cannot be said that there is no obligation to help, but the extent, the manner, and the timing is up to the honest judgment of the parties." After a vigorous, but one-sided debate, the Senate ratified the treaty in July, 82 to 13.[71]

* * *

Washington's inordinate determination, following the Truman Doctrine, to assume unprecedented commitments to European stability clouded the issue of military preparedness. Indeed, the perceived presence of Soviet expansionism in the creation of the Marshall Plan, and even the North Atlantic alliance, produced little examination of the levels of military preparedness required to defend U.S. as well as European security. The ubiquitous verbalization of Soviet ambitions, at times embracing immense regions of the world, created no real sense of military urgency at all. Rather, the exaggerated perceptions of danger that rationalized the Truman Doctrine, and the containment decisions that followed, confronted the military services with the admonition that they learn to survive with lower appropriations. This encouraged the service chiefs to concentrate less on an overarching design for the country's defense than on maximizing their share of the dwindling military budget.[72]

What underwrote the avoidance of precision in strategic planning was the increasing reliance of atomic weapons. President Truman revealed the military potential of the bomb when he reported to the nation on September 2, 1945, that it was "too dangerous to be loose in a lawless world." He announced that the United States and Britain would not reveal the secrets of the bomb until world leaders had created the means to control atomic power effectively. But at the Moscow Conference of December, Secretary of State James Byrnes was prepared to seek an agreement with the U.S.S.R. on the international control of atomic energy, convinced that the U.S. monopoly had become a source of controversy.[73] Before the end of the year, American, British, and Soviet officials agreed to assign the task of managing the future of atomic power to the United Nations. In January 1946, the General Assembly created the UN Atomic Energy Commission and charged it with the responsibility to design a satisfactory formula for atomic weapons control. Secretary Byrnes appointed Acheson and David E. Lilienthal, chairman of the Tennessee Valley Authority, to prepare the U.S. position. The Acheson-Lilienthal Report of March 28, 1946, proposed an International Atomic Development Authority to govern all phases of the development and use of atomic energy. Truman selected financier and longtime presidential adviser Bernard Baruch to present the American proposal to the UN Atomic Energy Commission. The Baruch Plan, unveiled in June, differed from the Acheson-Lilienthal Report by providing for sanctions, not subject to veto, as well as a program of on-site inspection—without which the United States would not destroy its weapons or reveal its secrets. Andrei Gromyko, representing the U.S.S.R., rejected the Baruch proposal and countered with a Soviet plan similar to that of Acheson and Lilienthal. Determined to have guarantees based on an intrusive inspection system, the administration rejected the Soviet formula.[74]

While members of the UN Atomic Energy Commission argued hopelessly over matters of inspection and control, Washington understood that the Soviets were pushing their own atomic program. In August 1947, the Policy Planning Staff concluded that the United States could better protect its security by creating its own atomic arsenal than by pursuing some elusive agreement on inspection. Whereas the Joint Strategic Plans Committee of the Joint Chiefs did not anticipate war in the immediate future, it agreed that the country, supported by Britain, required the power to confront the Soviet Union with superior force.[75] By mid-1948, the Joint Chiefs predicted that the United States, in the event of war, would use atomic weapons in counterforce operations against the U.S.S.R. In September, the NSC, after consultation with other Washington agencies, accepted the necessity of an atomic strategy. In May 1949 a joint Army-Navy-Air Force committee, headed by General H. R. Harmon, concluded that "the atomic bomb would be a major element of Allied military strength in any war with the U.S.S.R., and would constitute the only means of rapidly inflicting shock and serious damage to vital elements of the Soviet war-making capacity."[76]

For Acheson, the decision to place Western Europe under an atomic shield did not deny the need of an effective NATO military establishment. "The first line of defense is still in Europe," he told the nation in August 1949, "but our European allies today do not have the military capacity to hold the line. The shield behind which we marshaled our forces to strike decisive blows for the common cause no longer exists.... [T]he United States is open to attack on its own territory to a greater extent than ever before." Because Europe's vulnerability increased the danger of war, military assistance to the NATO countries, augmented by a major U.S. armament program, would strengthen international peace as well as American security. By October, Acheson had pushed an elaborate mutual aid program through Congress.

The Mutual Defense Assistance Act of 1949 authorized the president to furnish military assistance to members of NATO, but only to countries that had requested such aid prior to the effective date of the law. Before receiving military aid, any recipient nation had first to enter an agreement with the United States that embodied specific defense obligations. The *Washington Post* lauded the new program as "nothing more or less than an attempt to put more power behind peace and freedom than the Soviet Union can bring to the support of its aggressive ventures."[77]

* * *

Shortly after the failed London Foreign Ministers Conference, Western representatives reconvened in London to dispose of the German question. At issue was a trizonal fusion of the Western zones, leading to currency stabilization, a joint policy for the Ruhr, and, ultimately, the creation of a constitutional West German state. On March 7, 1948, France agreed, with security guarantees, to the program of converting the three Western zones into an independent West German republic. The London Conference on Germany, following detailed planning, issued a statement, on June 7, which authorized a Constitutional Assembly in Germany to prepare a constitution for a federal German government by September 1. The Ruhr would remain in Germany, but a six-nation International Authority would regulate its production of steel and coal. On June 17, the French National Assembly accepted this reversal of French policy toward Germany. On the following day the Western occupying powers announced a currency reform for their three zones.

Soviet leaders were resigned to the division of Germany, but not to the consolidation of the Western zones into a potentially powerful anti-Soviet state.[78] The Kremlin had given priority to reparations but intended to use its position in Berlin to exert some control over the West German economy, including the Ruhr. Soviet responses to the Western maneuvers were predictable. As early as March 6, the Kremlin objected to the London Conference and warned that it would not accept its decisions. Later in March, the Soviets inaugurated measures to restrict traffic between the Western sectors of Berlin and the Western zones of occupation. General Clay warned Washington that any retreat from Berlin would expose the West to Soviet blackmail until Communism would run rampant. "I believe that the future of democracy," he wrote, "requires us to stay." The continuing Soviet restrictions culminated, on June 24, 1948, with the suspension of rail traffic and, by August, a complete blockade of surface access routes into the Western sectors of Berlin. The Western powers, refusing to concede their treaty rights in the city, resorted to a massive airlift to supply the beleaguered population. For the isolated West Germans in Berlin, the airlift came as salvation. In subsequent negotiations Stalin recognized the Western right of access, but hoped to prevent the establishment of a West German government by making this the price for lifting the blockade. The expanding airlift, however, quickly undermined the Kremlin's bargaining power. During the early weeks of 1949, Washington anticipated the integration of western Germany into the European economy. Under the impetus of currency reform, the western zones required larger markets. Clay, meanwhile, remained impatient over the slow progress in establishing a West German government and ending the Allied occupation. Kennan, already troubled by Germany's lack of democratic institutions, opposed the London formula of June 7 because it eliminated any possible agreement with the Kremlin and assured the division of Germany.[79] Kennan still favored a united, neutralized Germany, convinced that a divided country would incite German nationalism and discourage a Soviet retreat from the heart of Europe. Unfortunately, what guaranteed a divided Germany was less the London program than the profound economic, political, and social contrasts between the Soviet and Western zones.[80] State Department officials feared that an independent, neutral Germany might seek concessions from both blocs and regain a preponderant position in European life. The acquisition of markets and raw materials in the East, moreover, might lead Germany into the Soviet bloc. For Western leaders such strategic risks were unacceptable. The official American commitment to the London formula remained firm. The administration rejected the Policy Planning Staff's Plan A that advocated a four-power arrangement for the creation of a unified, demilitarized Germany.[81]

In January 1949, Stalin announced that he would lift the blockade in exchange for a suspension of the Western program for a West German state. But, in May, he lifted the blockade without any resolution of the German question. Western leaders now agreed to present the London program for Germany as a *fait accompli* at the forthcoming Paris Foreign Ministers Conference. At Paris the Western foreign ministers, overriding all Soviet objections, announced their acceptance of the London accords and proceeded to establish the Federal Republic of Germany. John McCloy replaced General Clay as the top U.S. official in Germany; the State Department assumed control of German policy.

Figure 5.2
Berlin Airlift provides milk for Berlin children (Courtesy: National Archives)

Stalin countered the American triumph in West Germany by creating the East German Democratic Republic as a member of the Soviet bloc. That decision completed the division of Europe.[82]

* * *

Such Western triumphs as the creation of the West German Republic and the North Atlantic Treaty Organization were only the most spectacular in a full spectrum of Soviet retreats. During the early weeks of 1947, Washington remained apprehensive over the continued presence of Communists in the French government. In May, however, Prime Minister Ramadier reorganized the French cabinet, determined, under U.S. pressure, to govern without the Communists. Ambassador Caffery warned Ramadier, as he noted in his diary, "[N]o Communists in government, or else." Thereafter Caffery continued to warn the administration that a Communist victory in France would carry the country into the Soviet orbit and threaten Western Europe, Africa, the Mediterranean, and the Middle East. During the Marshall Plan negotiations in Paris, Washington officials predicted that a French Communist victory would provide the Kremlin access to French and North African airfields and convert France into the bastion of a new Soviet "continental system."[83] By 1948, the persistent U.S. effort to excise the Communists from the Paris government had triumphed. Whatever the validity of American fears, the French Communist Party behaved in accordance with the country's democratic process, independent of Soviet influence. French Communists no less than Frenchmen generally were concerned with the welfare of their country, and, as members of the French government, they pursued no interests except those of France.[84]

If the French Communist Party created apprehension in Washington, the Italian Communist Party (PCI) appeared so threatening that U.S. officials pressed Italy from the outset to remove its members from government. The party's leader, Palmiro Togliatti, managed, with Socialist support, to establish a center-left coalition that lasted until 1947. Despite Togliatti's denials, Washington feared that a victorious PCI would turn Italy into a totalitarian Communist state bound to the Soviet Union. In May 1947, Marshall advised Ambassador James Dunn in Rome to promise Prime Minister Alcide De Gaspari needed economic assistance if he would remove all Communists from his government.[85] In June, De Gaspari eliminated the Communists—who responded with strikes and demonstrations. In late 1947, President Truman instructed Secretary of Defense Forrestal to assign Italy whatever military equipment it required to combat the Communist-inspired unrest. In preparation or the critical 1948 Italian elections, the National Security Council, in NSC 1/1, defined a program for meeting the PCI threat. Subsequent documents laid out the policies for implementation. Meanwhile, Marshall announced that a Communist victory would terminate all aid funds for Italy. Washington's varied economic pressures and election-eering efforts proved successful. The Italian vote, on April 18, brought the Christian Democrats to power. De Gaspari formed a new gov-ernment free of Communists and Socialists, prepared to lead Italy into the Western alliance.

For Stalin, Tito's defection in Yugoslavia was especially troubling. Kennan had predicted the Kremlin's eventual failure to control the countries of Eastern Europe, but he, like others, was surprised by the ease and swiftness of Yugoslavia's departure from the Soviet bloc. Stalin had recognized that country's superior orthodoxy by placing the Cominform's headquarters in Belgrade. Still the tensions in Soviet-Yugoslav relations had been continuous after Stalin refused to support Tito's wartime partisans or defend wartime Yugoslavia against the ravages of Soviet soldiers. Stalin, moreover, rejected Tito's proposed Balkan federation, with its subordination of Bulgaria and Albania, as well as Yugoslavia's membership in the ERP. During March 1948, Soviet-Yugoslav relations disintegrated as Belgrade authorities arrested partisans who favored the U.S.S.R. On June 28, the Cominform announced the expulsion of Yugoslavia, charging Tito with nationalist deviations. The announcement stunned U.S. officials who presumed that Tito, as one of Europe's most dedicated Stalinists, was bound to the Kremlin. The break, to Stalin's dismay, demonstrated that Communism had failed to erode the power of nationalism. It was now clear that the remaining Soviet satellites would be held by force or not at all. Washington and Belgrade established close economic ties before the end of the year.

After 1947, the Truman Doctrine carried the burden of U.S. con-tainment policy in the Middle East. In extending aid to Greece, official Washington regarded the Greek civil war a pivotal contest in "a world-side struggle between the United States and the Soviet Union." Fortu-nately for the pro-government forces, the guerrilla command opted for conventional warfare, enabling the government forces to capitalize on their superior numbers, organization, equipment, and public support to seize and hold territory. Still the resistance continued into 1949; some journalists on the scene predicted a stalemate. Victory remained elusive until Tito, on July 10, 1949, announced the closing of the

Yugoslav-Greek border and dismantling of guerrilla installations within Yugoslavia, denying the Greek guerrillas a necessary refuge. During August, the Greek army won a series of engagements, especially at Tsouka. The final battle, at Grammos in late August, drove the remnants of the guerrilla forces into Albania to end the fighting. In early November, the guerrilla leaders announced the end of military resistance. President Truman proclaimed victory on November 28.[86] Meanwhile, U.S. officers reorganized and modernized the Turkish army, vastly improved the country's military capabilities with shipments of equipment and aircraft, and constructed new roads and airstrips.[87]

* * *

Behind that remarkable succession of diplomatic triumphs lay the overwhelming predominance of American power, both economic and military. Washington gained its immediate objectives easily, consistently, even overwhelmingly, because Europe's postwar challenges gave the economic and military supremacy of the United States a special relevance. The war had transformed the country into an economic and technological colossus, even as it wiped out the remnants of the Great Depression. Geography dealt the United States a good hand. With Europe in ruins and the Soviet Union reeling from near disaster, the country's economic superiority was absolute. The war had rained destruction on every major power of Europe and Asia, destroying countless cities, factories, and rail lines. By contrast, the United States, with its many accumulating elements of power, had escaped unscathed. Its undamaged industrial capacity now matched that of the rest of the industrialized world. It possessed two-thirds of the world's capital wealth. Its technological superiority was so obvious that the world assumed its existence and set out to acquire or copy American products. During the immediate postwar years the United States reached the highest point of world power achieved by any nation in modern times. British writer Harold J. Laski wrote in November 1947:

America bestrides the world like a colossus; neither Rome at the height of its power nor Great Britain in the period of its economic supremacy enjoyed an influence so direct, so profound, or so pervasive.... Today literally hundreds of millions of Europeans and Asiatics know that both the quality and the rhythm of their lives depend upon decisions made in Washington. On the wisdom of those decisions hangs the fate of the next generation.[88]

Following a visit to the United States in 1948 and 1949, British historian Robert Payne observed, "No other power at any time in the world's history has possessed so varied or so great an influence on other nations. ... [T]he rest of the world lies in the shadow of American industry."[89]

Unable to achieve the reconstruction of a united Europe in accordance with its principles, the United States gained its marvelous triumphs where it mattered: the economic rehabilitation of Western Europe and Japan, the promotion of international trade and investment, and the maintenance of a defense structure that underwrote the containment effort and played an essential role in Europe's postwar burgeoning confidence and political development. Even as American military power reinforced the division of Europe, its economic power, working through international agencies for trade and monetary stabilization, contributed to the world's unprecedented economic expansion. The rebuilding of Western Europe (and Japan), and the advancement of the world's economy, remained the essence of the nation's postwar international achievement. Whether or not these policies were required to stop the advance of Soviet Communism, they brought confidence, and eventual prosperity, to tens of millions of people who had emerged from the recent war amid chaos, hopelessness, and ruin.[90]

Europe's remarkable recovery rested on far more than American financial power and leadership. Highly instrumental in the West's postwar advancement were the European contributions to the Marshall Plan and the encouragement of international trade and investment embodied in the Bretton Woods system, adopted in 1944. What added to the illusion of America's global supremacy was the wartime destruction of all the imperial structures that had once set the boundaries of U.S. influence. The war not only destroyed the power of Nazi Germany and Imperial Japan, it had also produced the final demise of the French and British empires. Indeed, the United States, after 1945, expanded into a worldwide power vacuum. As a result, Walter Lippmann observed, "we flowed forward beyond our natural limits. ... The miscalculation ... falsified all our other calculations—what our power was, what we could afford to do, what influence we had to exert in the world."

Western predominance in global affairs resulted not alone from its economic and military power; it flowed as well from Soviet weakness. Whereas the Western World at mid-century stood on the threshold of the most brilliant material development and prosperity in world history, the Soviet Union experienced incredible political sterility, stunted social and economic progress, and repression under its totalitarian governmental structure. The German assault, moreover, compelled the U.S.S.R. to bear a disproportionate share of the war's costs. Even as Soviet citizens rejoiced over their narrow escape from Nazi domination and their country's first wartime triumph in 125 years, they wondered why they had paid a far more exorbitant price for victory than the Germans had paid for defeat. The Kremlin's wartime failures and impositions on the Soviet populace resulted in astonishing death and destruction. Moreover, Nazi invaders destroyed more than two thousand towns and cities, demolished 31,000 factories, and slaughtered 20 million hogs and 17 million cattle—altogether one-fourth of the country's capital supply. The Soviet people suffered between 25 and 30 million deaths, while defeated Germany, despite the effectiveness of Allied warfare, lost far less than five million. The estimated 7.5 million dead Soviet soldiers numbered one in every twenty-two citizens. By contrast, the 292,100 U.S. military deaths numbered one in every 450 persons.[91] Despite such losses, Soviet officials quickly canonized the Great Patriotic War as a glorious victory; for many Soviet citizens it was a disgrace.

Stalin had long imposed on the U.S.S.R. a crippling, centralized regime, managed and controlled by the apparatus of the Communist Party through corruption, secret police, slave-labor camps, purges, and other agencies of coercion. The rulers in the Kremlin believed in vain that they could, through education, condition the minds of the survivors sufficiently to gain public allegiance. Stalin acknowledged the failure of 30 years of ideological and political indoctrination by turning more and more to propaganda and repression. The Cold War, with its heavy demands on production, served to justify his arbitrary power and inordinate impositions on the Soviet people. As American Communist leader Earl Browder explained, "Stalin needed the Cold War to keep up the sharp international tensions by which he alone could maintain such a regime in Russia."[92] The brutality, murders, and imprisonments, were not lost on the Soviet masses—the real victims of the Cold War era. The millions who conformed to the demands of Soviet life, and enabled the regime to rule with some efficiency, did so less from conviction than from necessity.[93]

Soviet totalitarianism seemed capable of maintaining a functioning economy, based on inefficient agriculture and a technologically backward industrial machine, at a low standard of living. Soviet intellectuals and economists remained irrelevant, powerless to recommend improvements because they lacked the freedom to explore, innovate, and instruct. But the authority of the Stalinist regime to invent history and determine truth could not hide the Communist structure's inefficiency and failure to match the performance of the Western World, either from those who lived under it or from foreign observers who experienced it. The Soviet economy, with its proficient military-related factories, sustained large and impressive armed forces. The Soviet victory over Germany demonstrated the country's capacity to wage total war. But the Soviets displayed their astonishing tenacity, not in an expansionist cause, but in defense of their homeland. Nothing in the victory over Germany suggested that the Soviet people, having experienced fully the terror and costs of modern war, would respond with equal valor to a needless war of aggression, fought on foreign soil for objectives fashioned by the whims of the Kremlin.[94] The war's destruction, moreover, had badly weakened the Soviet economic infra-structure, eliminating, at least temporarily, the country's capacity to sustain a major war.

Such profound limitations on Soviet action did not necessarily limit Stalin's ambitions. By subordinating civilian to military needs, the Kremlin hoped to avoid any concessions to the West until the natural flaws in capitalism would weaken the Western economies, mire them in depression, and unleash tensions and discord between the United States and the states of Western Europe. Such inviting conditions could enable the Kremlin to extend its influence, not by war, but by exploiting Europe's economic and political chaos. What doomed Stalin's plans for exploiting a weakened Europe was the unexpected and overwhelming U.S. commitment to the security and economic revival of Western Europe. By mid-century the U.S.S.R. faced the greatest manifestation of opposing power in the peacetime history of the world. The persistent Soviet diplomatic retreats were evidence enough that Europe's balance of forces had turned against it.[95]

* * *

Such ubiquitous demonstrations of Western superiority offered reassurance only to those who measured the Soviet threat by comparative levels of economic and military power. For American anti-Communists, whose central concern was Soviet ideological expansionism, the Soviet danger to Western security was only emerging. It was left for Soviet ideologue Andrei Zhdanov to confirm the conviction that the Kremlin's challenge lay less in military power than in Soviet-based international Communism. In his address at the Cominform's inaugural meeting at Wiliza Gora, Poland, Zhdanov accused the United States of trans-forming the Western nations into an anti-Communist bloc, composed of imperialist and "antidemocratic" forces. To meet that danger the

Soviet Union, joined by the "democracies" of Eastern Europe, would form an opposing bloc. Zhdanov thus divided the world into two competing ideological camps, reinforcing the already flourishing notion that the Soviet danger lay in the Marxist-Leninist advocacy of world revolution.

Zhdanov's strictures confirmed the convictions of many Americans that the struggle with the Soviet Union transcended the specific purpose of keeping the Soviets out of Western Europe and the eastern Mediterranean. It had become, what many Washington officials long presumed, a global confrontation between Communism and freedom, one unlimited in scope and magnitude. The immediate danger lay in the chaotic economic and political conditions that prevailed in broad regions of Europe and Asia, offering unlimited opportunities for Soviet ideological exploitation. The doubtful validity of liberal ideas and capitalist institutions in a revolutionary world suggested that much of Eurasia and its resources might still escape the West and fall into the clutches of the Kremlin.

Despite Europe's essential stability, by 1948 some American officials could detect no visible limits to Soviet expansionism. The National Security Council's study, NSC 7, dated March 30, 1948, defined the Kremlin's global challenge in precisely such terms:

The ultimate objective of Soviet-directed world communism is the domination of the world. To this end, Soviet-directed world communism employs against its victims in opportunistic coordination the complementary instruments of Soviet aggressive pressure from without and militant revolutionary subversion from within.... The Soviet Union is the source of power from which international communism chiefly derives its capability to threaten the existence of free nations. The United States is the only source of power capable of mobilizing successful opposition to the communist goal of world conquest.[96]

With its control of international Communism, the U.S.S.R. had engaged the United States in a struggle for power "in which our national security is at stake and from which we cannot withdraw short of national suicide." Already, declared NSC 7, Soviet-directed world Communism, not Soviet power, had turned Poland, Albania, Hungary, Bulgaria, Rumania, and Czechoslovakia into satellites; it posed a direct threat to Italy, Finland, and Korea; it had prevented peace treaties with Japan, Germany, and Austria; it had rejected an agreement on atomic energy in the United Nations. "The Soviet world," ran the document's survey of Soviet gains, "extends from the Elbe River and the Adriatic

Sea on the west to Manchuria on the east, and embraces one-fifth of the land surface of the world."[97]

Such definitions of the Soviet danger created a vast dichotomy between the gigantic fears of Soviet expansionism, shared by countless Americans, for which ultimately no defense seemed adequate, and remoteness of any discernible military threat, reminiscent of Napoleon or Hitler, outside the Soviet periphery. In August 1948, the Policy Planning Staff drafted a more precise and promising statement of American strategy, embodied eventually in NSC 20/1. This document advocated a program to contract Soviet power and influence until the Kremlin could no longer endanger the interests of the Western World. To that end, NSC 20/1 distinguished between the Soviet Union, its power and ambitions, and the world Communist movement. Outside the U.S.S.R., the document declared, the Kremlin wielded power directly in Eastern Europe and indirectly in the revolutionary parties beyond the satellite regions. The document assigned the United States the task of separating the Soviet Union from Third World revolutionary movements by destroying the myth that revolution could create some new order of peace and economic progress. Discontented intellectuals who comprised the core of Communist leadership outside the U.S.S.R., NSC 20/1 advised, listened to Soviet preachments for reasons that would cause them to respond to other programs that promised salvation. The United States, therefore, would not succeed in destroying the ideological attractiveness of Moscow abroad until it had removed "the sources of bitterness which drive people to irrational and utopian ideas of this sort."[98]

NSC 20/1 acknowledged the special difficulties in undermining Soviet control of Eastern Europe. Still so vulnerable appeared the Soviet satellite empire to overextension and fragmentation that even the goal of liberating that region seemed well within the reach of a countering strategy. NSC 58, of September 1949, argued more emphatically that Western security required the elimination of Soviet influence from the countries of Eastern Europe because they, in varying degrees, were "political-military adjuncts of Soviet power."[99] Yugoslavia's defection from the Soviet camp demonstrated that stresses in Soviet-satellite relations could lead to a disruption in Soviet domination. By increasing these stresses, the United States might enable other states to extricate themselves from Soviet control. This could be achieved, predicted NSC 20/1, "by skillful use of our economic power, by direct or indirect informational activity, by placing the greatest possible strain on the maintenance of the iron curtain, and by building the hope and vigor of

Western Europe to a point where it comes to exercise the maximum attraction to the peoples of the east." How the United States would execute these attractive and cost-free means the document did not say. Washington had no intention of inciting war. To win without war, NSC 20/1 cautioned the government to "do everything possible to keep the situation flexible and to make possible a liberation of the satellite countries in ways which do not create any unanswerable challenge to Soviet prestige."[100]

In NSC 20/4, approved by the president on November 24, 1948, the National Security Council presented the last version, before mid-century, of its continuing effort to define a promising Cold War strategy. The danger remained unchanged. "Communist ideology and Soviet behavior," the document began, "clearly demonstrate that the ultimate objective of the leaders of the USSR is the domination of the world." In recognizing that any military expansion over Eurasia would tax Soviet logistic facilities and strain the Soviet economy, the document again attributed the danger to political strategies that would permit the U.S.S.R. to expand without war. This placed the burden of Soviet expansionism in the strength of the international Communist movement and its perfected techniques of infiltration and subversion. Such psychological and political warfare, threatening U.S. institutions and security without military force, demanded a varied resistance sufficient to assure its failure. "Soviet domination of the potential power of Eurasia, whether achieved by armed aggression or by political subversion," NSC 20/4 warned, "would be strategically and politically unacceptable to the United States." Such lurking dangers gave the United States no choice but to promote the gradual retraction of Soviet power and influence until they ceased to be threatening. Again the United States would achieve that goal without war by placing massive political and economic strain on the Soviet imperial structure.[101] Such cost-free, ill-defined means for victory acknowledged only dangers so imprecise that they defied effectual policy implementation.

Strangely, Tito's defection from the Kremlin produced no reevaluation of U.S. strategy. Tito's successful escape from the Soviet bloc demonstrated that the Kremlin's control did not extend beyond the reach of Soviet armies. Indeed, in supporting Tito's Stalinist Yugoslavia, the United States acknowledged the nonexistence of a Kremlin-centered Communist monolith. Still the Soviet-Yugoslav split, despite its profound historic implications, failed to challenge the chief American Cold War assumption that all Communists were subservient to the Kremlin. That other Eastern European and Balkan states did not immediately defect was no demonstration of the binding power of ideological affinity; it merely confirmed the Kremlin's regional monopoly of power. Nowhere could the Soviet Union's imposition of Communist rule transform the occupied populations into citizens of the Soviet world. Such historic complexities were lost in the rigid ideological framework that forced all variables into line.[102] America's Cold War ideology of liberation denied the power of nationalism—the innate desire of peoples to be their own masters —as the driving force in the affairs of the world.

* * *

In the events of 1948 and 1949, especially in the Czech and Berlin crises, the Cold War in Europe reached its peak. At the same time, the rapid succession of Western victories and Soviet retreats, added to Western Europe's astonishing recovery, created the foundations of a profound East-West stability across Europe. Behind the corresponding U.S. consensus was the supposition that the United States had formulated a consistent, coherent body of external policies designed to protect Western Europe from the danger of both Soviet power and Soviet-based international Communism. That body of policy toward Europe had evolved slowly and haltingly through endless debates within government. Acheson acknowledged the absence of both knowledge and agreement when the process began. As time passed, he recalled, "our preliminary ideas appeared more and more irrelevant to the developing facts and attitudes, purposes, and capabilities of other actors on the scene." As the administration, through piecemeal decisions, established the main lines of policy, Kennan moved steadily from the center to the periphery of the process. At the core of the internal debate were deeply conflicting views of the Soviet threat and the best means of confronting them. Kennan never denied his abhorrence of Soviet totalitarianism but never ceased to stress the limits of effective U.S. action in confronting it. By 1949, Truman's top leadership, sharing the Cold War insecurities, had disposed of Kennan's spectrum of restraining views. Backed by an overwhelming public consensus, it accepted the guiding principle of military containment. By mid-century that acceptance created consistency as well as predictability in policy formulation. That consistency appeared most forcibly in Washington's persistent rejection of Kennan's views on both NATO and Germany.[103]

If America's purpose in Europe was the stabilization of a divided continent, the United States, by 1950, had achieved its goal. The United States, alone or with its allies, would not change the *status quo* in Europe; the Soviets had no power to do so. The Western capitals were not inclined to recognize the Soviet empire in Eastern Europe openly, but they had long coexisted with what they publicly abhorred, knowing both that the expanding economic power of the West did not require a free Eastern Europe, and that any direct effort to undo the Soviet hegemony might result in disaster. With the major antagonists compelled to accept existing conditions, Churchill, Kennan, and others called for negotiations with Moscow to adjust differences, relieve tensions, and perhaps stall a threatening arms race.

Delay would serve no purpose. In a report to Marshall of March 1948, Kennan observed that the successful stabilization of Europe would permit the United States, for the first time since Germany's surrender, to enter negotiations with the Kremlin, both to gain a mutual withdrawal of forces from Europe and to acknowledge the acceptability of a stable, if divided, continent.[104] Similarly, Churchill declared before the House of Commons as early as January 1948: "I will only venture to say that there seems to me to be a very real danger in going on drifting too long. I believe that the best chance of preventing a war is to bring matters to a head and come to a settlement with the Soviet government before it is too late." Two years later Churchill put his case before the House of Commons with even greater urgency. The Western position, he predicted, would become weaker. "Therefore," he concluded, "while I believe there is time for further effort for a lasting and peaceful settlement, I cannot feel that it is necessarily a long time, or that its passage will progressively improve our own security."[105]

For Acheson and official Washington, Western power had eliminated the need for negotiation with the Kremlin. Confronted with inflexible will over West Berlin, the Soviets had retreated. Following the show of Western unity at the Paris Foreign Ministers Conference in June 1949, Acheson announced that the West had gained the initiative in Europe and could thereafter anticipate eventual Soviet capitulation. On June 23 he informed the press:

[T]hese conferences from now on seem to me to be like the steam gauge on a boiler. . . . They indicate the pressure which has been built up. They indicate the various gains and losses in positions which have taken place between the meetings, and I think that the recording of this Conference is that the position of the West has grown greatly in strength, and that the position of the Soviet Union in regard to the struggle for the soil of Europe has changed from the offensive to the defensive.[106]

Settlements, when they came, would simply record the corroding effect of Western power on the ambitions and design of the Kremlin. For Acheson negotiation recorded facts; it did not create them. Meanwhile NATO, backed by the destructive power of the United States, would sustain the military division—and thus the stability—of Europe with a vengeance; it would not do more.

CHAPTER 6

The Cold War in East Asia

At the Pacific war's end in August 1945, Soviet armies in Manchuria were stark reminders that Russia was a Pacific power, with interests in East Asia spanning more than a century. As journalist Harold Isaacs observed in May 1945, "Straddling the vast distances between the Baltic and the Sea of Japan, the new Russia will symbolize the greatest geopolitical fact of our times: not Europe and Asia as separate entities, but Eurasia, the greatest single land mass on the face of the earth." That month the *New Republic* observed that the Soviet Union was the only member of the Big Three with an actual geographical presence in East Asia.[1] Still, in the autumn of 1945 that seemed to matter little. The United States was overwhelmingly the predominant power in the western Pacific. To preserve the country's strategic advantage that flowed from Japan's approaching defeat, U.S. officials pressed the allies for permanent rights to the captured Japanese mandated islands. At the San Francisco Conference, the United States secured control of the Japanese bases through a trusteeship arrangement.[2] Following the Japanese surrender in September, Washington viewed Okinawa as a potentially powerful military base off the Asian coast. Even as Americans contemplated the problems of Far Eastern reconstruction, they could detect no dangers to their security lurking amid the ruins.

Victory over Japan, it seemed, had assured a peaceful Orient. For half a century that country had been the major, if not exclusive, threat to Western interests in the Pacific world. But already the United States had destroyed its army and navy, burned out its cities and factories, and reduced its possessions to the four islands that comprised its pre-imperial territories. In September 1945 Japan came under the direct control of U.S. post-surrender policies, designed to insure "that Japan will not again become a menace to the United States or to the peace of the world."[3] Under the direction of General Douglas MacArthur, supreme commander of the Allied Powers (SCAP), occupation authorities, in executing the provisions of the Potsdam Declaration, methodically assaulted every source of nationalistic indoctrination and centralized authority to create a new climate of political and intellectual freedom. Japanese schools were freed of centralized control. SCAP destroyed what remained of the Japanese war machine, placed the country's industrial capacity under the severest scrutiny and control, and eliminated Japan's top wartime leadership. The Japanese constitution, which became effective in May 1947, pledged Japan to international cooperation, with a police force limited to the requirements of internal order.[4] By demanding primacy in the design and management of occupation policy, the United States converted the northern Pacific into an American lake.

U.S. officials had hoped to liberate all Korea from Japanese rule unilaterally, but Stalin's decision to dispatch Soviet forces into Korea, in pursuit of Russia's historic interests in that country, compelled the United States to accept a line dividing the peninsula at the 38th parallel, a line otherwise without historical or political significance.[5] The Soviets established a predominantly Communist regime in the north; the United States returned Syngman Rhee, the famed Korean nationalist long in exile, to lead the south. At the Moscow Conference of December 1945, U.S. and Soviet negotiators agreed to an international trusteeship for Korea as the surest means of uniting the country under conditions satisfactory to all parties—except Koreans everywhere who rejected the principle of trusteeship as an unnecessary big-power impediment to their country's full independence as a united people. The Joint Soviet-American Commission on Korea began its deliberations in March 1946, but it could never discover a formula for creating an independent, sovereign nation that would overcome the pervading Soviet-American ideological conflict over Korea's political and economic future. Koreans, north and south, frustrated and angered over their country's continued division, harbored ambitions to reunite the peninsula with force.

Unfortunately, Washington's apparent success in protecting the country's strategic interests throughout the western Pacific did not assure Far Eastern stability. Japanese expansionism had not been the only challenge to the West's historic hegemony in the Orient. Asian nationalism was another. Whereas the United States possessed the power to harness Japanese ambition, it could not, however, complete its military dominance of the western Pacific, return the Far East to its prewar passivity toward Western domination, or regulate the forces of nationalism. As early as the fall of Singapore in 1942 the London *Economist* warned: "There can be no return to the old system once Japan has been defeated." During subsequent months other East Asian analysts repeated that prediction.[6] Asian nationalism, evolving slowly throughout the century, was fundamentally a quest for political independence. Until the outbreak of war in the Pacific, the colonial regimes maintained their authority against scattered nationalist forces. Emerging from the Pacific war confident, organized, and armed, Asia's native leaders, exploiting the anticolonialist emotions unleashed by Japan's wartime successes, began their final assault on the old order. The decolonization of Asia had begun.

Most nationalists found their emotional and intellectual resources in Western notions of racial equality and self-determination. A significant minority, characterized by such revolutionary leaders as China's Mao Zedong and Indochina's Ho Chi Minh, discovered their intellectual authority in the anticolonial writings of Marx and Lenin. As a Chinese nationalist, Mao, in his long crusade to gain control of China, sought to free his country from the myriad of unequal treaties the Western powers had imposed on a defenseless China. Ho, as an Indochinese nationalist, had sought the independence of his country through a peaceful concession at the Versailles Conference of 1919. With the conference's refusal to apply self-determination to the victorious Allied empires, Ho, remaining in Paris as an angry, frustrated Indochinese nationalist, found his support for Indochinese liberation in the anti-imperialism embodied in socialist doctrine. The writings of Lenin especially, he recalled, gave him the courage to pursue the cause of Indochinese independence despite France's tight hold on its Southeast Asia empire.[7] With Japan's defeat in August 1945, nationalist pressures began to undermine Asia's still-existing imperial structures. The colonial powers soon discovered that empires requiring large occupying forces to repress rebellious populations were exceedingly expensive to maintain. By 1947, Britain, exhausted by war, had granted independence to India, Pakistan, Burma, and Ceylon. The days of the French and Dutch empires in Southeast Asia were numbered. Thus Japan's defeat marked the beginning of the end for the Western colonial empires in Asia and the emergence of perceived dangers to Asian and American security scarcely predictable when the processes of disintegration began.

* * *

For President Franklin D. Roosevelt, France's empire in Southeast Asia was especially deplorable. Through a trusteeship arrangement he hoped to prevent France's return to Indochina. By early 1945, however, he faced the opposition of State Department officials who argued that the United States should not meddle in Europe's colonial affairs. At Yalta, Roosevelt assured both British and French leaders that the United States would request trusteeships only where the colonial powers approved. He spoke candidly of French Indochina's future to newsmen on February 23: "For two whole years I have been terribly worried about Indo-China. I talked to Chiang Kai-shek in Cairo, Stalin in Teheran. They both agreed with me. . . . The thing I asked Chiang was, 'Do you want Indo-China?' He said, 'It's no help to us. We don't want it. They are not Chinese. They would not assimilate into the Chinese people."[8] Already Paris had made known its determination to return to Southeast Asia. Charles de Gaulle warned Washington in March that if the United States opposed France's plans for Indochina there would be "terrific disappointment and nobody knows to what it may lead. . . . [W]e do not want to fall into the Russian orbit; but I hope that you do not push us into it."[9] Under French, British, and State Department pressure, the Truman administration gradually extended France a free hand in Indochina and gave up whatever leverage it had to control the region's future.[10] At Potsdam the United States granted the British operational control over the southern half of Indochina. France quickly announced its decision to replace the British forces and reestablish control over its former colony.[11] Following the French reoccupation of Saigon, French Minister of Colonies Paul Giacobbi announced on September 25: "I believe the situation in Indo-China is now in hand."[12]

Such optimism was short-lived. France reentered Indochina only to face an organized and determined Communist-led independence movement. During the war Ho Chi Minh had taken control of the League of Vietnam Independence, known as the Vietminh. This organization comprised the chief repository of Indochinese nationalism. Other groups, such as the rival Vietnamese Nationalist Party and the Revolutionary League, favored Indochinese independence, but none had the numbers, the discipline, or, more importantly, the organization to challenge the dominance of the Vietminh. This enabled Ho to gradually compel all Indochinese nationalists to support his cause or accept French rule.[13] When Ho returned to Indochina in the spring of 1945, both his Communist associates and officers of the U.S. Office of Strategic Services (OSS), who knew him well, viewed him primarily as an intense nationalist.[14] In August, Bao Dai, the puppet king of Annam under France and Japan alike, readily abdicated to the Vietminh.[15] Following Japan's surrender in September, Ho proclaimed the independence of Indochina. Having won the support of OSS agents because of his wartime anti-Japanese activities, Ho, between October 1945 and April 1946, addressed a series of notes to Washington asking for U.S. recognition and support. He reminded Washington that India and the Philippines were soon to receive their independence; Indochina expected no less.[16] The letters went unanswered. Washington could not respond without insulting the French government, still in official control of Indochina.

Paris could not ignore the Vietminh's growing strength. On March 6, 1946, French officials signed an accord with Ho Chi Minh that granted France the right to return to northern Vietnam. In return, France recognized Ho's Democratic Republic of Vietnam, with its capital of Hanoi, as a free state in the French Union. The arrangement had no future. Bao Dai, residing in Hanoi, reminded de Gaulle what the French really faced in Indochina: "You would understand better if you could see what is happening here, if you could feel this yearning for independence that is in everyone's heart, and which no human force can any longer restrain." Moreover, he noted, should you reestablish a French administration here, it will not be obeyed. Every village will be a nest of resistance, each former collaborator an enemy, and your officials and colonists will themselves seek to leave this atmosphere, which will choke them."[17] Undaunted by France's precarious position, Washington, in April, officially approved the French effort to regain control of all Indochina. Even as Ho prepared for trouble, he continued to anticipate U.S. support.[18] The armistice ended suddenly, on November 23, when the French high command at Haiphong ordered a bombardment of the city, killing thousands of Vietnamese. The long, bitter struggle for Indochina was under way.

Whether Washington's crucial decision to acquiesce in France's colonial war would ultimately trap the United States in the struggle for Indochina hinged on its perception of the Kremlin's role in Indochina's revolution. The process of entrapment began as early as November 1946 when U.S. Ambassador Jefferson Caffery warned the State Department that the French Foreign Ministry had "positive proof that Ho Chi Minh is in direct contact with Moscow and is receiving advice and instructions from the Soviets." That report, added to others, convinced some U.S. officials that Ho's success exposed Southeast Asia to Soviet encroachment. In December, Under Secretary Dean Acheson informed the American consul in Saigon: "Least desirable eventuality would be establishment [of] Communist-dominated, Moscow-oriented state [in] Indochina."[19] Secretary of State George C. Marshall reminded the embassy in Paris, on February 3, 1947, that the old empires were becoming a thing of the past; the French empire was no exception. "On the other hand," he observed, "we do not lose sight of the fact that Ho Chi Minh has direct Communist connection and it should be obvious that we are not interested in seeing colonial administrations supplanted by philosophy and political organizations emanating from and controlled by Kremlin."[20]

France's determination to defy Ho's nationalist crusade tested the State Department's powers of judgment. Abbot Low Moffat, joined by his associates in the Division of Southeast Asian Affairs, argued that Ho, as a native nationalist without significant ties to the Kremlin, was no threat to Asian or American security.[21] Moreover, he added, Ho would win. Similarly, Charles S. Reed, consul general in Saigon, predicted that the French, powerless to clear the countryside of insurgents, would lose. Vice Consul James L. O'Sullivan reminded Marshall from Hanoi that France faced a Communist-led rebellion, which it would not defeat, simply because it had refused to announce an independence program of its own.[22] Marshall, conscious of Washington's receding power of choice, ordered a State Department appraisal of Ho's relations with the Kremlin. The department's report of July 1948 established that Ho was a Communist, demonstrated by the support he received from Communist writers in France and elsewhere. Unable, however, to uncover any evidence of direct ties between Ho and Moscow, the report merely assumed that they existed.[23]

Those who accepted the necessity of supporting French policy desired only that France be wise and innovative enough to maintain the necessary control over Indochina's future. Under U.S. prodding, French officials agreed to negotiations with the Democratic Republic; Ho rejected the preconditions. But France, determined to protect its presence in Southeast Asia, refused to entice Ho to the bargaining table with a compromise offer. As the French High Commissioner, Emile Bollaert, explained in May 1947, "France will remain in Indochina, and Indochina will remain in the French Union."[24] Despite persistent warnings of disaster, Washington had become hostage to a faltering French policy that it could neither control nor desert. The State Department's report on Indochina of September 27, 1948, analyzed the country's dilemma precisely:

Our greatest difficulty in talking with the French and in stressing what should and what should not be done has been our inability to suggest any practical solution of the Indochina problem, as we are all too well aware of the unpleasant fact that Communist Ho Chi Minh is the strongest and perhaps the ablest figure in Indochina and that any suggested solution which excluded him is an expedient of uncertain outcome.[25]

In search of a native leader capable of bidding successfully against Ho for leadership of the anticolonial uprising, the French turned to Bao Dai, then residing in Hong Kong. Bao Dai had little support in Annam, almost none in Tonkin and Cochinchina, but Paris could discover no other Indochinese alternative to Ho Chi Minh. After lengthy negotiations, largely in Paris, French officials convinced Bao Dai to lead the new state of Vietnam. Their contract took the form of the Elysee Agreements of March 1949, promising eventual independence to Vietnam. France granted independence to Laos on July 19 and to Cambodia on November 8, designating both as neutral states between the Western powers and Indochina's revolutionary forces.[26]

State Department officials, whose reliance on France to save Southeast Asia from Kremlin influence had eliminated their freedom of maneuver, accepted Bao Dai as a necessity.[27] Acheson rationalized the critical decision to oppose Ho in favor of Bao Dai in a letter to the consulate in Hanoi on May 20, 1949:

Question whether Ho is as much nationalist as Commie is irrelevant. All Stalinists in colonial areas are nationalists. With the achievement of their national aims (independence) their objective necessarily becomes the subordination of the state to Commie purposes and the ruthless extermination of . . . all elements suspected of even the slightest deviation. . . . It must of course be conceded that the theoretical possibility exists of establishing a National Communist state on the pattern of Yugoslavia in any area beyond the reach of the Soviet army. However, the United States attitude could take account of such possibility only if every other possible avenue were closed to the reservation of the area from Kremlin control.[28]

What mattered to official Washington was keeping Indochina out of Communist hands. The American ambassador in Thailand advised Acheson that any failure of the Western powers to prevent a Soviet presence in Southeast Asia would result in "the whole of Southeast Asia [falling] victim to the Communist advance." Similarly Far Eastern expert Walton Butterworth assured Acheson that Ho, as a Communist, was seeking the extension of Soviet domination in Asia.[29] In September 1949 French Foreign Minister Robert Schuman reminded Acheson that France was fighting democracy's war against world Communism. Acheson agreed that Western security demanded a

French victory, but how the United States could offer aid to Bao Dai without appearing to underwrite French colonialism remained unclear.[30]

Other U.S. officials could detect no future for the "Bao Dai solution." For Reed, Bao Dai had no chance of success. Why, he wondered, should the United States follow the French to disaster? George M. Abbott, his successor in Saigon, advised Washington that the United States could not assure Bao Dai's success. The French, he concluded, would do well to grant Vietnam independence and leave. Charlton Ogburn, Division of Southeast Asian Affairs, complained in June that the Bao Dai solution assured a Communist victory in Indochina. "I think," he concluded, "we are heading into a very bad mess."[31] It was too late, observed State Department adviser Raymond Fosdick, to establish a cheap substitute for French colonialism in the form of the Bao Dai regime. "For the United States to support France in this attempt," he wrote, "will cost us our standing and prestige in all of Southeast Asia." To those in Washington who insisted that it was too late to do anything except support Bao Dai, Fosdick retorted: "It is never too late to change a mistaken policy." Because Ho was independent of both Russia and China, there was nothing to be gained by supporting French policy. "Whether the French like it or not," Fosdick concluded, "independence is coming to Indochina. Why, therefore, do we tie ourselves to the tail of their battered kite?"[32] Such predictions of disaster had no chance against the current wisdom that Vietnamese nationalism was no bulwark against the Kremlin's expansive power in Southeast Asia.

* * *

Behind the burgeoning fear of Communist expansion in Southeast Asia lay the larger issue of China. Throughout the Pacific war it had become increasingly clear that the United States would reap far greater success in saving the Nationalist government of Chiang Kai-shek from the invading Japanese than from its internal enemies, Mao Zedong's Chinese Communists. Under the pressures of war, the Chinese Communist Party's political ties to Moscow began to unravel. For Mao, the Soviet Union had ceased to offer a useful model. At the same time, he recognized the need of ideological and intellectual assurance, available only in the U.S.S.R. The Chinese Communists assumed that their wartime successes against Japan would compel Nationalist cooperation. But the sudden ending of the war in the summer of 1945 left Mao unprepared to deal with his Nationalist rivals. To compound his difficulties, Japanese units refused to surrender to the

Communists and, instead, turned what lands and weapons they possessed over to the Nationalists. Transported by American aircraft and naval vessels, Nationalist forces occupied northern China. For the Chinese Communists the Chinese-Soviet Pact of August 14 eliminated the prospect of Soviet support. The Nationalists, it seemed, had outmaneuvered them diplomatically, territorially, and militarily.

Washington viewed wartime China as the new Eastern power. At the Cairo Conference, in 1943, President Roosevelt promoted Chiang to the rank of world leader with the hope that China would contribute conspicuously to Asia's postwar stability. To assure a unified country, Roosevelt dispatched General Patrick J. Hurley to China, in 1944, to negotiate a coalition between the two Chinese factions. Hurley soon discarded the goal of a coalition government as unachievable, even undesirable. Only the Chinese elements that recognized Chiang Kai-shek, he argued, should receive American aid. Meanwhile, Chiang's wartime failures had convinced such Foreign Service officers as John Paton Davies and John Stewart Service that the Nationalist regime had no future in postwar China in competition with the highly disciplined Chinese Communists.[33] Convinced that Chiang had no intention of sharing power, Davies and Service predicted that U.S. support for Chiang would prevent the emergence of any effective government for China. George Atcheson, American chargé d'affaires in China, reported as early as February 1945 that Chiang's anticipation of U.S. support had made him, despite his weakness, unrealistically demanding.[34] General Albert C. Wedemeyer, commander of U.S. forces in China, was troubled by Nationalist incompetence and corruption. Still, for him Chiang's success comprised the only defense against the expansion of Soviet influence into China.[35] As late as November, when Hurley resigned, the formula for achieving a unified China under Nationalist leadership had proved agonizingly elusive.

Determined to create a strong, united, and democratic China, President Truman, in December 1945, dispatched recently retired General George C. Marshall on a special mission to China. Many in Washington believed that the Chiang Kai-shek's large, well-equipped, army seemed capable of defeating Mao's 300,000 veterans, and assure a unified China under Nationalist control.[36] During his first weeks in China, Marshall, through incredible patience and fairness, achieved a truce as well as some critical territorial agreements. Chiang, suspecting correctly that the United States would not desert him, had no intention of admitting Communists into a national government. When Marshall visited Washington briefly in March 1946, Chiang launched an attack on the Communist positions in Manchuria. Upon his return, Marshall, facing strong Nationalist resistance, failed in his effort to reinstate the truce.[37] As Marshall's official efforts at mediation ended in October 1946, Mao vowed to seek the victories on the battlefield that had eluded him at the

Figure 6.1
(L to R) Chou En-lai, Mao Zedong, and Ambassador Patrick Hurley (Courtesy: National Archives)

peace talks. Chiang accepted the challenge, declaring on December 31 that Mao's armies "will be annihilated within a year."[38] As the two Chinese contestants entered their final struggle for power, the Joint Chiefs of Staff warned that Chinese Communism was merely a tool of Soviet expansionism, with the Soviets threatening not only China but Indochina, Malaya, and India as well.[39] The United States, they agreed, faced the alternative of accepting the loss of East Asia or underwriting the Nationalist cause with every means short of armed intervention. One American officer in China explained:

The obvious Soviet aim in China is to exclude U.S. influence and replace it with that of Moscow. . . . Our exclusion from China would probably result, within the next generation, in an expansion of Soviet influence over the manpower, raw materials and industrial potential of Manchuria and China. The U.S. and the world might then be faced in the China Sea and southward with a Soviet power analogous to that of the Japanese in 1941, but with the difference that the Soviets could be perhaps overwhelmingly strong in Europe and the Middle East as well.[40]

Marshall regarded Mao a genuine Communist but independent of Moscow. In his farewell message, Marshall condemned Nationalists and Communists alike for their intransigence. He recognized Chiang Kai-shek's regime as the legal government of China, but resented its incompetence.[41] As secretary of state after January 1947, Marshall turned his attention to Europe. As the Nationalist armies continued to lose ground, Chiang pressed the administration for greater support, arguing, as did the French over Indochina, that he was protecting all Asia from Communist aggression. U.S. officials were conscious of Chiang's declining prospects as well as the high cost of sustaining him, but the suppositions of Moscow's growing influence in China ruled out any reevaluation of policy. To determine a feasible course of action, Marshall, in July, dispatched General Wedemeyer on another special mission to China. Wedemeyer, in his report of September 19, 1947, concluded that the regime of Chiang Kai-shek was corrupt, reactionary, and inefficient, with little prospect of success. No policy, he feared, would save it. But he continued: "If Chiang Kai-shek is a benevolent despot . . . or whether he is a Democrat or Republican, that is unimportant. The relevant and important facts are that the man has opposed Communism throughout his history." For Wedemeyer, Chiang could not be saved, but the United States had no choice but to save him. "A China dominated by Chinese Communists," he warned, "would be inimical to the interests of the United States."[42]

Official fears of Soviet influence in China began to mount. The National Security Council's interim report on China, completed in March 1948, noted that China had become significant, politically and militarily, because of its potential strategic dominance of East Asia. The report noted that the Chinese Communists, as the "instrument for the extension of Soviet influence," would, in time, "strengthen Communist movements in Indochina, Burma, and areas further south." State Department officials were no less concerned with the prospect of Soviet expansion into Asia. "In the Communist struggle for world domination," declared a departmental report, of September 7, 1948, to the National Security Council (NSC 34), " . . . the allegiance of China's millions is worth striving for . . . if only to deny it to the free world. In positive terms, China is worth having because capture of it would represent an . . . acquisition of a broad human glacis from which to mount a political offensive against the rest of East Asia."[43] Except for Soviet imperialism in China, the report concluded, the Chinese Communists would compromise no threat to Asia.

* * *

Such fears of Soviet expansion did not determine official U.S. policy. Marshall and his chief advisers questioned the mounting assumptions regarding Soviet influence in Chinese affairs. They could not, moreover, discover any strategy that would assure a Nationalist victory. " [W]e find it difficult to believe," reported Ambassador John Leighton Stuart in May 1948, "that [Chiang] is any longer capable of leadership necessary to instill new spirit into the people or that he has any intention of really instituting necessary reforms."[44] The Policy Planning Staff argued that Chiang's position was hopeless, but that China's destiny remained solely in Chinese hands. George F. Kennan, its director, predicted in a lecture at the National War College in May that, whatever the Kremlin's role in the Chinese revolution, it would decline as the Communists extended their control over China. "I am not sure," Kennan concluded, "that their relations with Moscow would be much different from those of China [the Nationalist government] today, because they would be much more . . . in a position to take an independent line vis-a-vis Moscow."[45]

Convinced that China did not endanger U.S. security, Kennan advised the administration to avoid all responsibility for what occurred in that country. Marshall adhered to that advice. In April, the administration, under extreme congressional pressure, accepted a $450 million appropriation for arms and economic aid to the Nationalist government.

Figure 6.2
(L to R) President Truman, Special Envoy George Marshall, Senators Vandenberg and Austin as Marshall returns from China (Courtesy: Harry S. Truman Library)

But, in August, Marshall rejected Ambassador Stuart's request for additional military equipment. In an October 1948 policy review, Marshall again bound the United States to the Nationalist cause, but he advised the administration to assume no economic or military commitment to China's future.[46] In December, he resisted the appeal of Madame Chiang Kai-shek, as well as her powerful supporters in Washington, for funds to cover Nationalist deficiencies.[47] The secretary reminded those who demanded the extension of the Truman Doctrine to China that China was not Greece; it was 45 times as large, with 85 times as many people.

Every promising U.S. approach to China had long evaporated. By 1949, the Nationalist regime was on the verge of collapse. Its armies, demoralized by faulty strategies in the field and known inefficiency and corruption in the government, were no match for the disciplined, highly-motivated forces of China's Communist leader, Mao Zedong. President Harry Truman explained to the cabinet why the United States would make no effort to save the Nationalists: "Chiang Kai-shek will not fight it out. ... It would be pouring sand in a rat hole under [the] present situation." Still the country had supported the Nationalist cause for so long that it possessed few policy options. The administration could still exhort Chiang to reform, but it was not free to threaten him with desertion if he refused. Nor could it publicize his regime's failures that accounted for American inaction.[48] "You cannot explain why you cannot do more," complained Acheson, "because if you do, you complete the destruction of the very fellows you are trying to help." Marshall summarized the administration's dilemma:

The Nationalist Government of China is on its way out and there is nothing we can do to save it. We are faced with the question of clarifying [this for] the American people and by so doing deliver the knockout blow to the National Government of China—or we can play along with the existing government and keep facts from the American people and thereby be accused later of playing into the hands of the Communists.[49]

In February 1949, the president called a small meeting at the White House to formulate some escape from the Chinese dilemma. Senator Arthur H. Vandenberg opposed desertion of the Nationalists. He proposed no action to prevent the looming Communist victory; he merely wanted Washington to avoid responsibility "for the *last push which makes it possible.*"[50] Truman and Acheson accepted Vandenberg's argument; the United States would continue to support the Nationalist government officially, while it waited for the dust to settle. As late as March 1949, Acheson advised Tom Connally, chairman of the Senate Foreign Relations Committee, against a large military appropriation for China.[51] The United States would not save Chiang Kai-shek, nor would it desert him.

Marshall's persistent refusal to launch some rescue mission in China raised a storm of protest from Chiang's American friends who trumpeted the Nationalist cause as the final barrier to the Communist conquest of Asia. For them such behavior was defeatist, if not treasonable. Moreover, it was inconceivable that the United States could not prevent the communization of China. This so-called China Lobby, an element totally unique on the world stage, shared an absolute, unshakable devotion to the Nationalist cause, as the regime that had maintained an open door to the China they loved. Their position at the core of American anti-Communism gave them incredible access to the country's fears and emotions. Ross Y. Koen, in his book, *The China Lobby in American Politics*, divided members of the group into two categories. One consisted of "individuals and groups, dependent upon a continuation of American aid to China," the other was made up of those who supported Chiang "for reasons of politics, ideology, or a particular set of assumptions regarding the requirements of American security."[52] For both groups, the interests of Chiang's Kuomintang party were paramount.

What characterized Chiang's American supporters was their incredible determination. One acknowledged leader of the China Lobby was the successful China trader Alfred Kohlberg, head of the American China Policy Association, who quite characteristically attributed the American problem in China to "stupidity at the top—treason just below."[53] Among the press lords who furthered the Lobby's crusade were Henry Luce of *Time-Life*, William Randolph Hearst of the Hearst newspapers, Roy Howard of the Scripps-Howard chain, and Robert McCormick of the Patterson-McCormick press. Among the leading pro-Chiang columnists were Joseph and Stuart Alsop. *Life* declared in December 1948 that the continuing collapse of Nationalist China imperiled the United States itself.[54] In Congress the key spokesmen for the Nationalist cause were Minnesota congressman Walter Judd and Republican Senators William F. Knowland of California, Styles Bridges of New Hampshire, Kenneth Wherry of Nebraska, William Jenner of Indiana, as well as Democratic Senator Pat McCarran of Nevada. Their terrorizing campaign comprised largely an unrestrained verbal assault on those who allegedly had failed in their duty to save the Nationalist regime. The administration exposed itself to endless charges of failure—even treason—when it failed to share the rationale for its declining faith in Chiang with its potential critics when the country had little choice but to accept its decisions. Despite their undying crusade to return Chiang to the mainland, the China Lobby and its supporters never advocated more than larger, risk-free appropriations for the Nationalist cause.

* * *

To explain why Chiang Kai-shek had failed to prevent the approaching Communist victory in China, the State Department, on August 5, 1949, released the famed China White Paper. The thousand-page document demonstrated profusely the failures of the Nationalist regime. It sought to reassure the nation that the grinding transfer of power in China was a legitimate expression of self-determination and no danger to American security. Acheson introduced the China White Paper with a 14-page letter of transmittal. "The Nationalist armies," wrote Acheson, "did not have to be defeated; they disintegrated." The United States, he continued, could have saved Chiang only with a "full-scale intervention in behalf of a Government which had lost the confidence of its own troops and its own people."[55] The White Paper summarized the administration's case:

The unfortunate and inescapable fact is that the ominous result of the civil war in China was beyond the control of the government of the United States. Nothing that this country did or could have done could have changed the result; nothing that was left undone by this country has contributed to it. It was the product of internal Chinese forces, forces this country tried to influence but could not.[56]

For those leaders and writers who had long agreed that the Nationalist cause was hopeless and its demise no threat to Asian security, the White Paper came as salvation. Here at last was official evidence that confirmed the accuracy of their judgments and convinced them that the world had no choice but to recognize the new Communist-led government of China. President Elpidio Quirino of the Philippines expressed much of the world's opinion when he declared that recognition of the Beijing regime was inevitable; the Chinese people had obviously accepted a Communist government that was firmly and permanently in control of the country. He concluded: "You can't help but recognize such a government."[57] British Foreign Secretary Ernest Bevin declared that his country would not procrastinate at the risk of endangering its chances of reaching a satisfactory *modus vivendi* with the new Chinese government.[58] In December 1949 and January 1950, Beijing received recognition from such Asian neighbors as Burma, India, Pakistan, Ceylon, and Afghanistan, as well as from Britain, Norway, Denmark, Israel, Finland, Sweden, and Switzerland.[59] The Netherlands followed in March. Other states—Australia, Canada, France, Italy, and the Philippines—expressed preference for recognition, but hesitated to defy Washington's opposition.[60]

Nowhere did the White Paper permit any change in official U.S. policy. What bound the Truman administration to Chiang was the official supposition that the Communist-led revolution to overthrow him was merely the initial phase of Soviet expansion into the Asian sphere. John Moors Cabot, U.S. consul general in Shanghai, warned, as early as February 1948, that if the Communists succeeded in winning control of China, they would "install in China a tyranny as subservient to

Russia . . . as Tito's." The State Department's China experts, in a memorandum of October 1948, concluded that Soviet policy was designed to establish control of China as firmly "as in the satellite countries behind the Iron Curtain."[61] In the White Paper's letter of transmittal, Acheson presumed that China had fallen victim to Kremlin control:

The Communist leaders have foresworn their Chinese heritage and have publicly announced their subservience to a foreign power, Russia, which during the last 50 years, under czars and Communists alike, has been most assiduous in its efforts to extend its control in the Far East. . . . [American policy] will necessarily be influenced by the degree to which the Chinese people come to recognize that the Communist regime serves not their interests but those of Soviet Russia and the manner in which . . . they react to this foreign domination."[62]

Writers in both Britain and the United States condemned the official effort in Washington to place responsibility for the outcome of the Chinese civil war on the Kremlin. If the United States, as the White Paper proclaimed, could not control developments in China, why, asked the *Manchester Guardian Weekly*, presume that the Kremlin could do so? The Chinese masses revealed no loyalty to the Soviet Union.[63] Such accusations, wrote Johns Hopkins scholar Owen Lattimore, revealed the administration as "relentlessly anti-Russian as the most fire-eating Republican."[64] The White Paper's total rejection of the new regime as the legitimate and established government of China closed the door to better U.S.-Chinese relations. Mao responded to the White Paper with five vituperative commentaries, noting cynically that China had been overrun by foreigners who had enslaved the Chinese people. He wondered only from where the foreigners had come.[65]

The State Department, in its recital of Chiang's many failings, made no countering effort to moderate U.S. relations with the victorious Communists. Acheson scarcely had accommodation in mind when he told the Senate Foreign Relations Committee in October 1949 that "the fundamental starting point in our relations with China" was the fact that the new Chinese government was "really a tool of Russian imperialism in Asia." George Kennan repeated that theme over CBS when he accused the Chinese Communists "of deceiving the Chinese people and of inducing them to accept a disguised form of foreign rule."[66] No documents in the White Paper revealed Chinese independence from Moscow. There was no explanation of why the administration ignored the sound advice of the wartime Foreign Service officers in China who unerringly predicted the Nationalist collapse.[67]

For Chiang Kai-shek's friends in Washington, the White Paper appeared less a valid explanation of official policy than an apology for its failure. Senator Kenneth Wherry and other Republicans charged that the White Paper was "to a large extent a 1,054 page whitewash of a wishful, do-nothing policy which has succeeded only in placing Asia in danger of Soviet conquest with its ultimate threat to the peace of the world and our own national security."[68] Hurley called it "a smooth alibi for the pro-Communists in the State Department who have engineered the overthrow of our ally . . . and aided in the Communist conquest of China."[69] Republican floor leader in the House, Joseph Martin, titled the White Paper "An Oriental Munich." John Foster Dulles termed it "an attempt to explain and excuse past failures." Congressman John Davies Lodge asserted: "Apparently the Administration would rather lose a continent than lose a little face."[70]

Members of the China Lobby termed the China White Paper a document of profound dishonesty. They accused the administration of distortion and special pleading, of omitting documents that revealed official errors in judgment. They resented the countless unflattering depictions of the Nationalist regime, although no credible observer of the Chinese scene denied the evidence of Nationalist incompetence.[71] Nothing in the White Paper convinced them that Chiang was responsible for the Nationalist failure to hold the mainland. The China Lobby responded to the White Paper with renewed determination to rid the government of its anti-Nationalist elements, especially those it held accountable for the Communist success.

Recalling Acheson's comment on "letting the dust settle," 21 Senators, in June 1949, signed a letter to the president, protesting any contemplated recognition of China's Communist government. In early 1950, Senator Arthur Vandenberg advised the administration that any move toward recognition would have rough going as long as the Chinese mistreated U.S. officials in China.[72] It mattered little. Chiang Kai-shek, despite his approaching collapse in China, possessed almost uncontestable control over U.S. policy in East Asia.

During 1949, U.S. relations with the Chinese Communists disintegrated completely. Acheson had given the Chinese Communists the choice between friendship with the U.S.S.R. and friendship with the United States. Mao, in his "lean to one side" speech of June 1949, revealed his choice by publicly allying China with the U.S.S.R. In an imperialistic age, said Mao, a people's revolution could not secure the benefits of victory without help from international revolutionary forces. Whatever Washington's assumptions of Chinese subservience to Soviet influence, Chinese-Soviet relations remained exceedingly barren. The Chinese had long discovered that they could achieve victory without Soviet support. They understood that the U.S.S.R. pursued its own interests, and that any Soviet concerns generated by the Chinese civil war were of secondary importance. Stalin distrusted Mao as he did all strong non-Soviet Communists. He viewed China as a primitive state, with a brand of Communism that reflected its backward, peasant society. He continued to deal with the Nationalists and even advocated a coalition government for China. Anastas Mikoyan's secret mission to China, in January 1949, produced no firm offers of assistance. Only when Mao's later successes assured a Communist victory did Stalin shift his allegiance to the Chinese Communists.[73]

At the end, the final collapse of Nationalist rule in China carried U.S. policy down with it. Mao Zedong proclaimed the People's Republic of China on October 1, 1949, atop Tiananmen gate in Beijing. The State Department continued to recognize the exiled Republic of China on Formosa or Taiwan as the official government of all China. Washington and Beijing had reached a relationship as hostile and rigid as any in modern times.

* * *

Mao's triumph in China, demonstrating graphically the expansive might of Soviet ideology, seemed to place what remained of East and Southeast Asia in jeopardy—and always, as in China, through ideological, not military, conquest. Edwin F. Stanton, writing from Bangkok, admonished Washington that Soviet psychological pressures, unless countered, would cause "the whole of Southeast Asia [to] fall a victim to the Communist advance, thus coming under Russian domination without any military effort on the part of Russia."[74] In November, Foreign Service Officer Karl Lott Rankin noted that China itself had become an expansive power. He warned from Hong Kong that the new Beijing regime would now attempt, through subversion, to extend its influence across South and Southeast Asia. He outlined the extent of its ambition:

Now that communist control of China proper is all but assured, it may be taken for granted that efforts will be redoubled to place communist regimes in power elsewhere in Asia. . . . China may be considered weak and backward by Western standards, but . . . in Eastern terms, communist China is a great power, economically, militarily, and politically. Supported by communist dynamism, China might well be able to dominate not only Indochina, Siam, and Burma, but eventually the Philippines, Indonesia, Pakistan, and India itself.[75]

Such dangers besetting Asia, all emanating from the alleged Soviet conquest of China, quickly exposed Washington's deepest fears. The noted National Security Council Document NSC 48/1, dated December 23, 1949, described fully the terrible significance of events in China: "The extension of Communist authority in China represents a grievous political defeat for us; if southeast Asia also is swept by communism we shall have suffered a major political rout the repercussions of which will be felt throughout the rest of the world, especially in the Middle-East and in a then critically exposed Australia." To the NSC, the Soviet Union, through its alleged control of China, had become "an Asiatic power of the first magnitude with expanding influence and interests extending throughout continental Asia and into the Pacific.[76] Such presumptions of expanding Soviet power in Asia, all without the necessity of conquering and occupying Soviet armies, discounted totally the role of nationalism, with its single-minded quest for self-determination, in the affairs of Asia.

The fears and challenges that globalized the American confrontation with the Soviet Union had found their chief affirmation in East Asia. Whereas in Eastern Europe the West faced an unmovable Soviet occupation, in East Asia the U.S.S.R. had neither conquering nor occupying armies. There the presumption of Soviet expansion demonstrated dramatically, not the Kremlin's military might but its alleged power to expand through its command and exploitation of local Communist revolutions. In attributing to the Soviet Union the totally unprecedented capacity to pursue a career of global conquest across Asia and throughout the Third World, without reliance on armed force, U.S. officials, by mid-century, could recognize no limits to the Kremlin's expanding power and ambitions. U.S. official responses, however, never conformed to the dangers so perceived. Because the Communist movements in postwar Asia were invariably indigenous and defiant of Soviet control, they would present no dangers to Western security precise enough to permit the creation of effective countermeasures. Washington would never confront the Kremlin directly over any proclaimed Soviet-backed Communist expansion outside Europe.

This denial of nationalism as the driving force in Chinese behavior sustained the debate over Titoism as a program for achieving, in China, a repetition of what had occurred in Yugoslavia. For those in Washington who viewed the disintegration of Sino-American relations tragic but reversible, the possibilities of Chinese Titoism, freeing Beijing from its allegiance to Moscow, offered an opportunity to salvage something from the Communist victory. Some U.S. officials advocated the promise, to Beijing, of trade and diplomatic relations. Others favored a more coercive approach, designed to drive China deeper into the Soviet embrace until the Chinese reeled at the cost and sought escape in the arms of the United States. That solution required simply the creation of problems for China that its Kremlin ties could not alleviate.[77]

Washington's discourse on the possibilities of Titoism rested on the questionable presumption of a binding Moscow-Beijing relationship, one dominated by the Kremlin. For that presumption the Yugoslav experience provided no precedent. There was no monolith. The supposition that Communist ideology created some special affinity among Communist states suggested that Tito's break from Moscow, in June 1948, was unusual, perhaps unique. Actually, Tito's easy assertion of Yugoslavia's independence from Stalin's authority demonstrated again the absence of Kremlin hegemony beyond the reach of Soviet armies. If the Kremlin could establish no forcible control over neighboring Communist-led Yugoslavia, it is not clear how it could do so over a Communist government in a huge, distant, self-centered, sovereign, historically antagonistic, and highly nationalistic country such as China, especially without a huge bureaucracy backed by an overpowering army. A country that had regarded itself the center of the world for five thousand years was not inclined to recognize any superiority in Soviet civilization, wisdom, or power. The Chinese Communist Party was indigenous, both organizationally and ideologically; it owed little or nothing to the Soviets for its successes. As a device for manipulating Sino-Soviet relations, Titoism—like U.S. policy in Asia generally—denied the force of nationalism and the reality that China was always free to pursue its external relations in accordance with its own interests.

George Kennan and John Paton Davies, his associate on the Policy Planning Staff, led a counterattack on the official denial of nationalism as Southeast Asia's natural defense against Soviet or Chinese expansionism. Southeast Asia had never been of major concern to Kennan. But Davies had long regarded the region of primary importance to the Western World, both strategically and economically. At Bangkok's diplomatic conference in June 1948, which he attended as a State Department representative, Davies discovered that American officials from China to India seemed determined to tie all Southeast Asia into a regional bloc against Soviet expansionism, much as the United States was attempting to do in Europe. In July, Davies presented his rebuttal to the Policy Planning Staff. For him, Southeast Asia's security rested, not on military defenses, but on the power of nationalism, then driving the independence movements throughout the region. The Soviets, he noted, always supported nationalist causes while the United States appeared to oppose them in deference to the interests of the colonial powers. For Davies, the United States would serve its concern for Southeast Asian security far better by identifying its interests with the struggles of those seeking to overthrow colonial regimes, whether those regimes belonged to European allies or not.

Kennan applied Davies's advice to Indonesia where nationalist leaders—Sukarno, Hatta, and Sjahrir—had declared the independence of the Indonesian republic as early as August 1945. Japan had encouraged the Indonesian nationalists by giving them high wartime positions and leaving behind a well-armed and well-led independence movement. As in Indochina, Washington favored the continuation of colonial rule and refused to take the proclamation of the Republic of Indonesia seriously. The Dutch, like the French, had never relinquished their sovereignty over their colonies. Stanley Hornbeck, U.S. ambassador to the Netherlands, took up the Dutch cause, in December 1945, by warning Washington that the disappearance of Dutch rule in Indonesia would create a vacuum that would invite external encroachments.[78] Walter A. Foote, former consul in Batavia, reported to Washington repeatedly that the Indonesian people wanted peace, not independence.[79] As American relations with the U.S.S.R. and China continued to deteriorate, U.S. support for the Dutch became increasingly firm.

In October 1947, Frank Graham, former president of the University of North Carolina, arrived in Indonesia with his associate, Charlton Ogburn, as a member of the UN Committee of Good Offices in search of a peaceful solution of the Indonesian conflict. The committee achieved nothing, but the two Americans discovered much. In November Ogburn informed the State Department that the Indonesians demanded unqualified independence and that the Dutch were destined to lose. The longer that independence was delayed, Graham and Ogburn warned, the worse the political strife would become.[80] Robert A. Lovett, acting secretary of state, reminded Graham that U.S. support for the Indonesian nationalists would undermine the Dutch government and damage the American position in Europe.[81] In June 1948, Coert du Bois, Graham's successor, informed Washington that unless the Dutch recognized Indonesia's independence quickly they would lose all their economic advantages in the islands. The republicans, he predicted, would rule well and cooperate with the Dutch—who were over demanding.[82]

Washington now turned on the Dutch. Lovett, reflecting the new approach, informed the Dutch on September 17 that "Indonesian nationalism must be accommodated in a just and practical way as a condition precedent to dealing with Communism in that area."[83] Kennan, also convinced that further Dutch resistance would lead to chaos exploitable by Communists, predicted, in December, that a Communist victory would lead to the fall of Thailand and Malaya and "sweep westward through the continent to Burma, India, and Pakistan." An independent Indonesia, on the other hand, would anchor "that chain of islands stretching from Hokkaido to Sumatra which we should develop as a politico-economic counter-force to communism on the Asiatic land mass."[84] During succeeding months the U.S. demand for the fulfillment of Indonesian aspirations was continuous. When the Dutch government again insisted on a commonwealth arrangement that the nationalists had long rejected, members of Congress threatened to cut off all Marshall Plan aid. Without hope of victory and facing global opposition, the Dutch negotiated a truce and, at The Hague Round-Table Conference of August–October 1949, awarded independence to Indonesia.[85] Washington's acknowledgement of Indonesian nationalism as the ultimate defense against Communist encroachment came hard, but, unlike in Indochina, it came with telling effect.

It was left for India's Jawaharlal Nehru to challenge the full spectrum of U.S. Cold War assumptions in Asia. Nehru's forceful acceptance of nationalism as the driving force in Asian affairs denied the relevance of Communism to Asia's quest for independence. The Communist regimes of Asia, Nehru argued, were legitimate expressions of self-determination, not, as Washington proclaimed, the creations of Soviet expansionism. As early as September 1946, Nehru rejected his country's involvement in the burgeoning East-West conflict. "India," he said, "will follow an independent policy, keeping away from the power politics of groups aligned one against the other." Instead, it would uphold the right of dependent peoples to have governments of their own.

Until the threatened fall of Nationalist China in the summer of 1949, India's external outlook mattered little to Washington. U.S. officials saw that an independent India might play the stabilizing, pro-Western role in Asia that they had once held out to China. Nehru accepted an invitation to visit the United States, arriving in Washington on October 11, 1949. In talks with U.S. officials, he refused to consider any proposal at the expense of India's established neutralism.

Nehru denied that Asia was endangered by the Communist-controlled states of China, Indochina, or even North Korea. He advised Acheson that the French adherence to the pro-Western Bao Dai regime in Indochina was doomed to failure and that U.S. policy would sink with it. Ho Chi Minh, Nehru argued, was a Communist, but no danger to Asian security. He announced that India would soon recognize the Communist government of China—which it did in December. The Chinese government, he asserted, was stable and nothing would supplant it. Such devotion to nationalism, such expressions of moderation and confidence, were alien to Washington. Acheson admitted Nehru's importance to India and Asia. "Nevertheless," he recalled in his memoirs, "[Nehru] was one of the most difficult men with whom I ever had to deal."[86]

* * *

Strangely, the Communist threat to East Asia was so confined to the realm of rhetoric that it scarcely raised the question of regional security. But in February 1948, Kennan advised the State Department "to see what parts of the Pacific and Far Eastern world are absolutely vital to our security."[87] On March 14, he wrote from Manila that the United States had no overall strategy for the defense of the western Pacific. American bases and forces in the region comprised no coordinated system of protection against anyone. Kennan suggested to Marshall that the United States anchor its western Pacific defenses to Okinawa—a recommendation, he added, that had the full approval of General MacArthur and other American officers in the region. For Kennan, Okinawa would be only the most advanced base in a U-shaped security zone that reached from the Aleutians to the Ryukyus, the former Japanese mandated islands, and Guam. American air and naval forces at Okinawa seemed sufficient to prevent the assembling and launching of any amphibious force from the central Asian mainland. Following Philippine independence, in July 1946, the Manila government, under Manuel Roxas, granted the United States permission to recover its former bases. To Kennan, however, it was not clear whether the United States maintained its Philippine bases to defend the islands, support operations elsewhere, or for no reason at all.[88] Kennan saw no need to include Japan and the Philippines in any American defense perimeter, provided that the islands could be neutralized and their independence assured.

By 1947, Japan had achieved political stability within its new free environment, but not a strong economy. The country had no protection other than that supplied by U.S. forces. In October, Kennan warned the State Department that Japan would not achieve the economic power required for a proper national defense without a major revision in allied occupation policy.[89] He advocated the elimination of some economic controls, permitting Japan's industrial potential to become a force for progress and stability in Pacific affairs. The continued breakup of Japan's industrial combines, he complained, served no recognizable purpose and prevented economic growth.[90] Shortly before departing for Japan in March, Kennan reminded Marshall that the occupation had achieved its objectives as defined in the Potsdam Declaration.

Kennan's study trip to Japan overlapped William Draper's mission to examine economic conditions in that country. Draper, like Kennan, arrived with an agenda: to demonstrate the necessity for Japan's economic recovery. Kennan's report of March 25, 1948, recommended a shift from reform to the preparation of Japan for the occupation's termination.[91] The Draper Committee report of April, complementing Kennan's, advocated the termination of MacArthur's reform measures, the encouragement of foreign investments, and the rebuilding of Japan's merchant marine.[92] In May, the United States appropriated $150 million for Japan's economic reconstruction. Kennan's report, slightly revised, emerged in October as official U.S. policy, changing the thrust of the occupation from reform to recovery.[93] MacArthur's acceptance of the new policy was so reluctant, the changes so imperceptible that many observers were scarcely conscious of them.[94]

Kennan had no desire to see Japan integrated into American strategy for the defense of the western Pacific until it could fulfill its own security obligations. MacArthur agreed with Kennan that Japan should not be incorporated into the American defense perimeter. Those who disagreed won the argument; Japan soon entered heavily into American plans for regional defense. The Joint Chiefs of Staff recognized Japan's strategic location for staging possible action on the Asian mainland.[95] By June 1949, the Joint Chiefs agreed that the minimum U.S. position "in the Far East vis-a-vis the U.S.S.R., one to which we are rapidly being forced, requires at least our present degree of control of the Asian offshore island chain." To that end they proposed that the United States maintain its bases and forces in Japan.

While the administration accepted the necessity of an island perimeter defense in the western Pacific, it made the fundamental decision to avoid any commitment to the defense of South Korea. In June 1949, as the last American troops left South Korea, the Joint Chiefs concluded that an American police action in Korea would involve an over-commitment of the country's manpower and resources in the Far East. "From the strategic viewpoint," ran their report, "the position of the Joint Chiefs of Staff regarding Korea ... is that Korea is of little strategic value to the United States and that any commitment ... of military forces in Korea would be ill-advised and impracticable in view of the potentialities of the over-all world situation and of our heavy international obligations."[96]

Similarly, the administration rejected any commitment to the defense of Formosa. The Cairo and Potsdam conferences had agreed that Formosa belonged to China. In late 1949, however, U.S. officials moved quickly to prevent China's new regime from gaining control of the island. To conceal their purpose of separating the island from the mainland, they agreed to promote Formosan autonomy. The State Department dispatched Livingston T. Merchant to analyze the island's political future. Merchant predicted that Chiang Kai-shek would dominate Formosa. Convinced, however, that the Nationalist government would remain incompetent and unpopular, he advised Washington to disassociate itself from the exiled regime. Many State and Defense Department officials, warning that a possible Communist conquest of the island would endanger the nation's strategic position in the western Pacific, preferred to keep the island militarily neutral. They agreed with the administration that the American commitment to the Philippines, Okinawa, and Japan was sufficient to protect the western Pacific against Communist expansion.[97]

In late December, Senator Knowland of California, returning from a trip to Formosa, urged the administration to send a military mission to the island. Early in January, he released a letter from former President Herbert Hoover that declared that the United States should continue to support the Nationalists and, if necessary, extend naval protection to Formosa and the Pescadores. Truman replied, on January 5, that the United States had no intention of becoming involved in China's civil war by committing American forces to protect the Nationalist government. Economic aid would continue but "no military aid or advice."[98] Defending the administration's Formosa decision, Acheson that day reminded the Senate Foreign Relations Committee of the dangers in supporting the Nationalists on Formosa, a cause for which few Americans would care to fight. He informed Knowland that U.S. resistance to the Chinese Communists had ended, and that Congress must be prepared to accept Formosa's collapse.[99]

Already the administration had determined that Communist expansion in Asia not move beyond China. In July 1949, Acheson appointed a review committee under Philip C. Jessup to examine U.S. policy in Asia. Any new approach, he advised, must "make absolutely certain that [we] are neglecting no opportunity that would be within our capabilities to achieve the purpose of halting the spread of totalitarian communism in Asia." He instructed Jessup to take, as his assumption, the fundamental decision that "the United States does not intend to permit further extension of communist domination on the continent of Asia or in the Southeast Asia area."[100] This crisis mood, and the containment of Soviet expansion in Asia that it demanded, found its ultimate expression in the National Security Council Staff Paper NSC 48/2, approved by the president on December 31, 1949. The paper accepted the premise that in East Asia the United States faced "a coordinated offensive directed by the Kremlin."[101] The document defined the full range of policies designed to defend the vast regions of Asia against that danger. It advocated the treatment of China as a hostile country, but one vulnerable to economic sanctions and not permanently lost to the Soviet camp. To exploit any rifts between Stalinists and other elements in China, the United States would avoid a posture toward Communist China harsher than it reserved for the U.S.S.R. itself. The United States would continue to support South Korea and Formosa through the United Nations as well as through diplomatic and economic means, but not with "overt military action . . . so long as the present disparity between our military strength and our global obligations exists." The Asian offshore island defenses would focus on Japan, Okinawa, and the Philippines. Elsewhere the United States would seek to strengthen regional security against Communist aggression and subversion by providing "political, economic and military assistance and advice where needed." Toward the remaining colonial areas, the United States would attempt both to satisfy the fundamental objectives of nationalist movements and to minimize the strain on its colonial allies. In Indochina, the United States would encourage the French to lift all barriers to Bao Dai's success. Nowhere did NSC 48/2 contemplate conflict in the containment of Asian Communism.[102] But it anticipated the gradual reduction, and eventual elimination, of "the preponderant power and influence of the USSR in Asia to such a degree that the Soviet Union will not be capable of threatening from that area the security of the United States." If the document appeared utopian, it assumed that the major arena of East-West conflict was Europe, that the pressures in Asia were largely political and psychological, and that the Soviets did not contemplate military aggression in Asia. The prescriptions of

NSC 48/2 scarcely recognized any troublesome dangers in the vast region of East Asia.

By early 1950, the American high command had adopted the concept of a perimeter defense for the western Pacific. Acheson acknowledged that decision publicly when, in his National Press Club speech of January 12, 1950, he proclaimed a defense perimeter that ran "along the Aleutians to Japan and then . . . to the Ryukyus . . . [and] from the Ryukyus to the Philippine Islands."[103] Acheson's exclusion of both Korea and Formosa from the perimeter reflected established policy. Supported as he was by the Joint Chiefs, MacArthur, and Truman, the secretary was puzzled that anyone would accuse him of innovation in his National Press Club statement. The perimeter defense presumed that bases on the Asian mainland were both unnecessary for American security and an over-commitment of U.S. power in the Pacific. Administration officials doubted that even a hostile China could launch a successful amphibious attack against the island defenses. Acheson reminded the Senate Foreign Relations Committee that the United States had far greater security interests in Europe than in the Far East, and could not sustain a global defense structure. "We cannot scatter our shots equally all over the world," he warned. "We just haven't got enough shots to do that. . . . If anything happens in Western Europe the whole business goes to pieces, and therefore our principal effort must be on building up . . . the strength of Western Europe, and so far as Asia is concerned, treating that as a holding operation."[104]

CHAPTER 7

The National Security State

For those who accepted the full range of American Cold War assumptions, two events of late 1949 shattered the dream of a stable East-West equilibrium. The Communist victory in China, adding perhaps a half billion people to the Communist bloc, loomed as a disastrous miscarriage of the U.S. policy of containment. Official rhetoric warned that Mao's triumph exposed millions elsewhere to Chinese encroachments. If the Communist conquest of China elicited only a limited U.S. response, for countless citizens of the United States and Western Europe it vastly diminished the security of the non-Soviet world. But the worst was yet to come. In late August 1949, the explosion of a Soviet atomic device terminated abruptly the American atomic monopoly on which all Western military strategies against possible Soviet aggression relied. Clearly, it seemed, the West's external security policies required an overhaul.[1] To minimize the impact of the Soviet atomic explosion on both the American mind and the American military budget, the administration discounted its significance. The explosion, the president assured the press, had not taken the government by surprise. "The eventual development of this new force," he declared, "was to be expected. This probability has always been taken into account by us." Dean Acheson repeated that assurance, reminding the press that the administration, in its atomic policy, had anticipated the Soviet scientific triumph. Newsmen seemed to accept these assurances, but some writers noted, with concern, that the Soviet achievement came three years before predicted.[2] Nothing could deny, moreover, that Soviet weapons development, in time, would place American cities in jeopardy.

It was precisely such fears that the administration sought to prevent. The president had informed reporters as early as October 1948 that the United States could not afford military budgets of $14–$15 billion a year. The rationale for limited military expenditures was implicit in the Report of the Committee on the National Security Organization (the so-called Eberstadt Committee) of January 1949. The report asked the armed services to recognize that American strength resided as much in the health of the nation's economy as in the status of its military defenses. The Eberstadt Committee warned that the projected $15 billion defense budget for 1950 was already "imposing strains on the civilian economy and on the underlying human, material, and financial resources on which effective military strength depend."[3] Much of the press agreed with the committee's concern for financial restraint. The *New York Times'* military expert, Hanson W. Baldwin, concluded on January 16, 1949, that the higher levels of military expenditures, if continued, would ruin the country's economy.[4] Truman's ceiling of $15 billion received the full support of key Washington officials, including Louis Johnson who succeeded Forrestal as secretary of defense in March 1949. On October 30, the president signed a $15.6 billion defense appropriation. For fiscal 1951 the administration accepted a ceiling of $13.5 billion, with promises to pursue the downward course to $10 billion.[5]

Throughout 1949, the president's moderate defense program faced an increasingly critical press, compelling him to explain its adequacy. On May 22 the *Washington Post* called for the creation of a bipartisan commission on national security to determine whether the Truman defense economies endangered the country's security. Congressman Carl Vinson questioned the impact of the president's economy program on the effectiveness of the armed forces. He took up the defense issue in the House Armed Services Committee, instituting an investigation that carried into 1950. Vinson concluded that, in his judgment, the administration's "economy scalpel has not only carved away some service fat, but has cut—deeply in some areas—into sinew and muscle of the armed services."[6]

The requirement of having sufficient atomic weapons, to offset Soviet conventional capability, had driven the United States into a one-sided quest for atomic supremacy long before the Soviet atomic test. Following the explosion—on August 29, 1949—Secretary of the Air Force W. Stuart Symington reminded the administration that the country's unprecedented vulnerability to major destruction required a stronger deterrent in the form of an expanded atomic arsenal and a more effective delivery capability.[7] Meanwhile, the Joint Chiefs of Staff endorsed the development of a thermonuclear, or hydrogen, bomb.

Such noted physicists as Edward Teller and Ernest O. Lawrence, as well as Atomic Energy Commission members Lewis L. Strauss and Gordon Dean, promoted the nuclear bomb program, convinced that it had some technical feasibility. The Joint Chiefs, in its statement of January 13, 1950, concluded that the super bomb, if deployed, could serve the cause of peace by vastly increasing the country's deterrent capability. Moreover, the decision not to build the bomb would not prevent the Soviets from doing so.[8] On the issue of the bomb's potential destructiveness, the Joint Chiefs' memorandum concluded: "[I]t is difficult to escape the conviction that in war it is folly to argue whether one weapon is more immoral than another. For, in the larger sense, it is war itself which is immoral, and the stigma of such immorality must rest upon the nation which initiates hostilities."[9] Unfortunately, throughout the history of modern war, that stigma was often difficult to assign. Truman responded sympathetically to the Joint Chiefs' memorandum.

Not all in Washington agreed. On January 20, George Kennan submitted his personal critique to Acheson, questioning the decision to base strategy on weapons of mass destruction. Were the weapons, he asked, to be used in war or merely as instruments of deterrence? If their purpose were to discourage an attack on the United States, nuclear weapons would be redundant. If they were to assure maximum destruction, then their use would be as threatening to democracy as any other form of government. The modes of warfare, wrote Kennan, could not dismiss a nation's obligation to human welfare. "The weapons of mass destruction," he concluded, "do not have this quality. . . . They fail to take account of the ultimate responsibility of men for one another, and even for each other's errors and mistakes." Kennan believed that a system of international atomic control, however imperfect, would serve the country's interests better than reliance on weapons of mass destruction.[10] Neither Kennan's arguments nor those of others failed to impede the super bomb momentum in Washington. On January 31, the president directed the Atomic Energy Commission "to continue its work on all forms of atomic weapons, including the so-called hydrogen or super-bomb."[11]

* * *

On the day that he announced his thermonuclear bomb decision, the president called on the departments of State and Defense to "undertake a re-examination of our objectives in peace and war, and of the effects of these objectives on our strategic plans, in light of the probable fission bomb capability . . . of the Soviet Union."[12] During the next two months the State-Defense Review Group created the noted document NSC 68. For Acheson it was one of the most important documents in American history. As a statement of advocacy, NSC 68 reflected the determination of Acheson and his associate, Paul Nitze, Kennan's successor as director of the Policy Planning Staff, to prepare the administration and the country for a vastly expanded defense posture. Nitze entered the task of framing the document, convinced that the United States would either enhance its own and allied military capabilities or lose the peace.[13]

Designed to kindle the nation's insecurities, NSC 68 comprised the final and most elaborate attempt of Truman's Cold War elite to arrive at a definition of an adequate national defense policy. This document, like its predecessors, described the danger of Soviet expansionism in global, limitless terms. It concluded that the U.S.S.R., "unlike previous aspirants to hegemony, is animated by a new fanatic faith, antithetical to our own, and seeks to impose its absolute authority over the rest of the world." Conflict had become endemic, waged by the Soviets through by violent and nonviolent methods in accordance with the dictates of expediency. "The issues that face us," NSC 68 continued, "are momentous, involving the fulfillment or destruction not only of the Republic but of civilization itself." The Kremlin design called for subversion of the entire non-Soviet world. "To that end," the document warned, "Soviet efforts are now directed toward the domination of the Eurasian land mass. The United States, as the principle center of power in the non-Soviet world and the bulwark of opposition to Soviet expansion, is the principal enemy."[14] Only by recognizing such dangers could the America frame an adequate defense.

"These risks," warned NSC 68, "crowd in on us, in a shrinking world of polarized power, so as to give us no choice, ultimately, between meeting them effectively or being overcome by them." To confront the Soviet challenge, NSC 68 advocated "a substantial and rapid buildup of strength in the free world ... to support a firm policy intended to check and roll back the Kremlin's drive for world domination."[15] However grave the danger, NSC 68, like its predecessors, assumed that the United States, with "calculated and gradual coercion," could unleash the forces of destruction within the Soviet empire. Washington had no reason to curtail its overall objective of frustrating the Kremlin design. Rather than pursue unconditional surrender, however, the United States would seek Soviet acceptance of "the specific and limited conditions requisite to an international environment in which free institutions can flourish, and in which the Russian people will have a new chance of working out their own destiny." In this necessary effort to limit Soviet ambitions to the needs of Soviet citizens and the requirements of a peaceful world, the United States could anticipate support even within the U.S.S.R. "If we can make the Russian people our allies in this enterprise," NSC 68 predicted, "we will obviously have made our task easier and victory more certain." In the process of inducing change, the United States would avoid, as far as possible, any direct challenge to Soviet prestige and "keep open the possibility for the U.S.S.R. to retreat before pressure with a minimum loss of face."[16] However grave the dangers portrayed in this most terrifying of documents, their elimination was assured without risk or war.

Nitze and Acheson defended the document's exaggeration as a necessity. Nothing less, they insisted, would enable them to establish the need for a fully militarized containment policy. It was essential, Acheson recalled, that a public official, seeking to carry a point, adopt arguments "clearer than truth." For Acheson, NSC 68's purpose "was to so bludgeon the mass mind of 'top government' that not only could the president make a decision but that the decision could be carried out."[17] Charles Bohlen admitted that the document exaggerated the Soviet threat, but believed that the international situation justified its oversimplification.[18] Dictatorial governments, NSC 68 lamented, could act with speed and secrecy, whereas democracies could not. The United States, therefore, could compensate for its natural vulnerability only if it maintained "clearly superior overall power in its most inclusive sense."[19] The authors of NSC 68 were not troubled by the lack of evidence regarding the specific location and nature of the dangers. For Nitze, the problem lay simply in the Marxist-Leninist notion that Communist socialism was destined to triumph everywhere. It was the very abstractness and universality of the threat that rendered it so awesome.

NSC 68 itself warned that a program for the rapid buildup of military strength would place heavy demands on the American people, requiring courage and sacrifice. "Budgetary considerations," the document concluded, "will need to be subordinated to the stark fact that our very independence as a nation may be at stake."[20] What ultimately made the higher military expenditures both possible and feasible was the Keynesian view of national economic management as advocated by Leon Keyserling, chairman of the president's Council of Economic Advisers. Keyserling convinced those who advocated expansion of the military program that the government could resort to deficit financing and stimulate the entire economy without injury to the nation's welfare.

Although it embodied a full response to Soviet expansionism, NSC 68 anticipated neither war nor peace, but rather the continuation of global conflict until the Kremlin chose to accept the implications of its declining world role. That minority of Americans who doubted the United States could dominate the U.S.S.R. without war pressed Acheson to explain the Western buildup of power. In confronting his critics, Acheson rationalized his preoccupation with power as a temporary condition, preparatory to an eventual resolution of the Cold War largely on Western terms. Until the U.S. advantage was sufficient to produce precisely that result, Acheson preferred that the West avoid any negotiations. The very notion of a global conflict in a fluid power relationship, he asserted, rendered all diplomatic settlements elusive, meaningless, and perhaps dangerous. Any accommodation that recognized the existing spheres of influence would merely encourage the Soviets in their pursuit of world domination.[21] To deflate the notion that power had become an end in itself and gave the nation's defense policies, especially after the hydrogen bomb decision, a needed sense of purpose, Acheson developed the promising concept of negotiation from strength. He first developed the theme at a press conference on February 8, 1950:

We have seen ... that agreements reached with the Soviet Government are useful when those agreements register facts. ... So it has been our basic policy to build situations which will extend the area of possible agreement; that is, to create strength instead of weakness which exists in many quarters. ... Those are illustrations of the way in which, in various parts of the world, we are trying to extend the area of possible agreement with the Soviet Union by creating situations so strong they can be recognized and out of them can grow agreement.[22]

Acheson's concept of negotiation from strength meant, in practice, no negotiation at all. It mattered little. NSC 68 assumed that the United States could create conditions that would compel the Kremlin to accept capitulation.

NSC 68 remained a secret document, but its precepts flowed through the official speeches and correspondence of the time. Throughout the spring of 1950, Acheson took the premises of NSC 68 on the road. What drove Kremlin policy, he told the American Society of Newspaper Editors in April, was not a traditional struggle for power, but a fanatical, expansive ideology. The danger was especially pervading because the Soviets had singled out the United States as the only country that stood between it and dominion over the entire world. "We are faced with a threat," Acheson continued, "in all sober truth I say this—we are faced with a threat not only to our country but to the civilization of which we live and to the whole physical environment in which that civilization can exist."[23] Soviet military power demanded an effective deterrence. But to commit U.S. air, naval, and land forces to the elimination of the global threat that Acheson described encumbered them with burdens that defied the creation of a rational policy.

* * *

Throughout the early months of 1950, U.S. officials perfected their rationale of Soviet expansionism in East Asia. Acheson, in his National Press Club speech of January 12, stressed the relationship between Asian Communism and Soviet imperialism. "Communism," he said, "is the most subtle instrument of Soviet foreign policy that has ever been devised, and it is really the spearhead of Russian imperialism." The Kremlin's victory in gaining China's allegiance demonstrated "the true function of communism as an agent of Russian imperialism."[24] For Acheson the Sino-Soviet Treaty of Friendship, Alliance, and Mutual Assistance, signed in Moscow during February 1950, demolished all doubt that the China had become a puppet of the Moscow Politburo. He warned the Chinese that they would bring grave trouble on themselves if they were "led by their new rulers into aggressive or subversive adventures beyond their borders."[25]

Actually, the seven weeks of negotiations in Moscow revealed that all was not well in the Mao-Stalin relationship. Throughout the long negotiations, the Chinese and Soviet leaders were at the breaking point, held together largely by their mutually tense relations with the United States. When Mao reached Moscow in December 1949, Stalin kept him in a dacha outside the city. The Sino-Soviet pact itself committed the two countries to the consolidation of their economic and cultural ties. The Kremlin promised China credits of $300 million, spread over five years, and relinquished earlier concessions over Manchurian railroads and ports. Nothing in the treaty implied binding ties between Moscow and Beijing; nor as a defensive pact, primarily against Japan, did it threaten aggressive action against anyone. Under what conditions—and against whom—the pact would function remained unclear.[26]

But to Acheson the Soviet control of China was complete. When China appeared to be achieving true national independence, he told the Commonwealth Club of California in March, its leaders were forcing it into the Soviet orbit. "We now face the prospect," he warned, "that the Communists may attempt to apply another familiar tactic to use China as a base for probing for another weak spot which they can move into and exploit." He reminded Asians that they "must face the fact that today the major threat to their freedom and to their social and economic progress is the attempted penetration of Asia by Soviet-Communist imperialism and by the colonialism which it contains."[27] In New Delhi, on March 27, Ambassador Loy Henderson chided India's leaders for not cooperating with the United States in confronting the "powerful forces in the world which feed on human poverty and suffering." Upon his return from East Asia, Ambassador Philip Jessup, on April 13, explained Asia's new importance. Asia had become critical, he proclaimed over ABC, "because Soviet communism is clearly out to capture and colonize the continent." Asians everywhere relied on the United States for their defense.[28] Such official assumptions of Soviet power and expansionism called for a strategy that would diminish, if not eliminate, the danger. Such a strategy, however, lay far outside the country's interests and capabilities.

The persistent charges of failure in past U.S. China policy suggested that the real foundation for Communist success in East Asia lay somewhere in Washington. An English journalist, in an April 1950 letter to columnist Walter Lippmann, observed that the United States, in American eyes, was "by definition incapable of being defeated. The United States has nevertheless been defeated in China. Since the United States cannot be defeated, it must have been defeated by treachery, [and] therefore, somewhere in the high command there must be a Soviet spy to explain the otherwise impossible fact that the United States has suffered a diplomatic defeat."[29] It was left for Senator Joseph R. McCarthy of Wisconsin not only to give life to the continuing crusade to return Chiang Kai-shek to the mainland, but also to relieve the American people of the burden of taxes and possible war. In his sensational speech at Wheeling, West Virginia, in February 1950, McCarthy charged that the State Department, especially its Far Eastern Division, was infested with Communists. Chiang, he asserted, had been the victim, not of revolutionary changes in China, but of a Communist conspiracy in Washington "on a scale so immense as to dwarf any previous venture in the history of man." McCarthy invented the scapegoat of collective treason and employed it, wrote scholar Hans J. Morgenthau, "to reconcile the delusion of our omnipotence with the experience of limited power."[30]

Republican leaders, especially members of the China bloc, endorsed McCarthy's charges because they had become indispensable to their anti-Communist crusade in China. These charges also exposed the State Department, Foreign Service, and the administration to limitless attack. U.S. diplomats in wartime China had predicted China's Communist future with incredible accuracy, but it was a future unbearable to the country's pro-Chiang legions. The inclusion of their reports in the White Paper sealed their doom and undermined the State Department's Asian bureau in the process.[31] Gradually the assault simmered down to a persistent flaying of Acheson. Many of the attacks on Acheson and the State Department were textually similar to the pro-Chiang charges leveled earlier by Alfred Kohlberg and other members of the China Lobby.[32] Through McCarthy, the country's pro-Chiang elements gained profound influence on American attitudes toward China.[33] They would discover soon enough that their dominance of the American mind was irrelevant to the course of events in China.

* * *

In Indochina the United States maintained its firm attachment to French policy under the continuing assumption that Ho Chi Minh, no less than Mao, was a puppet of the Kremlin. In January 1950, both Moscow and Beijing recognized Ho's newly-established Democratic Republic of Vietnam. Acheson declared that the Soviet recognition of Ho's government revealed him "in his true color as the mortal enemy of national independence in Indochina."[34] Similarly Charles W. Yost, director of the Office of East European Affairs, warned that Soviet recognition strengthened the Soviet presence in Southeast Asia and made Indochina "the focal point of the most intensive and determined Communist pressure." The French Assembly, on January 29, granted autonomy to Vietnam within the French Union, but informed Washington that it had no intention of granting Vietnam full independence. Nevertheless, in February, the United States recognized the French-backed Bao Dai government of Vietnam. Thereafter the notion that the Paris-chosen native aristocrat had better claims to Vietnamese leadership than Ho Chi Minh and would ultimately triumph became official doctrine in Washington. In March, Livingston Merchant reminded the State Department that another Communist triumph on the Asian mainland "could be expected adversely to affect our interests in India, Pakistan and even the Philippines." On April 14 the Joint Chiefs defined Indochina as "a vital segment in the line of containment of communism stretching from Japan southward and around the Indian Peninsula. The security of . . . Japan, India, and Australia . . . depends in a large measure on the denial of Southeast Asia to the Communists." On June 8, Assistant Secretary of State Dean Rusk informed the Senate Foreign Relations Committee that the war in Indochina was not a civil war but a war "captured by the Politburo. It is part of an international war, ... and because Ho Chi Minh is tied in with the Politburo our policy is to support Bao Dai and the French in Indochina."[35] Such fears bound Washington to the French cause.

On February 16, the State Department sent a mission to Indochina, under Robert Allen Griffin, to determine French-Indochinese military requirements.[36] Washington acknowledged no choice but "to support the legal government of Indochina or to face the extension of communism over the remainder of the continental area of Southeast Asia and possibly westward." Acheson feared that the beleaguered French might quit the Asian scene and permit Communism to flood all Southeast Asia. In March, the secretary informed the Senate Foreign Relations Committee of the danger that the French might attempt to transfer the burden of Indochina to the United States. "We want the French to stay there," he said, ". . . the French have got to carry [the burden] in Indochina, and we are willing to help, but not to substitute for them."[37] Unless the colonial powers succeeded in protecting their colonies, Acheson warned, the Western position in Asia would collapse.

To keep France in Southeast Asia, the Joint Chiefs, in April, recommended military assistance. On May 1, Congress approved a $10 million military aid program for Indochina. Then on May 8, Acheson negotiated an arrangement with Foreign Minister Schuman whereby France and Indochina together would carry the responsibility for the requisite Communist defeat. Acheson defined it for the press, "The United States Government, convinced that neither national independence nor democratic evolution exist in any area dominated by Soviet imperialism, considers the situation to be such as to warrant its according economic aid and military equipment to the Associated States of Indochina and to France in order to assist them in restoring stability and permitting these states to pursue their peaceful and democratic development."[38] Much of the press accepted the administration's program as a necessary precaution. The New York Times editorialized, on May 9, that "Indochina occupies a critically strategic position—if it falls to the Communist advance the whole of Southeast Asia will be in mortal peril."

For many U.S. officials, Formosa remained the essential barrier to Communist adventurism off the Asian mainland. Senator William F. Knowland warned Acheson that the administration, in denying any responsibility for Formosa's safety, "was pursuing a policy of grave danger to the American people." For Rusk, Formosa was the key to the defense of the western Pacific and Southeast Asia. Late in May, he recommended neutralization of the island to keep it out of Communist hands. "If we do not act," he wrote, "it will be everywhere interpreted that we are making another retreat because we do not dare risk war. . . . But sometimes such a risk has to be taken."[39] General Douglas MacArthur observed, in mid-June, that Okinawa and the Philippines were especially vulnerable to attack from Formosa. He warned that Formosa, under Kremlin control, would be "an unsinkable aircraft carrier and submarine tender ideally located to accomplish Soviet offensive strategy and at the same time checkmate counteroffensive operations by United States Forces based on Okinawa and the Philippines."[40] Still Truman and Acheson were not prepared to underwrite the defense of Formosa from a possible Chinese attack.

* * *

What troubled many contemporary analysts was the absence of evidence that Soviet imperialism was the essential catalyst in Asia's political upheaval. National governments, whatever their ideologies, had never willingly bargained away their sovereignty or slavishly anchored their policies to the dictates of other countries. Far Eastern expert Owen Lattimore condemned the popular assumption that China had fallen under Soviet control. His vigorous denial appeared in the *Nation* on September 3, 1949, "China is a fact. The Chinese Communists are a fact. It is a fact that Russian strength remains concentrated and deployable, and that no detectable part of it has been diverted or committed to China." Walter Lippmann, speaking before the Chicago Council on Foreign Relations on February 22, 1950, reminded his audience: "While it is true that we have lost our power and for the time being most of our influence in China, it by no means follows that Russia has won control of China or has achieved an enduring alliance with China."[41] Experts agreed that the driving force for change in Asia was nationalism. There was, as Philippine statesman Carlos Romulo informed a Harvard audience in June 1950, an unwillingness among U.S. officials to view Asia through Asian eyes, a view, he averred, that would reveal the presence of nationalism behind every Asian social and political movement.[42] The Soviets understood that no country had ever conquered China, and that any untoward effort to influence policy in China would face repulsion.[43] It was absurd, declared the *Manchester Guardian Weekly*, to "confuse the China of Mao Tse-tung with the satellites of Eastern Europe."[44] Mao's Communist regime, riding the crest of a powerful nationalist uprising, was more nationalist than the Chiang's Kuomintang.[45]

For the aroused Chinese masses, Communism simply carried the promise of a more comfortable, satisfactory existence, a promise that the Kuomintang never made convincingly.[46] John K. Fairbank, Harvard's noted China expert, criticized Washington for failing to distinguish between China's massive social upheaval and its highly ideological political revolution. Mao's power, Fairbank noted, was based less on ideology or coercion than on an alignment with a social revolution that far antedated the rise of the Communist crusade.[47] Nathaniel Peffer, Columbia University's eminent Asian scholar, observed that the United States had not escaped the penalty of its massive miscalculations in China. While the world concluded that nothing would save the Nationalist regime, the United States, Peffer charged, continued to deepen is moral commitment to Chiang, squandering its influence and goodwill in Asia and antagonizing China's victors in the process. It was natural, he concluded, that the United States be kicked out of China.[48]

Critics challenged, as well, the notion that a Soviet threat to Indochina demanded the potentially exorbitant price of supporting France. Few observers believed that the French effort to gain the necessary native support through the creation of the Bao Dai regime would succeed. Only if the French transferred genuine sovereignty to Indochina, critics agreed, would the Bao Dai regime have any chance of survival. As French writer J. R. Clementin observed in September 1950, "[I]t is impossible to name a single Vietnamese nationalist leader with enough authority to take many partisans along with him. This is the crux of the problem."[49] The French themselves had little interest in the Indochina war; half the French troops were African Senegalese. The native population would no longer support any military unit commanded by a French officer.[50] Critics wondered why the United States would continue to support a cause of such little promise. In May, Fairbank openly protested Washington's continuing commitment to the French as one more misguided sign of policy creation without reference to the Asians.[51] Shortly before he left the State Department in late August 1950, Kennan, in a memorandum prepared for Acheson, addressed Indochina's future with incredible prescience. "In Indochina," he wrote, "we are getting ourselves into a position of guaranteeing the French in an undertaking which neither they nor we, nor both of us together, can win." He advised the secretary that a preferable course would permit "the turbulent political currents of that country to find their own level," even if this resulted in the spreading of Vietminh authority over the whole country. Vietnam, believed Kennan, had no relationship to the larger question of global competition between the United States and the U.S.S.R.[52]

Even for the administration the situation in Southeast Asia required a new evaluation. In June, Acheson agreed to the dispatch of survey mission to the area, led by State Department official John Melby and General Graves B. Erskine, commandant of the First Marine Division. The Melby-Erskine mission left Washington on July 7 for Saigon, Singapore, Bangkok, and Manila. Since Indochina was still a French colony, U.S. relations with that unhappy land were handled through the French Foreign Office. Melby discovered that the French commander in Indochina, General Marcel Carpentier, was an old friend from Brazil days. They proceeded to converse freely in Portuguese. On July 25, Melby reported his conversation to William Lacy, head of the State Department's Southeast Asia desk:

[The Vietnam] problem cannot be solved by military means alone. French by proper application force can break [the] back of Viet Minh military strength, but basic problem it represents will crop up again in same or other form. Hatred of French is so deep-seated and traditional that [the] French [are] incapable of selling that political, economic, and propaganda follow-up required to make military successes stick. Only Vietnam can do this and Bao Dai, though intelligent and aware of problem seemingly lacks requisite determination and training. Some new and vitalizing element should be injected into [the] situation within [the] predictable future. . . . All Viets secretly pleased with [Vietnamese] success in bogging down [the] French since distaste for white man [is] greater than any other fear.[53]

Acheson and other Washington officials listened to Melby's report but rejected it. It was less troublesome to rely on the French, whatever the limited promise of that strategy. On October 8, the Viet Cong defeated the French in a major battle.

Amid Washington's official confidence, the burgeoning fears of Soviet expansion in the Far East had no effect on the country's Pacific defenses. Military appropriations did not rebound with the rise of Mao. On April 9, the Policy Review group submitted NSC 68 to the president. The document dwelled on the country's profound insecurity, but it presented no detailed program, no cost estimates, no specific plans or timetables for rearmament. Truman acknowledged the document, but refused to endorse it. It would mean, he complained, a doubling or tripling of the military budget. That he would not allow.[54] In June, the administration approached Congress for a billion-dollar military aid appropriation; Congress refused to touch it. Both the administration and Congress, whatever their fears of Soviet expansion in Asia, still regarded the danger of direct military aggression remote. Until mid-1950, the administration avoided formal alliances or extensive troop deployments in the Far East. It made no commitment to defend South Korea. President Syngman Rhee, a petty dictator, had long been an embarrassment. As late as June 19, the visiting John Foster Dulles, special adviser to the State Department, reminded Rhee that the agreements between the United States and South Korea did not include common action against direct attack, or aid against indirect aggression. Still, Washington's assumption of a Kremlin-based threat to Asia rendered the avoidance of armed resistance to any Communist-led aggression difficult, if not illogical.

* * *

Containment's test came with remarkable suddenness on June 25, 1950, when the U.S. ambassador in Seoul, South Korea, informed the State Department that North Korean forces had invaded the South. Washington presumed that the Kremlin had ordered the North Korean assault to inaugurate its advance into the western Pacific. The invasion confronted Truman and his advisers with the immediate opportunity to teach the Communists a lesson and reinforce American regional defenses. At the president's Blair House meeting on June 25, General Omar N. Bradley, chairman of the Joint Chiefs of Staff, declared that "the Korean situation offered as good an occasion for action in drawing the line as anywhere else." Admiral Forrest P. Sherman, Chief of Naval Operations, agreed. "The present situation in Korea," he said, "offers a valuable opportunity for us to act."[55] On June 26 Charles Bohlen added the warning that "all Europeans to say nothing of the Asiatics are watching to see what the United States will do." One day later Truman informed those gathered around his council table that "we could not let [the Korean] matter go by default."

In his address of June 27, the president listed his immediate responses to the Korean crisis. To protect Formosa from possible Communist occupation, he dispatched the Seventh Fleet to the Formosa Straits. He ordered additional military assistance to the Philippine government as well as to the French and Associated States of Indochina.[56] So popular were the president's Korean decisions that Acheson and members of Congress assured him that his burgeoning war required no formal congressional approval.[57] The UN Security Council, with the U.S.S.R. absent, voted unanimously, on June 27, to support the U.S. effort in Korea.

Washington scarcely knew how to define the enemy in Korea. Was it North Korea, China, or the Soviet Union? For North Korea the war had become a necessity; all previous efforts to unify the peninsula peacefully had failed.[58] North Korea was an independent state; its leader, Kim Il Sung, was no puppet of the Kremlin. But North Korea was a patron of the U.S.S.R., which had established its government and built its political and military structure.[59] Stalin approved the North Korean invasion, largely to deflate U.S. prestige in East Asia by bringing South Korea into the Communist sphere. North Korea initiated the war, but Stalin was sufficiently involved to eliminate the notion that it was a simple civil war. Kim Il Sung anticipated a victory so sweeping that the United States would have no occasion for entering the struggle. For Stalin, this assurance was critical; he regarded the Korean peninsula of minor strategic significance. Determined to avoid any fighting, he sought to limit the Soviet stakes to aid and advice.[60] Both Soviet and North Korean ambitions were expansionist, but they never extended beyond the territorial limits of the Korean peninsula.

In his June 27 address, the president defined the Soviet danger: "The attack upon Korea makes it plain beyond all doubt that Communism has passed beyond the use of subversion to conquer independent nations and will now use armed invasion and war."[61] Despite the assumption of Soviet responsibility, Washington officials presumed that the United States could fight and win a limited war against North Korea without engaging any Soviet forces. The order of June 29 permitted air operations into North Korea, but insisted that they remain clear of "the frontiers of Manchuria or the Soviet Union."[62] Except for the Cold War presumption of Soviet global ambitions, Washington seemed incapable of recognizing the war for what it was: a struggle to decide the future of the Korean peninsula. Kennan viewed the Soviet move into Korea an isolated attack with limited objectives, but one worth engaging. For him the incorporation of even South Korea into the Communist orbit would be "wholly disruptive of our prestige in Asia."[63] However limited both American and Soviet aims in Korea, official U.S. rhetoric continued to transform the conflict into a global struggle fought on Korean soil. At times it denied that the war belonged to Korea at all.

Washington placed enormous faith in China's refusal to join the presumed Soviet-driven aggression. China's entry would expose Formosa to capture, and with it Chiang's exiled Republic of China. In his prepared address to the Veterans of Foreign Wars in August,

MacArthur warned that, in hostile hands, Formosa's military potential would neutralize American's Western Pacific defense system. For him the United States would defend Formosa or it would retreat to the western shores of North America and expose Japan, the Philippines, Indonesia, Australia, and New Zealand to the enemy.[64] Washington officials agreed that U.S. policy should aim at the severing of Soviet-Chinese ties, but for the moment, Bohlen acknowledged in August, the United States could not afford to predicate its policy "on the expectation of Communist China splitting away from the Soviet world."[65] Still Acheson hoped that Beijing would confirm its independence with a public disclaimer. He revealed his confidence in the good judgment and resistance of the Chinese to Soviet pressures in a CBS telecast of mid-September 1950. For the Chinese to enter the war, he said, would be sheer madness. "And since there is nothing in it for them," he added, "I don't see why they should yield to what is undoubtedly pressure from the Communist movement to get into the

Figure 7.1
General MacArthur (center) at Inchon Landing, September 15, 1950 (Courtesy: National Archives)

Korean row." At the same time Judd advised Congressman J. William Fulbright that any anticipation of a Sino-Soviet break was "leaning on a weak reed."[66]

U.S. and South Korean forces had been in long, disastrous retreat to the Pusan Perimeter—at the bottom of the Korean peninsula— when General Douglas MacArthur's successful Inchon landing, on September 15, sent the North Korean forces into rapid flight. The general, who gained a reputation for infallibility at Inchon, urged a military advance in to North Korea to unify the peninsula under South Korean President Syngman Rhee. In agreement with MacArthur, John M. Allison, director of the Office of North East Asian Affairs, denounced any U.S. failure to cross the 38th parallel—the previous line of demarcation—as a compromise with clear moral principles. "When all legal and moral right is on our side," he asked, "why should we hesitate?" State Department officials Dean Rusk and John Foster Dulles supported the move.[67] Washington ordered MacArthur to cross the 38th parallel; his forces did so on October 8. The initial object of containing the North Korean invasion had changed into a policy of liberation. After MacArthur's forces crossed the parallel, the United Nations endorsed the American rollback decision.

Early in October, the Indian ambassador in Beijing, K. M. Panikkar, advised the world that Chinese forces would enter the struggle if UN troops, other than those of South Korea, crossed the 38th parallel. Truman refused to take the warning seriously. The problem, he wrote in his memoirs, was Panikkar's known sympathy for the Chinese cause. At their October 15 meeting on Wake Island, MacArthur assured the president that the Chinese would not risk predictable disaster by entering the war. As MacArthur's forces approached the Yalu on November 26, the Chinese entered North Korea 300,000 strong, overwhelming the UN forces to create a new, costly and unwinnable war.

For the critics of rollback, the initial UN decision to underwrite the war was solely for the purpose of restoring the Republic of Korea to its pre-invasion status. As the *Economist* observed, "Any moral obligations to South Korea were fully discharged when the 38th parallel was reached."[68] Kennan termed the crossing of the parallel a venture into uncertainty. For him, stopping at the parallel would serve U.S. prestige far more surely than pursuing a military rollback. Acheson acknowledged in his memoirs that he had erred badly in advising Truman to pursue rollback. He lacked, he wrote, a sense of what was far enough in a contest for prestige. The mighty clash at the Yalu did not serve the interests of either contestant; neither the United States

Figure 7.2
**Jacob A. Malik, Soviet UN representative casts only dissenting vote to the reso-
lution calling on the Chinese Communist to withdraw troops from Korea
(USIA; Courtesy: National Archives)**

nor China achieved the objectives that led to the confrontation. The
miscalculations of November 1950 were profound. To prevent them,
both contestants required a highly competent and dedicated ambassador in the capital of the other. For them and for the world, the price
of China's nonrecognition became exorbitant.

* * *

China's intervention seemed to demonstrate not only Beijing's
irrationality but also its absolute subservience to Moscow. "Those
who control the Soviet Union and the international Communist movement," Acheson warned the country in a nationwide radio address on
November 29, "have made clear their fundamental design." Truman
declared on the following day, "We hope that the Chinese people will
not continue to be forced or deceived into serving the ends of Russian
colonial policy in Asia."[69] On December 7 the president informed the
visiting British Prime Minister Clement Attlee that the government of
China was "actually a Russian government." He hoped that time would
bring the Chinese "to realize that their friends are not in Siberia but in
London and Washington."[70] Even the *New York Times* proclaimed on
December 8: "The Chinese Communist dictatorship will eventually go
down in history as the men who sold out their country to the foreigners,
in this case the Russians, rather than as those who rescued China from

foreign 'imperialism'." If the new assault in Korea was successful, ran a White House press release, "we can expect it to spread through Asia and Europe to this hemisphere. We are fighting in Korea for our own national security and survival."[71]

That month the nation's acute state of insecurity unleashed a number of recommendations to strengthen the country's defenses. On December 1, the president hinted at a national resort to nuclear weapons. He proceeded to create the Federal Civil Defense Administration. Acheson informed the joint State-Defense meeting that the UN Security Council was in a virtual state of panic. Senator Stuart Symington of Missouri suggested greater national austerity to increase resources for national defense.[72] Two days later, Nitze suggested that the United States should forget China and concentrate on the Soviet Union. On December 9, Nevada and California began planning for 1.5 million refugees from Los Angeles in the event of a Soviet atomic attack. Five days later, New York Governor Thomas Dewey asked for total national mobilization, with a third of the country's productive capacity devoted to national defense.[73] On December 16, President Truman declared a state of national emergency.[74] Two days later, Pacific Northwest skiers moved to organize 5,000 skiers as a potential guerrilla force to defend the mountain passes against an invasion.[75] On December 21, Senator Pat McCarran established the Senate Internal Security Subcommittee. On December 24, the Georgetown University Vice President, Edmund A. Walsh, defended a preventive atomic attack against the U.S.S.R.[76] And on December 30, MacArthur suggested to the Joint Chiefs that the United States evacuate Korea and declare war on China.[77]

Clearly, the impact of East Asian events on the American mind throughout 1950 transformed the Cold War from a stable, diminishing confrontation across Europe into a global struggle for the world, centering now in East Asia. Early in 1951, Dean Rusk, speaking in Philadelphia, delineated fully the new dimensions of the Cold War:

The year 1950 was a very significant year in our postwar development and, it may very well be, in the history of the world. I do not suggest that Soviet Russia has changed ... but during 1950 it entered a new phase in its aggressive program, a phase marked by at least two important factors. First, it has clearly shown that it is prepared to wage war by satellites so far as that becomes desirable to further its objective—not only wars by small satellites such as the North Koreans but full-fledged war by Communist China, a major satellite. Second, the Soviet Union has shown that it is itself prepared to risk a general war and that it is pushing its program to the brink of general war.[78]

At the policy level such fears were irrelevant, for U.S. officials never confronted the Kremlin on its alleged wars by satellites. Neither Washington nor any other government could devise a program to counter dangers so perceived. For the world, the troublesome issues of East Asia were more limited and precise, and they focused on China and Indochina not the Soviet Union.

What troubled British and American critics especially was the continued refusal of Washington to establish peace with China. British Prime Minister Attlee's agenda in Washington, during December, focused precisely on that question. It included firm opposition to renewed war in Korea, either through the unleashing of MacArthur or the resort to atomic weapons. He urged the administration to recognize the new Chinese government, to accept its membership in the UN Security Council, and to support a negotiated solution of the Formosan and Korean issues.[79] For those who endorsed recognition, it no longer seemed reasonable to deny mainland China a major voice in Asian affairs.[80] Instead, following the events of November, Washington moved to intensify the tensions by imposing a total trade embargo on the Chinese mainland and proposing a resolution in the United Nations condemning China as an aggressor. For the critics, both decisions—largely for domestic consumption—would knowingly aggravate U.S.-Chinese animosities without purpose or perceivable end.[81]

* * *

The mounting Korean crisis seemed to demand a restructuring of the country's defense establishment. As Acheson expressed it, the North Korean invasion revealed fully the dangers that the country faced. Its impact on the budget was immediate and profound. The president's initial request, in July 1950, for $10 billion in increased defense authorization for fiscal 1951 passed unanimously without debate. That was the first of four requests that, by December, carried the year's military appropriations from $13.5 billion to $48.2 billion. The administration formally adopted NSC 68 on September 30, 1950. That document, the president and National Security Council agreed, would guide U.S. policy for the next four or five years, with implementation coming as quickly as possible.[82] Subsequent modifications of the program culminated in NSC 68/4, adopted in December, which called for "an effort to achieve, under the shield of the military buildup, an integrated political, economic, and psychological offensive designed to counter the current threat to national security posed by the Soviet Union."[83]

Despite the Korean War's profound impact on official thought, U.S. military planners continued to regard Europe the key to global peace and stability, requiring ever larger commitments of money and manpower for defense against the Soviet threat. For countless Americans, however, the notion of a peacetime obligation to European security remained unacceptable. The Republican opposition—much of it traditionally isolationist—crystallized around the leadership of Senator Robert A. Taft of Ohio, chairman of the Senate Republican Policy Committee. To Taft and his supporters, the administration exaggerated the danger. For five years, observed North Dakota's Usher Burdick, Western Europe had been exposed to overwhelming Soviet forces; still the Kremlin had not been troublesome. For Taft, a proper U.S. strategy would emphasize atomic deterrence as well as naval and air defenses of the United States itself. On December 20, 1950, former President Herbert Hoover, in a national radio and television broadcast, elaborated the standard isolationist theme that the United States avoid a commitment to Europe's defense and "preserve this Western Hemisphere Gibraltar" through reduced expenditures and balanced budgets.[84]

This emerging national debate focused on two issues: the increase in the number of permanent U.S. divisions in Europe from two to six, and the authorization of $7.5 billion in economic and military assistance under the Mutual Security Act of 1951. The president defended the administration's program in an address to the nation on December 15:

I am talking to you tonight about what our country is up against. Our homes, our Nation, all the things we believe in are in great danger. This danger has been created by the rulers of the Soviet Union. . . . The future of civilization depends on what we do. . . . All of us will have to pay more taxes and do without things we like. . . . We must . . . work with the other free nations to strengthen our combined defenses . . . build up our own Army, Navy, and Air Force, and make more weapons for ourselves and our allies.[85]

Truman appealed to Congress to reject partisanship and stand together as Americans in support of measures essential for the country's security. To Republican arguments that the U.S. security required neither additional troops in Europe nor additional expenditures for mutual defense, administration Democrats retorted that those who opposed the administration would carry the responsibility for the West's profound vulnerability.

National insecurities seemed to assure the administration's command of Congress. Still, Lovett and others recommended the creation of a nonpartisan group of distinguished citizens to defend the measures before Congress. Harvard President James B. Conant agreed to head the so-called Committee on the Present Danger. The Committee, consisting of twenty-five leaders in American life, announced its existence in the *New York Times* on December 13, 1950. Its inaugural statement set the tone of its crusade in behalf of a stronger national defense: "The aggressive designs of the Soviet Union are unmistakably plain.... Unless an adequate supplement for the atomic potential of the United States is brought into existence, the time may soon come when all of Continental Europe can be forced into the Communist fold."[86] The Committee's play on national insecurities kept pace with the countering Republican denials that the country faced any dangers. The public stature of its members guaranteed the Committee its share of the headlines. Following the president's State of the Union address in January 1951, the *New York Times* carried the Committee's warning: "A menacing despotic power, bent on conquering the world, has twice in recent months in Korea resorted to aggression.... Europe is the next great prize Russia seeks." Beginning in March, the Committee began a series of weekly radio broadcasts over the Mutual Broadcasting System.[87] By the spring of 1951 the administration had captured the public mind. On April 4 the Senate approved the sending of additional troops to Europe, 69 to 21. The debate over military and economic aid continued through the summer and autumn. The Senate approved the $7.5 billion mutual security measure on October 2—56 to 21. The House concurred three days later.

European as well as American leaders saw the chief deterrent to Communist expansion in the collective forces of the North Atlantic community. In May 1950, John J. McCloy, retiring high commissioner for Germany, declared that German troops were required for the defense of Europe. In September, the foreign ministers of the United States, Britain, and France, responding to the shock of the Korean War, agreed that the creation of a national German army would serve the best interests of both Germany and Western Europe. They authorized the German government at Bonn to establish its own foreign office and enter into diplomatic relations with foreign countries. In December, the NATO Council unanimously asked President Truman to select a supreme commander. Truman named General Dwight D. Eisenhower, then president of Columbia University, to the task of translating NATO military plans into armed forces in being.

France opposed the incorporation of West Germany into NATO's military structure, convinced that a revived Germany, militarily strong and free to pursue its historic ambitions, would unleash unwanted tensions across Europe. To assure its security against an armed Germany, France proposed the creation of a European Defense Community (EDC), a supranational body within NATO that would limit and control Germany's contribution to Europe's defense. The EDC proposal, as finally adopted by the NATO governments in May 1952, ended the allied occupation of Germany and provided for a German contribution of twelve divisions to Europe's defense, with all military units above division level under multinational control. Equally important for French security, EDC would deny Germany the right to manufacture aircraft, heavy ships, or atomic, chemical, and biological weapons without unanimous NATO Council approval. Germany ratified EDC despite the widespread fear among Germans that NATO membership would challenge Soviet security interests sufficiently to guarantee Germany's permanent division.[88]

* * *

Meanwhile the Truman administration addressed the continuing evolution of Asia's Communist monolith, centering in the Kremlin. Truman reminded the American people in his State of the Union message of January 1951, "Our men are fighting . . . because they know, as we do, that the aggression in Korea is part of the attempt of the Russian communist dictatorship to take over the world, step by step."[89] In April the president again warned the nation that behind the millions of Chinese stood "the tanks, the planes, the submarines, the soldiers, and the scheming rulers of the Soviet Union." It was left for Rusk and Dulles to carry the fears of Soviet aggression in the Far East to their ultimate conceptualization. These top spokesmen for the State Department accepted, without question, the existence of a global monolithic Communist enemy, with its center in Moscow. For them Stalin's studies of Leninism had revealed the possibility of weakening the West mortally through alliance with Asia's liberation movements. In February Rusk condemned the Soviet Union's Asian strategy of "preaching nationalism and promising utopia." It was the Soviet appeal to nationalism that had allegedly converted China into a Soviet puppet. "By the test of conception, birth, nurture, and obedience," Dulles declared in May, "the Mao Tse-tung regime is a creature of the Moscow Politburo, and it is on behalf of Moscow, not of China, that it is destroying the friendship of the Chinese people toward the United States."[90] On May 17, Truman, in NSC 48/5, acknowledged China's close attachment to the U.S.S.R. as well as the U.S. objective of reestablishing its independence.[91]

This concept of a Kremlin-controlled monolith created the ultimate rationale for denying China both UN and American recognition. The Beijing regime, Rusk explained, was not the government of China. "It does not pass the first test," he said. "It is not Chinese." During December 1950, Acheson warned British Prime Minister Attlee that any compromise with the Beijing regime on the matter of UN recognition would undermine the government on Formosa and render the mainland Chinese more aggressive. "We should make it a policy," he said, "not to recognize the enemy's gains." Truman, through his UN ambassador, Warren R. Austin, took the first long step toward barring Beijing from the United Nations and thereby isolating it from the main currents of world politics. On January 24, 1951, Austin urged passage of the U.S. resolution that condemned Beijing as an aggressor in Korea. Except for that aggression, said Austin, there would be no fighting in Korea. On February 1, the General Assembly adopted the U.S. resolution by a vote of 44 to 7.

Korea and Indochina, where the principle of containment was under direct assault, made special demands on American resources. In defense of Korea, the United States supported not only its own army, now engaged in a debilitating, stalemated war, but also a South Korean army—one of the largest in the non-Communist world—at a cost of almost $1 billion a year. Official American concern focused as well on Southeast Asia where the Indochinese people, Rusk declared, were in danger of being "absorbed by force into the new colonialism of a Soviet Communist empire." In December 1950 the United States signed a special Mutual Defense Assistance Agreement with France, Vietnam, Cambodia, and Laos for the defense of Southeast Asia.

Although Paris had revealed no capacity to dispose of Ho Chi Minh, administration officials demanded that France maintain primary responsibility for the Indochinese war until the Vietminh ceased to serve the cause of Moscow and Beijing. French reports of success rendered the reliance on France for victory promising enough. From Saigon, the French commander boasted that Vietminh defeats were becoming decisive. On June 18 Acheson informed the press that the military situation in Indochina was developing favorably, with national armies assuming a larger share of the burden. "The process of organizing Asiatic armies to halt Asiatic Communism," added the *New York Times'* Hanson W. Baldwin, "has been well-begun in Indo-China." The State Department *Bulletin*, on June 30, reported the "unanimous satisfaction over the vigorous and successful course of military operations." On August 2, the *New York Times* editorialized: "The actual military position is getting better, not worse."[92] To assure continued French successes, Washington supported Paris with heavy annual expenditures.[93] Washington eventually underwrote 80 percent of the cost of the French effort in Indochina. During 1952, the bulk of military assistance went to four countries regarded especially vulnerable to Communist aggression: the Republic of China, the Republic of Korea, Indochina, and Japan.

During 1951, the United States negotiated a series of alliances to strengthen its containment program for East Asia. Japan emerged as the key to the new alliance system. In March, Dulles returned from the Far East with his recently negotiated Japanese peace treaty. The time has come, he announced, to transform a defeated enemy into a prosperous and stable ally. To encourage Japan's economic development, the treaty imposed no restrictions on Japanese commerce and industry. It stripped Japan of its island possessions, but it acknowledged Japan's right to self-defense and provided for future Japanese rearmament. The United States retained the right to land and naval bases on Japanese territory. Not all accepted the Japanese treaty with equanimity. Remembering their narrow escape from Japanese invasion in 1942, the Australian and New Zealand governments demanded special security guarantees from the United States before they would sign the Japanese treaty. U.S. officials joined representatives of Australia and New Zealand in signing the ANZUS pact in San Francisco in September 1951. Shortly thereafter, the Asian countries, in special ceremonies at San Francisco, approved the Japanese treaty. Late in August, the United States offered a bilateral defense treaty to the Philippines. The Senate approved the new Pacific pacts overwhelmingly in the spring of 1952. In these agreements the United States undertook no obligation except to consult in the event of an aggression.

For Washington the American interest in opposing Asian Communism had become a "given," rarely if ever explicated, rarely questioned by those charged with the conduct of national policy. Early in 1952, the National Security Council issued a statement on "United States Objectives and Courses of Action with Respect to Southeast Asia." It presented the following proposition: "Communist domination, by whatever means, of all Southeast Asia would seriously endanger in the short term, and critically endanger in the longer run, United States security interests." What those security interests were neither that document nor any that followed defined. Instead, the document went on to warn: "In the absence of effective and timely counteraction, the loss of any single country would probably lead to relatively swift submission to or an alignment with communism by the remaining countries of [Southeast Asia]. Furthermore, an alignment with communism in the rest of Southeast Asia and India, and in the longer term, of the Middle East . . . would in all probability progressively follow. Such widespread alignment would endanger the stability and security of Europe."[94] That language of despair created a paranoia, shared by military and civilian officials alike, that overlooked such fundamental determinants as culture, interest, and nationalism in the affairs of Asia.

* * *

Following the adoption of NSC 68 in September 1950, the United States sought, not a balance, but a preponderance of power. "[T]o seek less than preponderant power," Nitze averred, "would be to opt for defeat. Preponderant power must be the object of U.S. policy."[95] After 1950, the United States sought military capabilities sufficient to defend Europe, the Middle East, and East Asia with little support from Britain and France. Behind that pursuit of global containment was the astonishing outpouring of planes, tanks, and other equipment from American factories. By early 1953, the volume was almost seven times that of three years earlier. This augmentation of U.S. strategic power focused primarily on the Air Force and the atomic arsenal. The unprecedented peacetime levels of military production enabled Washington to furnish equipment to NATO and other allies, long promised but not delivered. Outside Europe, the guns and supplies went largely to those at war with Communist-led forces in Korea, Indochina, and Formosa. During 1951 and 1952, U.S. covert operations designed to forestall possible Communist aggression increased sixteenfold. Much of that activity, limited and ineffectual, attempted to sow discord in Eastern Europe and weaken the Kremlin's hold on that region.[96] A fearful public entrusted Washington with enormous power to fight the Cold War, confident that it would protect the nation's security while avoiding unnecessary trouble.

For most advocates of preponderance, containment, as the term implied, remained largely defensive. Its object was essentially that of stabilizing the Cold War world, protecting the immense body of interests that Soviet policy had not touched, and enabling Western civilization to continue its postwar evolution in what was, after mid-century, a remarkably secure environment. Behind the walls of military preponderance, Washington officials sought the economic and political progress of Western Europe, as well as the conversion of Germany and Japan into prosperous, democratic friends. Such policies presumed that the issue between the United States and the U.S.S.R. was imperialism, not revolution.[97] This rendered the Soviet danger, measurable by interest and power, subject to Western military constraints. What actual dangers the U.S.S.R. posed to Europe's peace defied any accurate appraisal. Preponderance in itself would not produce change or assure any triumphs for self-determination in Eastern Europe, but it would add an essential element of stability to a situation long established.

What military preponderance meant for containment in Asia remained exceedingly elusive. Asian Communism was indigenous and not necessarily expansive; it presented no discernible military challenges. Not even China had made any effort to extend its control beyond its traditional borders. In Korea, where the issue was international aggression, allied military successes had gained no more than a costly stalemate in a small, peripheral arena bordering the sea. Korea, troublesome enough, stood in sharp contrast to the immensity of the Asian continent. Yet the United States, in supporting the French, had already trapped itself in a doubtful Indochinese struggle for national unification in the name of containment.[98]

The U.S.S.R., no less than the United States, had a dubious future on the Asian continent; both China and Indochina remained outside its grasp. A strong, unified China, bordering the Soviet Union's long Asiatic frontier, had been a nightmare to Russian governments for centuries. The words of Russia's famed foreign minister, Sergei Sazonov, uttered in 1912, still had meaning: "Germany is interested in China as a market and she fears China's disintegration. . . . Russia, on the contrary, as a nation bordering China, and with a long, unfortified frontier, cannot wish for the strengthening of her neighbor: she could therefore view with equanimity the collapse of modern China."[99] The Soviet quest for a truce along Korea's 38th parallel discounted the presumptions of a Kremlin design on the entire Pacific basin. The Soviets had recognized the price of war in the western Pacific.[100] There would be no more Koreas. Asia belonged to the Asians. To challenge that reality, as Korea and Indochina demonstrated, would be costly indeed.

Such profound limitations on the use of force scarcely assuaged the insecurities of those Americans for whom coexistence presaged disaster. For them the Kremlin's historical dialectic— which assured the global triumph of Communism—underlay the Soviet drive for world domination. As a determinant of policy, anti-Communism overlooked the fact that the Communist world was rent by conflicting nationalisms, and that much of the Communist bloc harbored no allegiance to the Kremlin at all. Anti-Communism defined dangers so universally, yet so capriciously, that it defied the creation of policy. Any crusade against Communism would extend the country's security interests and proclaim national objectives beyond the capacity of U.S. military power, at any level of effectiveness, to achieve.[101] Amid such limitations Washington never developed any program designed to free Eastern Europe, China, or the Soviet Union from Communist control. By 1952 the United States had gained a position of leadership and influence in world affairs unprecedented in modern times. The American empire did not involve formal political control over other states, but rather comprised, as Geir Lundestad aptly defined it, "a hierarchical system of political relationships, with one power clearly being much stronger than any other."[102] American influence eventually encompassed not only Germany and Japan but also, through alliances and economic aid, Western Europe, Australia, and New Zealand, as well as Latin America. Built on consent, the American empire reflected a body of mutual advantages that sustained the relationship. Such countries as France accepted U.S. leadership and all that it entailed, grudgingly but profitably.[103] Nowhere did the assent rest on total agreement with U.S. policies or their assumptions of danger. For Europeans, the challenges that mattered were largely European, and those challenges Western leaders had faced with enough resolution and success to stabilize the continent. As the European powers, always in control of their decisions, regained, after mid-century, much of their former confidence, their cooperation required ever-greater American concessions. Europeans and Asians alike rejected overwhelmingly Washington's fears of Soviet expansionism in Asia, a region where U.S. policies remained largely unilateral.

Washington's repeated responses to danger demanded human and material resources of sufficient magnitude to create the National Security State. Fighting the Cold War at a cost of $50 billion a year had become, by 1952, the dominant business of government, commanding much of the nation's energy, substance, and talent. State and Defense, the CIA, and the Federal Bureau of Investigation developed powerful bureaucratic interests in the existence of a Soviet threat. National insecurities conferred huge appropriations and influence on these agencies and their officials. So pervasive was the Cold War in national affairs that it required no less than a bipartisan establishment, as well as a broad intellectual milieu, in which policy-makers of different ideological, political, and emotional hues could work together in reasonable agreement.

Outside government were the arms manufacturers, writers, scholars, and politicians for whom the Cold War offered purpose, security, satisfaction, and often superb remuneration.[104] Many of the new national security managers were international bankers and their lawyers, men who could associate easily with the political and business elite of Europe. The New York Council on Foreign Relations gave them a social and intellectual identity, fostered their conservative views of international affairs, and propelled them into positions of leadership in Washington where they found policies sufficiently congenial to enter the country's Cold War elite.[105] That elite succeeded in building and sustaining a powerful consensus, with the American people prepared to underwrite the hundreds of billions—eventually trillions—required to maintain the military levels that the perceptions of danger seemed to require. Not without reason, President Truman left office in January 1953, firm in the conviction that the future belonged to the West and not to the Communist world.[106]

CHAPTER 8

High Tide: The Eisenhower Years

Dwight D. Eisenhower's accession to the presidency in January 1953 confirmed the American Cold War consensus. Through six years of continuous conflict with the U.S.S.R., the nation's Cold War elite had effectively conditioned the country's citizenry to acclaim any anti-Soviet maneuver emanating from Washington. Still, under the Truman leadership containment had emerged as a highly conservative program designed to sustain, not undo, the world that the power revolution of the previous decade had created. The administration had long accepted the reality of a divided Europe. Within the national consensus was also broad support for national efforts to prevent any Soviet expansion into Western Europe or regions of Asia regarded vulnerable to Communist exploitation. To meet this yet still-elusive Soviet challenge, Americans overwhelmingly sustained the national commitment to NATO and the anti-Communist elements in China, Indochina, and Korea. With the Korean War, moreover, they underwrote the massive rebuilding of the nation's armed forces.[1]

What rendered the evolving containment policies of the Truman administration vulnerable to political assault was the absence of a precise strategy for victory. It was left for John Foster Dulles, noted Republican spokesman on foreign affairs, to challenge the Truman administration's refusal to contest the Kremlin's continuing dominance of the captive states. Dulles was the grandson of John Watson Foster, Benjamin Harrison's secretary of state, and the nephew of Robert Lansing, secretary of state under Woodrow Wilson. He had been secretary to the Chinese delegation at The Hague Peace Conference of 1907 and adviser to the American delegation at Versailles in 1919. He had served as special assistant in Truman's State Department and had lauded the Democratic administration for its foreign policy achievements. Detecting the possibilities of a Republican victory in 1952, however, he resigned his State Department post in March and immediately assumed command of the Republican crusade against the conservatism in Truman's containment policies.[2]

Life magazine, on May 19, 1952, published Dulles's article "A Policy of Boldness," which condemned the Truman-Acheson concept of limited power and added a new, ambitious element to the Republican program. The country's external policies, Dulles charged, were too far-flung, extravagant, and expensive. They were not designed to win the Cold War but rather to live with peril, "presumably forever." Clearly the free nations required a better choice than that of "murder from without or suicide from within." But Dulles had discovered an alternative that would stop aggression even as it reduced the danger of war. "There is one solution and only one," he argued; "that is for the free world to develop the will to organize the means to retaliate instantly against open aggression by Red armies, so that if it occurred anywhere, we could and would strike back where it hurts, by means of our own choosing." Dulles promised more. The free world, he believed, could turn to the political offensive by developing a *dynamic* foreign policy based on *moral* principles. Today, Dulles charged, the captive nations "live close to despair because the United States, the historic leader of the forces of freedom, seems dedicated to the negative policy of containment and stalemate." American policy, he continued, should no longer sponsor the Iron Curtain through containment but seek the "liberation" of those living under compulsion, making "it publicly known that it wants and expects liberation to occur."[3]

Early in July, Dulles embodied his views in the Republican platform. He termed Teheran, Yalta, and Potsdam scenes of "tragic blunders" that abandoned the friendly peoples of Eastern Europe to Communist aggression. He promised a program that would "mark the end of the negative, futile and immoral policy of 'containment' which abandons countless human beings to a despotism and Godless terrorism which in turn enables the rulers to forge the captives into a weapon for our destruction." Under Republican direction, the United States would "become again the dynamic, moral and spiritual force which was the despair of despots and the hope of the oppressed."[4] Finally, Dulles promised that the new Republican administration would achieve its purposes under the goal of a "balanced budget, a reduced national debt, an economical administration and a cut in taxes." Eisenhower proclaimed his adherence to liberation on August 25 before the American Legion convention: "We can never rest—and we must so inform all the world ... that until the enslaved nations ... have in the fullness of freedom the right to chose their own path, that then, and then only, can we say that there is a possible way of living peacefully and permanently with Communism in the world."[5] For Dulles as well, liberation would create the essential conditions for world peace. "The only way to stop a head-on collision with the Soviet Union," he warned in late August, "is to break it up from within."[6]

Recalling the Truman administration's refusal to challenge the Kremlin's control of Eastern Europe, European writers feared that Eisenhower was inviting trouble with Moscow. Paris's *Ce Soir* accused him of inaugurating a needless crusade against the Soviet Union. For Britain's *Manchester Guardian* the Republican goal of liberation simply presaged war. The London *Daily Mirror*, wondering what Eisenhower had in mind, asked Republican leaders to "consider the effects of their oratory beyond the American borders."[7] Other European critics noted that Eisenhower's aggressive approach to the U.S.S.R. was notably lacking in means. The *Economist* (London) observed on August 30, 1952, "Unhappily 'liberation' applied to Eastern Europe ... means either the risk of war or it means nothing. ... 'Liberation' entails no risk of war only when it means nothing."[8] The *Economist*'s Washington correspondent concluded that Republican declarations on liberation were fundamentally a quest for minority votes and so divorced from policy that Eisenhower and Dulles would do well to drop the subject. Unless Republican leaders intended to give armed support to the peoples of Eastern Europe, Truman declared at Parkersburg, West Virginia, they were deceiving their fellow citizens and "playing cruel, gutter politics with the lives of countless good men and women behind the Iron Curtain."[9] Republican editors, however, assured Europeans and Americans alike that Eisenhower contemplated peaceful liberation, largely through psychological warfare. An Eisenhower administration, Dulles averred, would never encourage a premature revolt. "There are countless peaceful ways," he added, "by which the task of the Russian despots can be made so unbearably difficult that they will renounce their rule. That was shown in Yugoslavia."[10]

At the Senate committee hearings on his appointment as secretary of state on January 15, 1953, the committee chairman inquired of Dulles what his new, dynamic policies of liberation entailed. Dulles assured the Senators:

[W]e shall never have a secure peace or a happy world so long as Soviet Communism dominates one-third of all the peoples that there are. ... These people who are enslaved are people who deserve to be free . . . and ought to be free because if they are the servile instruments of aggressive despotism, they will eventually be welded into a force which will be highly dangerous to ourselves and to all the free world. Therefore, we must always have in mind the liberation of these captive peoples. . . . It must be and can be a peaceful process, but those who do not believe that results can be achieved by moral pressures by the weight of propaganda, just do not know what they are talking about.[11]

President Eisenhower, in his first State of the Union message of February 2, 1953, promised that his administration would never acquiesce in the enslavement of captive peoples. To that end he repudiated the Yalta and Potsdam agreements which, Republican critics insisted, had brought Soviet dominance to millions of Europeans. He would ask Congress to join in "an appropriate resolution making clear that this Government recognizes no kind of commitments contained in secret accords which condoned enslavement."[12] Pro-liberation columnist David Lawrence rejoiced that a congressional resolution would now enable the new president to bring freedom to the peoples of Eastern Europe. Freda Kirchwey retorted in the *Nation* that Eisenhower could achieve no more in Eastern Europe than had Truman.[13] On February 26, Dulles explained the resolution before the House Foreign Affairs Committee. "The aim," he said, "is to make totally clear the integrity of this Nation's purpose in relation to the millions of enslaved peoples in Europe and Asia."[14] The proposed resolution, however, condemned Soviet behavior rather than President Roosevelt's alleged sellout at Yalta; Senate Republicans rejected it even as they demanded that the administration fulfill its promises to the captive peoples.[15]

Dulles reaffirmed the administration's commitment to liberation when he addressed the American Society of Newspaper Editors in April. Unless the United States assured the captive peoples that it did not accept their captivity, he warned, it "would unwittingly have become partners to the forging of a hostile power so vast that it could encompass our destruction."[16] Only the reduction of the Soviet presence in Eastern Europe, Dulles warned, would sustain the established lines of demarcation. Dulles never explained how psychological warfare would achieve the peaceful withdrawal of Soviet military power from Eastern Europe.

* * *

What was lacking in the goal of liberation was the definition of policy toward the U.S.S.R. itself. Dean Acheson and other Truman officials had rationalized the country's rapidly expanding defense efforts after mid-century as a prerequisite for successful negotiations. By 1953 the Marshall Plan, the creation of the West German Republic, and the formation of NATO, all backed by the economic and military supremacy of the United States, had halted the perceived landslide to disaster. In Europe containment had apparently won. Convinced that Western power vis-a-vis the Soviet Union would never be greater, Winston Churchill, who had returned to power in October 1951, believed the time propitious for high-level conversations with Stalin. On New Year's Eve 1952 he set out on the *Queen Mary* to bid Truman farewell and to reestablish, by capitalizing on his wartime association with president-elect Eisenhower, London's former ties with Washington. During his days in New York, Churchill formed a distinct dislike for Dulles, whose influence on Eisenhower he regarded pernicious. He gained nothing in his exchanges with Eisenhower, who insisted that the American policy of treating every country as a sovereign equal ruled out any special relationship with Britain. Nor did the president-elect reveal any interest in talks with Kremlin leaders.[17]

With Stalin's death on March 5, 1953, his successor, Georgi Malenkov, argued for peaceful coexistence and new measures to guarantee it. On March 11, Churchill reminded Eisenhower that Stalin no longer presented an impediment to improved East-West relations. The judgment of future generations would be harsh, he warned, if the West made no effort to establish something better "than a series of casual and dangerous incidents at the many points of contact between the two divisions of the world." Eisenhower was not impressed, warning Churchill that a meeting would merely unleash another Soviet propaganda barrage.[18] On April 5, Churchill acknowledged that negotiations would demand alertness but, he added, "we think, as I am sure you do also, that we ought to lose no chance of finding out how far the Malenkov regime are prepared to go in easing things up all around." Churchill informed Washington, on April 21, that he was considering a personal contact with the Kremlin. The president objected. "Premature action by us in that direction," he admonished the prime minister, "might have the effect of giving the Soviets an easy way out of the position in which I think they are now placed." Churchill sent Eisenhower the draft of a proposed letter to Molotov. "Foster and I have considered it deeply . . . ," the president responded. "We would advise against it."[19] Churchill dropped his plans for a meeting with the Soviets, but concluded a speech before the House of Commons, on May 11, by appealing for an "easement" in Western relations with the U.S.S.R. and a new approach to end the misunderstandings dividing East from West.

It was a mistake, he declared, to assume that negotiations could settle nothing merely because they could not settle everything.[20]

Eisenhower and Dulles were not amused. Neither were the London and Washington foreign policy establishments. Dulles made clear his displeasure at Europe's generally favorable response to Soviet appeals. "I think there's some real danger of our just seeming to fall in with these Soviet overtures," he cautioned. "It's obvious that what they are doing is because of outside pressures, and I don't know anything better we can do than to keep up these pressures right now." Dulles assured the National Security Council, on March 31, that the United States, by squeezing the already overextended Soviet regime, might force its collapse. "We must not relax this pressure," he said, "until the Soviets give promise of ending the struggle. . . . [T]he American effort must not now be abandoned."[21] The East German riots of June 1953, followed in July by the execution of Lavrenti Beria, notorious head of the Soviet secret police, convinced Dulles that the Soviet empire was seething with discontent and that greater Western pressure could break Soviet control of East-Central Europe. "This is the kind of time when we ought to be *doubling* our bets, not reducing them—as all the Western parliaments want to do," he informed the cabinet on July 10. "This is the time to *crowd* the enemy—and maybe *finish* him, once and for all." At the same time Dulles assured the nation: "[T]he Communist structure is over-extended, over-rigid and ill-founded."[22]

Clearly such burgeoning expectations of easy victory, when contrasted to the realities of international politics, required some reexamination of national policy. To that end the president, in June 1953, arranged a top-secret policy study, code-named Project Solarium. His 18 participants formed three separate task forces, with the dominant Task Force A led by George Kennan. The deliberations covered six weeks. Following the detailed reports on July 16, Eisenhower summarized the findings and demonstrated a keen appreciation of the limitations imposed on national policy by a resistant world. In the end, he favored a national security policy that differed little from that of Harry Truman, one which emphasized containment over liberation.[23] On July 30, the NSC staff prepared a document on national strategy based on the Solarium deliberations. The new policy directive emphasized the need of a powerful retaliatory capability, strong and independent allies, selective foreign assistance, and a public declaration of the lines beyond which any Soviet bloc advance would bring war. A summary guideline recommended "selected aggressive actions of a limited scope, involving moderately increased risks of general war, to eliminate Soviet-dominated areas within the free world and to reduce Soviet power in the Satellite periphery."[24] Yet in a draft policy statement on September 30, the NSC concluded that "the detachment of any major European satellite from the Soviet bloc does not now appear feasible except by Soviet acquiescence or by war."[25]

During July, Churchill again anticipated talks that might lead to a relaxation of the Cold War. Foreign Secretary Eden and most of the Foreign Office continued to emphasize containment, convinced with American leaders that, in time, Western diplomats could approach the Kremlin from a position of total military superiority. Churchill feared that such expectations would result less in diplomatic triumphs than in endless years of hatred and hostility. The prime minister was distressed to learn that cabinet member Lord Salisbury, who visited Washington in July, had found Eisenhower "violently Russophobe, greatly more so than Dulles, and ... personally responsible for the policy of useless pinpricks and harassing tactics the U.S. is following against Russia."[26] Churchill had long pressed Eisenhower for a Western summit meeting in Bermuda. Washington finally agreed to an early December date. Shortly before his departure for Bermuda, Dulles assured a House committee that the United States would welcome the opportunity to settle specific questions with the Soviet Union, but, he added, "We do not look on the conference table as a place where we surrender our principles, but rather as a place for making principles prevail."[27]

At the first plenary session on December 4, Churchill, following an intensely anti-Soviet speech by the French foreign minister, presented his "double dealing" policy of confronting the Soviet Union with strength while holding out the hand of friendship. Eden regarded the speech a disaster. Eisenhower followed with a coarse and violent rebuttal. Denying that Soviet policy had any new look, the president declared "Russia was a woman of the streets and whether her dress was new, or just the old one patched, it was certainly the same whore underneath. America intended to drive her off her present 'beat' into the back streets." Colville noted in his diary: "I doubt if such language has ever been heard at an international conference. Pained looks all round."[28] The conference moved on to other subjects. There would be no offer of negotiations. Instead, the Bermuda declaration repeated the U.S. rejection of the *status quo* for Eastern Europe: "We cannot accept ... the present division of Europe. Our hope is that in due course peaceful means will be found to enable countries of Eastern Europe again to play their part as free nations in a free Europe."[29]

Already the Eisenhower-Dulles revisionism had turned to the issue of German reunification. West Germany loomed as the continent's most powerful country; for political reasons, many feared, its government would not accept as permanent the Soviet subjugation of 17 million East Germans. American leaders entertained little hope of immediate reunification, but they were determined to protect West German interests by preventing Europeans from using the East Germans as pawns in an East-West settlement. As early as July, Eisenhower declared that an honorable European peace would require the reemergence of a united German republic. "The continued partition of Germany," Dulles noted in September, "is a scandal. It is more than that. It is a crime. . . . [I]t is not only wrong to the Germans; it is a menace to the peace."[30] Dulles, with allied approval, made German unification the central issue at the Berlin Conference of February 1954. "I am firmly convinced," he said, "that a free and united Germany is essential to stable peace in Europe." Dulles condemned the Soviets for perpetuating the division of Germany by holding the East German regime in power against the will of the German people. Dulles denied that such a government had the right to negotiate with the West Germans on equal terms.[31] Dulles's goal of unification through free elections sustained the public illusion that rollback remained the administration's irreducible objective.

* * *

Eisenhower's Washington accepted the existence of a massive Soviet threat, one based on impressive conventional and atomic preparedness and control of the international Communist apparatus with its alleged power to penetrate, divide, and weaken the free world. At the same time the administration's ubiquitous demands for Soviet capitulation to American principles, calling for compliance without compensation or even serious negotiations, seemed to deny that the U.S.S.R. was a problem at all. Washington officials no longer anticipated war with the U.S.S.R. in the immediate future, perhaps never. The president, moreover, backed by Secretary of the Treasury George M. Humphrey, was determined to fulfill the campaign pledge of reduced taxes and balanced budgets. As early as February 1953, he announced his intention of tailoring military power to fiscal requirements. "Our problem," he said, "is to achieve military strength within the limits of endurable strain on our economy." In March, the president responded to a request of the service chiefs for additional appropriations by wondering "whether national bankruptcy or national destruction would get us first."[32] In his Defense Reorganization message of April 30, he announced major changes in defense policy, "which would continue to give primary consideration to the external threat but would no longer ignore the internal threat."[33] After three months of study, the administration, in late April, recommended budget reductions of $8 billion for fiscal year 1954, to create a situation of "maximum military strength within economic capacities."[34]

In late April, the president approved NSC 149/1 that provided for a review of the size and structure of the military. During subsequent weeks the Joint Chiefs of Staff agreed that the country was overextended and lacked the manpower to maintain its global defenses. To avoid abandoning Europe and other strategic areas, Arthur W. Radford, Chairman of the Joint Chiefs, recommended that the United States place greater reliance on its growing nuclear arsenal.[35] Eisenhower added another dimension to the emphasis on nuclear weapons, and the expanding retaliatory striking force, when he observed that the challenge to strategy lay in deterring, not winning, a war with the Soviet Union. But he noted in a memorandum to Dulles, on September 8, that hydrogen weapons could serve as a deterrent only if the United States was prepared to initiate a nuclear war.[36] In early October, the president endorsed NSC 162 with its emphasis on nuclear strategy, but acknowledged again "nothing would so upset the whole world as an announcement . . . of a decision to use these weapons." At an NSC meeting on October 13, Dulles suggested that the State and Defense departments define the areas where the United States could reasonably use nuclear weapons to cut defense costs. At the end of October, the New Look assumed final form in NSC 162/2; nuclear weapons and the effective means for their delivery had become the foundation of national strategy.[37]

Dulles soon elevated the military New Look into a broad strategic concept. In his address of January 12, 1954, to the New York Council on Foreign Relations, he emphasized the "deterrent of massive retaliatory power" to supplement the earlier reliance on conventional ground forces. The United States, he warned, would now "depend primarily upon a great capacity to retaliate, instantly, by means and places of our own choosing." The new strategy would eliminate future Koreas, because no government would engage in aggression knowing that its urban centers might be reduced to rubble. But Dulles promised more. "If we persist in the courses I outline," he said, "we shall confront dictatorship with a task that is, in the long run, beyond its strength. . . . If the dictators persist in their present course, then it is they who will

Figure 8.1
President Eisenhower and Secretary of State Dulles (Courtesy: Dwight D. Eisenhower Library)

be limited to superficial successes, while their foundations crumble under the tread of their iron boots."[38]

Dulles's new doctrine gave his critics a field day. Military analyst Hanson W. Baldwin charged the administration with "putting a price tag on national security." To military writers everywhere the concentration on nuclear weapons narrowed the freedom of choice to inaction or the mushroom cloud. Matthew B. Ridgway, Army Chief of Staff, reminded the administration that future wars would involve conventional, not nuclear, power, and that the reductions in force levels would prevent the country from meeting its overseas commitments.[39] Dulles replied to his critics in the April 1954 issue of *Foreign Affairs*. "The essential thing," he wrote, "is that a potential aggressor should know in advance that he can and will be made to suffer for his aggression more than he can possibly gain by it." Dulles denied that the capacity to retaliate instantly imposed the necessity of unleashing nuclear power in every instance of attack and concluded, "it is not our intention to turn every local war into a general war."[40]

Treasury Secretary Humphrey insisted that the United States had no business getting into little wars. "If a situation comes up where our interests justify intervention," he said, "let's intervene decisively with all we have got or stay out." For some the new threat of massive retaliation restored the strategic initiative to the United States and assured victory in any future contest outside Europe without the commitment of ground forces. "The doctrine is a departure from the policy of 'containment' which we have heretofore followed in recent years," observed Senator William Knowland in March 1954. "It is clear, therefore, that this Administration intends to change our defense emphasis to a point where we are no longer dependent on merely reacting to Soviet initiative within limits planned and desired by the Kremlin."[41]

At no time did the administration deny the importance of the NATO allies in defense planning for Europe. The issue of Europe's defense centered on the continued refusal of the French Assembly to ratify its own government's proposal for the European Defense Community (EDC). Through 1953 and the early months of 1954 Dulles continued to force the issue of EDC ratification on both the French Assembly and the French people. Anticipating a French rejection of EDC, the U.S. Senate, by a vote of 88 to 0, threatened a unilateral American approach to German rearmament. The Senate Armed Services Committee made clear its determination to cut future aid to France unless that country ratified EDC. In August, the French Assembly delivered its predictable *coup de grace* to EDC —a resounding defeat for American policy. Dulles reacted with scarcely a murmur; American interests in Europe would permit no "agonizing reappraisal."[42]

Britain's Anthony Eden resolved the crisis by committing four British divisions to the continent "as long as the majority of the Brussels partners want them there." The English Channel had ceased to be a special guarantee of British security. Eden saved NATO by placing curbs on Germany satisfactory to the French. Suddenly the Western Europeans shared a renewed spirit of unity. President Eisenhower lauded the prospective accord as perhaps "one of the greatest diplomatic achievements of our time."[43] During October 1954, the foreign ministers met in Paris to approve the new agreements with Germany. Chancellor Konrad Adenauer of West Germany granted the necessary concessions—the Federal Republic would not manufacture "any atomic weapons, chemical weapons or biological weapons." The Supreme Allied Commander in Europe maintained direct control over Germany's military forces. The United States received what it had long desired: the full integration of West German power into the

Western alliance. In May 1955 West Germany became the fifteenth member of NATO.[44] The Soviet Union responded to the new challenge by organizing its Warsaw Pact across Eastern Europe. The division of Europe and Germany was complete.

* * *

Europe's very stability called for some accommodation among the great powers. As guest at the White House in June 1954, Churchill again sought Eisenhower's approval for a conference with the Soviets. Under pressure from Dulles, the president refused to attend, but offered no objection if the prime minister chose to meet with Malenkov and Molotov in Moscow. On the way home aboard the *Queen Elizabeth*, Eden persuaded Churchill to submit his proposed approach to Molotov for cabinet review in London. Upon reviewing Churchill's proposal, Lord Salisbury and other cabinet members threatened to resign if the prime minister persisted. This ended Churchill's long pursuit of a settlement with the Kremlin.[45] Yet by the year's end, the pressures on Eisenhower to engage the Soviets directly began to mount. The president acknowledged them in a press conference in early December 1954. "Let us recognize," he said, "that we owe it to ourselves and to the world to explore every possible means of settling differences before we even think of such a thing as war."

Throughout the early months of 1955, the demand for negotiations permeated the official statements of nations the world over. Thomas P. Whitney analyzed the phenomenon succinctly in the *New York Times Magazine* on May 22, 1955: "People everywhere are desperate for assurances of a long term peace so far denied them. They want to see everything tried, . . . including face-to-face meetings, not just of Foreign Ministers but of the men who give the Foreign Ministers their instructions." In April and May, after ten years of obstructionism, the Soviets signed a peace treaty with Austria; they retreated from Finland and recognized the government of West Germany.[46] With irresistible logic these promising elements in the international scene pushed both the United States and the U.S.S.R. into the Big Four summit conference at Geneva in July 1955.[47]

Geneva fulfilled the expectations of those who expected little except a pleasant atmosphere. The issues that separated East from West had not changed since Potsdam; nor had the demands of Soviet or American leaders. The Kremlin still sought no less than Western recognition of the Soviet hegemony behind the Iron Curtain; the West remained reluctant to grant it. But if the Geneva Conference failed to settle Cold

Figure 8.2
(L to R) Soviet Premier Nikolay Bulganin, Eisenhower, French Premier Edgar Faure, and British Prime Minister Anthony Eden at the Big Four Summit, 1955 (Courtesy: Dwight D. Eisenhower Library)

War issues across Europe, it permitted the leaders of Britain, France, the United States, and the U.S.S.R. to respond to the insecurities created by the appalling specter of nuclear war. "The United States," Eisenhower assured Soviet Premier N. A. Bulganin, "will never take part in an aggressive war." The president declared his trust of the Soviet leaders and credited them with a desire for peace no less sincere than that of the West. This was the image that the Soviets desired to create with their plea for peaceful coexistence. What gave the Geneva Conference significance was the unwritten agreement between the two superpowers that, under conditions of nuclear stalemate, they would settle their differences by means other than war.

Even more reassuring for the West were the internal developments transforming much of Soviet life. Nikita S. Khrushchev, who by 1956 had replaced Bulganin as Kremlin leader, sought greater legitimacy for the Soviet state by addressing both its past oppressions and the longing of the Soviet masses for the good life that the Communist system had promised for 30 years—but not delivered. Khrushchev gambled that he could secure greater allegiance for Communism by easing the Soviet grip. In line with this conviction, Khrushchev, addressing the Twentieth Party Congress in February 1956, denounced the Stalin cult of leadership and encouraged the critical thought already released by Stalin's death. He emphasized the need both to increase consumer production and to raise the Soviet standard of living.[48] Quickly the criticism, although muted, encompassed the very structure of the Soviet system itself. There would be various degrees of criticism—and efforts at repression—after the Kremlin established the principle that it could exist.[49]

Khrushchev's new economic program focused on gross industrial production and consumer goods. Long before 1960 the impact of Soviet economic growth was evident in the large cities of the U.S.S.R.— Moscow, Leningrad, Kiev, and Kharkov. Television aerials appeared on urban rooftops. More cars appeared on the streets and more merchandise, including foreign goods, in the stores. The country began to lose its provincialism as foreign visitors—students, delegations, and cultural exchange groups—brought new modes of dress and behavior. Khrushchev's attention to public needs enabled millions to improve their existence and think less of sheer survival. But, as Oxford University's Leszek Kolakowski phrased it, "The improvement in living conditions turned out to be politically dangerous. Far from appeasing the people, making them more docile, as certain Sovietologists expected, such measures slowly opened up a space for critical thinking, ultimately for rebellion."[50]

Even as the Twentieth Party Congress recognized Khrushchev's leadership, it underwrote the "New Look" in Soviet foreign policy by seeking to disarm the fears of Soviet aggression and acquiring greater support for the Soviet Union in the world's neutral and uncommitted states. The Kremlin's effort to strike a more assuring pose began under Malenkov, but attained its easygoing diplomatic style under Bulganin and Khrushchev. Without altering their basic objectives, the new Kremlin leaders set out to use diplomacy, economic aid, and propaganda to attract the Asia neutrals. By 1955 the Kremlin's post-Geneva diplomacy revealed amazing agility and vigor. It sought to exploit Arab nationalism by procuring Czech arms and offering to aid Egypt in building the Aswan Dam. During November and December, Bulganin and Khrushchev toured India, Burma, and Afghanistan, promising trade and economic assistance. By February 1956, the Kremlin leaders had offered trade and aid policies to Pakistan as well as to Latin America. The Twentieth Party Congress stressed "the rich opportunities which these developments opened up for Soviet initiatives on the world scene."[51]

The new Soviet emphasis on coexistence reflected not only the Soviet interest in avoiding war but also the conviction that the U.S.S.R. could achieve world leadership through peaceful competition. Khrushchev, in 1957, warned the West that the Soviet Union had declared war on the West in the field of peaceful production, adding: "We are relentless in this, and it will prove the superiority of our system." For millions of Europeans and Americans, Khrushchev's new emphasis on coexistence offered the prospect of diminishing conflict. Official Washington, however, detected little new or reassuring in an aggressive strategy based on suppositions of coming economic preponderance. Secretary Dulles warned Congress in March 1956 that the Soviet government, whatever its appeal to peaceful coexistence, continued "to pursue its overall aim of Communist domination." W. Averell Harriman declared in the *Atlantic Monthly* of April 1956 that the aim of the new strategy was "destruction of all we believe in and eventual world domination by Soviet Communism. This is 'peaceful coexistence,' Russian style."[52] Throughout the succeeding two years, administration officials and Soviet experts repeated the warning that the Soviet "new look" diplomacy comprised merely a risk-free method of achieving the well-established goals of Communist expansion by drawing the recipients of Soviet bloc aid "away from the community of free nations and ultimately into the communist orbit."[53]

Soviet spokesmen did little to dispel such fears. They announced repeatedly their belief in the Marxist-Leninist notion of ultimate Communist domination. Khrushchev's words especially were characterized by a disturbing rude arrogance. At a Kremlin reception in November 1956, he stated the oft-quoted but not exceptional phrase: "Whether you like it or not, history is on our side. We will bury you." Capitalism will perish, he predicted, just as feudalism had perished earlier. "All the world will come to communism," he declared in June 1957. "History does not ask whether you want it or not." The Soviet premier warned the West that the underlying Soviet purpose transcended the policies and actions of the moment. "People say our smiles are not honest," he once observed. "That is not true. Our smile is real and not artificial. But if anyone believes that our smile means that we have given up the teachings of Marx, Engels, and Lenin, he is badly mistaken."[54] Assured the eventual triumph of the Soviet system through industrial and technological superiority alone, Khrushchev persistently urged coexistence. "We want to live in peace and friendship with Americans," he observed in July 1959, "because we are the two most powerful countries and if we live in friendship these other countries will also live in friendship."[55]

Few American economists, however, accepted Khrushchev's prediction that Communism would bury capitalism. They agreed that the Soviet economy had grown more rapidly than those of the West, but they denied that the Soviet economy could outstrip that of the United States. Henry Cabot Lodge, U.S. representative in the United Nations, commented realistically on the Soviet economic challenge: "[I] do not dispute Chairman Khrushchev's right to challenge us. Nor am I worried by improving the lot of the Russian citizen. In fact I welcome it. But I dispute the accuracy of his prophecy. If we do what we are capable of doing, the Soviet Union will never surpass us." The United States, he added, should not shrink from economic competition. No one explained how productive capacity could lead to world domination. Nor would any triumphs of Soviet production cause the United States to falter and collapse. There was no diplomatic answer to Soviet boasts of expanding power and influence through increased productivity.[56]

* * *

Already the restlessness across Eastern Europe raised doubts that the Kremlin could long maintain its Eastern European hegemony. In most countries local Communist leaders kept the new pressures within bounds by making concessions. In Poland, however, the demand for change quickly resulted in the Poznan riots of June 1956. Dulles assured the Senate Foreign Relations Committee on June 26 that "Khrushchev is on the ropes and, if we can keep the pressure up ... there is going to occur a very great disintegration within the apparatus of the international Communist organization." To the Poznan marchers, American aspirations for liberation meant nothing; it was hunger and repression that drove them to rebel. In defying Poland's Communist regime, they looked to their own resources.[57]

When the growing instability produced an uprising in Hungary, the United States quickly became too involved to escape all responsibility. Secretary Dulles, from the beginning, identified American purpose with that of the revolting Hungarians. "These patriots value liberty more than life itself," he explained to the Dallas Council on World Affairs on October 27, 1956. "And all who peacefully enjoy liberty have a solemn duty to seek, by all truly helpful means, that those who now die for freedom will not have died in vain." Patriotism and the longing for freedom were at last breaking the Soviet grip.

"The weakness of Soviet imperialism," the Secretary continued, "is being made manifest. Its weakness is not military weakness nor lack of material power. It is weak because it seeks to sustain an unnatural tyranny by suppressing human aspirations which cannot indefinitely be hidden." Dulles invited the Hungarians, as they now achieved their independence, to draw upon America for aid in adjusting their economy to serve their needs.[58]

Boasts that American-encouraged aspirations for freedom were now rending the Soviet hegemony asunder were drowned out within a week as Soviet tanks slowly ground down Budapest's revolutionary forces. Some Hungarian leaders, having declared Hungary's neutrality and withdrawal from the Warsaw Pact, now sought aid. They quickly learned that Washington had no intention of inviting World War III. In acknowledging, at this moment of great urgency, that Hungary's independence was not a basic American interest, American officials rendered the concept of liberation a mockery. As one Budapest factory foreman said of Western broadcasts into Hungary, "The speakers in their studios in Munich had it easy; just talking, talking, talking. We did the fighting." Hungary demonstrated that policy, not guided by national interest, becomes irresponsible when put to the test.[59]

Amid its embarrassment, Washington turned to the United Nations. A Soviet veto eliminated the American condemnatory resolution, introduced into the Security Council on November 4. Immediately, the General Assembly, called into emergency session, passed the resolution calling on the U.S.S.R. to stop its armed attack on the people of Hungary and withdraw its forces from that country without delay. India's Prime Minister Nehru warned the Western states that such condemnation would only intensify the conflict; under moral pressure the Kremlin could not relent without the admission of wrongdoing. The neutralist spokesmen of India, Indonesia, and Burma remained unalterably opposed to the Assembly's efforts to turn the Soviets out of Hungary with words. That the UN resolutions saved no Hungarians seemed to make no difference in Washington as long as the Soviet Union stood properly condemned. Not even the support of a major uprising enabled the Western democracies to change the 1945 line of East-West demarcation. Yet American officials refused to accept even this lesson from the Hungarian debacle. Official policy statements continued to condemn the Soviets for their domination of Hungary. On the second anniversary of the Hungarian revolt, the State Department announced: "These actions of the Soviet and Hungarian Government in defiance of the UN ... have occasioned deep concern in the U.S. as elsewhere throughout the world. They cannot and will not be ignored." In December 1958, U.S. Ambassador Henry Cabot Lodge declared that the Hungarian people "must be relieved of that scourge of terror. ... If the existing tension is to be relaxed and the danger of still another tragic explosion ended, it will be necessary to end the injustice which causes the tension."[60] Each year the United Nations, under U.S. pressure, called on the new Hungarian regime of Janos Kadar to comply with its resolutions. By 1960, the rapidly declining percentage of nations willing to engage in the annual censure, it looked less and less like an effective moral judgment.

What the verbal adherence to liberation achieved, other than the continued disillusionment of those who took it seriously, was not apparent. Yet it was doubtful that the Kremlin would fully recover from the Hungarian experience; the courageous resistance of Budapest illustrated the widespread opposition that the Soviets faced throughout their Eastern European hegemony. Only Czechoslovakia's Communist government kept its populace immune from the liberalizing tendencies that plagued the Kremlin elsewhere in Eastern Europe. Hungary's Kadar regime made strenuous efforts to improve conditions within that country and eliminate the causes of discontent. Extensive Soviet credits, industrial raw materials, fuels, and food bolstered the shattered economy. Budapest's well-stocked shelves revealed a rising standard of living. But the general mood of resignation and depression in Hungary and elsewhere could not destroy the continuing quest for something better than physical survival. After Hungary, Soviet leaders would accept the growth of self-determination or subject themselves to increasingly costly and counterproductive policies of repression.

* * *

Undaunted by the U.S.-Soviet clash over Hungary, the Kremlin, in November 1957, launched a crusade for another summit with the Western powers. The Soviets still hoped to gain the recognition of their hegemony in Eastern Europe as an unchangeable element in European politics. To publicize his campaign for high-level talks, Khrushchev initiated an exchange of public letters with the heads of Western governments. The Eisenhower administration demanded that any future summits have adequate preparation, an agreed-upon agenda, and reasonable assurance of success. Washington was determined as well to seek prior approval of regional allies, registered in a pre-summit foreign ministers conferences. Soviet leaders argued that pre-summit conferences would eliminate the possibility of diplomacy among equals. Khrushchev's letter writing produced no results.[61]

Then on November 27, 1958, the Soviet leader challenged the allied status at its weakest point—West Berlin. In a note to the Western powers, he warned that the Soviet government was resolved to abolish the occupation regime in Berlin and enter negotiations designed to transform West Berlin into a demilitarized free city. Threatening a general war, he said that only "madmen" would "go the length of unleashing another world war over the preservation of privileges of occupiers in West Berlin." If at the end of six months the Big Four had reached no agreement, the Kremlin would turn over control of traffic into West Berlin to the East German government. West Berlin's extraordinary progress, reflecting the remarkable prosperity of West Germany, contrasted sharply with the drabness, distrust, and fear that characterized East Germany. That contrast rendered West Berlin both a dangerous Western showcase and a refuge for those who chose to escape the Soviet sphere. The city, moreover, was the one remaining open window through which the West could penetrate the Iron Curtain.[62] On December 31 the United States rejected the Soviet proposal of a free city of West Berlin. Facing a firm Western stand, Khrushchev, in January, called for a summit conference to discuss Berlin; he did not repeat his six-month deadline.[63]

During February 1959 the Western powers suggested a Big Four Foreign Ministers conference, with representatives from both East and West Germany. The Soviets agreed to a conference, scheduled to open in Geneva on May 11. Before it convened, Dulles resigned because of illness. Christian Herter, who succeeded him, presented the West's initial position at Geneva on May 14. It sought the unification of Berlin through free elections and a city council to govern Berlin until it became the capital of a united country. Two days later, Andrei Gromyko presented the Soviet plan, designed fundamentally to formalize the *status quo* across Central Europe. It proposed separate peace treaties with East and West Germany, permitting the two Germanies to maintain armed forces, but without nuclear weapons. The Big Four would withdraw from the two Germanies, dissolve the four-power occupation of Berlin, and leave Berlin a free city pending German unification and a final peace settlement. Herter and Gromyko quickly rejected each other's proposals. When the conference recessed on June 20, after seven weeks of fruitless talks, the Soviet and Western positions were as far apart as they had been at the beginning. When the conference reconvened in July, the two sides exchanged new proposals.

With the United States emphasizing the principle of self-determination, the conference remained deadlocked until its final adjournment on August 5.

Despite the seriousness of the Berlin crisis, the atmosphere in 1959 was more relaxed. Early that year Anastas Mikoyan, the dapper Soviet deputy premier, toured the United States and conferred with top leaders of government and industry. On June 28, Frol R. Kozlov, another deputy premier, arrived in New York to open the impressive Soviet Exhibit of Science, Technology, and Culture at the New York City Coliseum. In July, Vice President Richard M. Nixon opened the complementary U.S. exhibition in Moscow. It was in the kitchen of this exhibit that Nixon had his colorful exchange with Khrushchev. On August 3, President Eisenhower announced that Khrushchev would visit the United States. Khrushchev's tour of the United States received tremendous coverage by television, radio, and the press in Washington, New York, Los Angeles, San Francisco, and the Midwest. As the visit drew to a close, Eisenhower announced that the removal of Soviet's Berlin deadline had cleared the way for a summit conference and his own visit to the Soviet Union in the spring of 1960.[64] Khrushchev's visit left most Cold War issues as clouded as in the past. The Kremlin still sought nothing less than Western recognition of the territorial and political consequences of the Soviet victory in World War II.

President Eisenhower, on December 3, 1959, embarked on a tour of Europe, Asia, and North Africa. His purpose, he said, was to build "a better understanding of the United States and good will for us." The schedule called for visits to 11 countries in less than three weeks. In brief visits to Italy, Turkey, Pakistan, Afghanistan, India, Iran, Greece, Tunisia, Spain, and Morocco, with an interlude in Paris for a conference with Western leaders, the president appeared before millions. In Paris, the leaders of Britain, France, and Germany looked to the president for forceful and imaginative leadership to prepare them for the coming summit conference with Khrushchev; but Eisenhower had little to offer. Those who equated the cause of peace with the enthusiasm that greeted the president abroad tended to forget that it was the country's relations with the government in Moscow, not with the crowds of New Delhi, Paris, or Kabul that measured the status of world politics.[65]

The chief issues before the summit were the complementary challenges of Germany and European security. As the Western powers searched for proposals on which they could agree, events elsewhere decreed that the summit would never take place. Khrushchev announced on May 5, 1960, that the Soviets had downed a U-2 American spy plane over Soviet territory. When the administration denied the accuracy of the story, the Soviets announced that they had captured the pilot. Actually the president knew of the flights. He accepted full responsibility, but termed the flights an unfortunate necessity. Now Khrushchev, obsessed with the issue of American over flights, demanded a presidential apology. He informed Charles de Gaulle and British Prime Minister Harold Macmillan that he would scuttle the Paris summit unless Eisenhower apologized and punished those directly responsible. At the Paris Summit on May 16, de Gaulle planned to have Eisenhower open the summit as head of government. Khrushchev, however, interrupted the initial proceedings with a diatribe, revoked his invitation to the president to visit Moscow, and walked out to end the summit. Perhaps it mattered little; neither side was prepared to compromise any of its established positions. The Berlin issue, unresolved, would live to see another day.[66]

This persistent avoidance of accommodation reflected the fundamental conflict between self-determination and European security. Both the West and the U.S.S.R. moved through the Berlin crisis of 1958–1960 without concession or preparation for action. Behind the mutual restraint was the recognition among Western and Soviet leaders alike that the unresolved issues in Europe, including Berlin, were far less than vital and therefore better left unresolved than disposed of through war. Recognition of the East German government would not infringe on any vital Western interest. By 1960 the West had coexisted for 15 years with the East German regime, as well as all the Communist-dominated governments of Eastern Europe, without damaging consequences. The realization that German unification had no future in a divided, but stabilized, Europe gave rise in the late 1950s to the concept of "disengagement."

George F. Kennan gave it form and synthesis in his Reith Lectures over BBC in the late autumn of 1957, later published under the title, *Russia, the Atom, and the West*. Kennan accepted the traditional goals of Western diplomacy—the achievement of greater self-determination for the captive peoples, including those of East Germany. But any peaceful evolution toward self-determination, he argued, would require the voluntary withdrawal of Soviet occupation forces. Because the question of Soviet occupation could not be divorced from that of Soviet security, he recommended the disengagement of NATO forces from West Germany and a Western willingness to accept the neutralization of that country. Finally, he favored a nuclear-free band across Central Europe, an idea popularized by Adam Rapacki, Poland's Foreign Minister in January 1958.[67] Kennan's impact on European liberals was profound; German Social Democrats immediately produced a phased program of their own. They advised the Bonn government to negotiate unilaterally with the Kremlin. Disengagement, in short, questioned the fundamental decisions of the past that assumed that desired changes within the Soviet sphere, as well as the security of Western Europe, rested on the perpetuation of a hard military line of demarcation across Europe.

Dean Acheson's sweeping criticism of Kennan's thesis appeared in *Foreign Affairs*, April 1958. Acheson's arguments reaffirmed NATO's traditional commitment to military containment. He doubted that the West could ever pay the requisite price for a Soviet military retreat without weakening its own security. He challenged the notion that the U.S.S.R. could afford to evacuate its satellite states as part of a disengagement agreement. Furthermore, retiring Soviet forces would leave in their wake a group of unstable Communist regimes whose collapse the Kremlin could not tolerate without risking the overthrow of its entire system. It was equally improbable that the Soviets would accede to the absorption of East Germany into the economy and political structure of West Germany. Such an eventuality, Acheson warned, would bring the Soviets back into Central Europe in force. Finally, Acheson discovered the means of breaking up the Iron Curtain in NATO itself. A powerful and united Western Europe, he wrote, exerted a radiating influence on the Soviet sphere. It had prevented the total repression of Poland and Yugoslavia; in time it would subvert the entire Soviet structure.[68]

European conservatives shared Acheson's deep commitment to NATO and the security it offered. They regarded the Atlantic Alliance the primary achievement of postwar diplomacy, and attributed the amazing economic recovery of Western Europe to its existence. To them the Rapacki Plan for a nuclear-free zone was nothing less than a Soviet trap. "It would be folly," declared Paul-Henri Spaak, Secretary General of NATO, in June 1959, "and I venture to say criminal folly, to follow a policy which might lead to the departure of American troops from Germany." The neutralization of Germany, finally, would withdraw German forces and space from NATO, curtail the alliance's effectiveness, and forever consign its defense to nuclear weapons. "Deadlock and stalemate are certainly hard to endure," admitted one British official, "but to yield would be worse. We should all of us do well not to forget the lesson of the nineteen-thirties." Europe's stability, militarily reinforced, was not everlasting, but for the moment no alternative condition seemed as satisfactory.[69] Washington's concurrent refusal to concede any legitimacy to the Soviet view of security denied it the freedom to prepare the American people for the only kind of European peace available to them.[70]

* * *

For Eisenhower and Dulles, the non-European world they inherited from Truman remained the essential battleground of the Cold War. Conceding to the Kremlin full control of Communism's alleged expansive power in Asia, the new president, in early 1953, declared that the country stood in greater peril than any time in its history. Eisenhower confided to his diary of January 6, 1953, that world Communism was taking advantage of nationalist pressures and the "confusion resulting from the destruction of existing relationships ... to further the aims of world revolution and the Kremlin's domination of all people." Soviet leaders, "in mapping their strategy for world conquest," Dulles warned in November 1953, "hit upon nationalism as a device for absorbing the colonial peoples." The danger, Dulles continued, rested in the ability of Communist agitators to aggravate nationalist aspirations so that people would rebel violently against the existing order. Before the revolting nationalists could create a new stability, Communists would gain control of the nation and convey it into the Soviet orbit.[71] Ambassador Karl Lott Rankin in Taipei revealed the administration's entrapment when he reminded Ambassador George V. Allen in India, during July 1953, that the United States could maintain its anti-Beijing posture only by denying that Mao enjoyed any independence from Moscow. Whether or not this was true, wrote Rankin, the Chinese Nationalists on Formosa feared that Washington might accept it as true and thereafter follow the course of Britain and India. "Only so long as they are persuaded that Americans continue to regard Mao simply as a Soviet tool," ran Rankin's admonition, "will they feel reasonably assured as to our China policy."[72]

For the Eisenhower presidency, China had already received top billing. Chiang Kai-shek's countless supporters interpreted the Republican victory, with its promise of liberation, as a mandate for a policy that would reestablish Nationalist control over the mainland. Henry Luce's *Life* magazine asserted that a sound China policy would bind "free China's fate and policy to ours with hoops of steel." Members of the China bloc in Congress reminded the administration that war with China was inevitable and that the Nationalists were the last guardians of American security in the Orient. "Let us face one simple fact," William Jenner of Indiana warned the Senate. "There can be no American policy in the Pacific if the Communists are allowed to retain the heartland of Asia.... All American policy must start from a firm decision to reestablish the legitimate anti-Communist government on the China mainland." For William C. Bullitt, even a war to uproot Communist power in East Asia would require no more than "a concerted attack on the Chinese Communists, employing no American soldiers except those in Korea, but using the American Navy to blockade the China coast and the American air force to bomb appropriate targets, while assigning the great burden of the ground fighting to the Koreans and the Free Chinese."[73]

Dulles, conscious of the abuse that Acheson had suffered at the hands of Chiang's American friends, simply handed them control of U.S. China policy. Under Eisenhower, California's Senator Knowland emerged as Chiang's leading spokesman in the Senate; Congressman Walter Judd of Minnesota assumed command of the House's powerful Nationalist China bloc. These Republican stalwarts hoped that by preventing any widespread international recognition of the Beijing regime, they could return Chiang to the mainland and again open that country to American merchants, investors, officials, travelers, and scholars. Those who controlled U.S. official relations with China soon discovered that it was far easier to mould public sentiment than to build a policy. Even the national opinion that demanded Chiang's return to the mainland opposed war to achieve it.

Too responsible for military ventures against China, yet too fearful of public opinion to question the expectation of Chiang's imminent triumph, the Eisenhower administration adopted, in effect, a "two-China policy," recognizing the Republic of China on Formosa while coexisting satisfactorily with the mainland regime.[74] In practice the administration, to avoid trouble, refused to sanction any unleashing. Meanwhile nonrecognition of the mainland regime perpetuated the illusion of Beijing's eventual demise.[75] In meetings with his staff, the president expressed uneasiness over the U.S. commitment to the Nationalist regime. Journalist Robert J. Donovan, who attended staff meetings in preparation for his semiofficial history of the administration, recorded the president's lack of conviction "that the vital interests of the United States were best served by prolonged nonrecognition of China." "He had serious doubts," Donovan continued, "as to whether Russia and China were natural allies.... Therefore, he asked, would it not be the best policy in the long run for the United States to try to pull China away from Russia rather than drive the

Chinese ever deeper into an unnatural alliance unfriendly to the United States?"[76] The transcripts of Dulles's telephone conversations, however, reveal that Knowland and Judd reported every rumor or newspaper report that suggested a softening of official policy toward China. Dulles invariably reassured them that the administration would never compromise its opposition to the mainland regime.[77]

What magnified the danger of an unwanted involvement in the Chinese civil war was the Nationalist occupation of the offshore islands of Quemoy and Matsu, hugging the China coast. In September 1954, the mainland Chinese shelled the islands with the apparent intent of seizing them by force. Eisenhower cautioned Admiral Radford, who advocated a decisive American response: "We're not talking now about a limited brush-fire war. We're talking about going to the threshold of World War III. If we attack China, we're not going to impose limits on our military actions, as in Korea. Moreover . . . if we get into a general war, the logical enemy will be Russia, not China, and we'll have to strike there."[78] Eisenhower saw little reason for the United States to defend the offshore islands, yet his hesitant posture regarding the offshore islands quickly subjected the administration to criticism from the pro-Chiang bloc. Few Americans or Europeans regarded the U.S. commitment to the defense of Formosa unreasonable or particularly dangerous, but they questioned the wisdom of any commitment to the offshore islands. Except for the assumption that Chiang, to perpetuate his regime, required the offshore islands as symbolic stepping-stones for his return to the mainland, the American involvement in the Formosa Strait had no apparent purpose. Walter Lippmann detected danger in this assumption: "If, as a matter of fact, the internal strength of Nationalist China rests on the fantasy that Chiang Kai-shek will someday return to China, we are headed for trouble."[79]

In the Formosa Resolution of late January 1955, Congress authorized the president to resist any effort to capture the offshore islands if it appeared that the assault was an initial move against Formosa itself. "Clearly, this existing and developing situation," the president agreed, "poses a serious danger to the security of our country and the entire Pacific area and indeed to the peace of the world."[80] When newsmen questioned Eisenhower, in March, on his apparent decision to employ nuclear weapons in defense of the offshore islands, the president responded: "Now in any combat where these things can be used on strictly military targets and for strictly military purposes, I see no reason why they shouldn't be used just exactly as you would use a bullet or anything else." Analysts observed that even the tactical use of such weapons around Amoy would have killed an estimated 12–14 million Chinese civilians.[81] Eisenhower escaped the crisis by resisting the appeals of Radford, Dulles, and others for stronger responses to the Chinese shelling. The Communists were content to leave the Nationalist forces on the islands.

In August 1958, the Chinese resumed the shelling of Quemoy to create another crisis. Dulles looked on in disbelief, troubled that the Chinese might attempt to take the island. On September 4, he traveled to Newport, Rhode Island, where Eisenhower was vacationing, with a carefully prepared statement that represented the views of the Pentagon, the CIA, and the State Department. Dulles predicted that the loss of Quemoy would lead to the loss of Formosa; this, in turn, would expose the entire U.S. defense barrier in the western Pacific to destruction. The United States, he concluded, had no choice but to defend the island. Dulles recommended that Washington, if it could not dissuade the mainland Chinese from invading, prepare to use nuclear weapons. The world might object, but a swift, total victory would soon cause it to forget. After suggesting a few minor changes in the text, Eisenhower accepted the Dulles proposal and authorized the secretary to release it to the press.[82]

Washington embarked on another unilateral policy in Asia that had little or no support abroad.[83] On September 29, Senator Theodore F. Green, chairman of the Foreign Relations Committee, questioned the importance of Quemoy to the defense of Formosa and the United States. The president responded that a successful attack on Formosa would drive the United States from the western Pacific. To prevent that, the country had no choice but to protect the status of Quemoy and Matsu. "We must not forget," Eisenhower concluded, "that the whole Formosa Straits situation is intimately connected with the security of the United States and the free world."[84] Some writers praised Eisenhower for engaging in a successful game of bluff, apparently defending the Nationalist cause at no cost.[85] Such a bluff, if called, would have left the United States in the inextricable dilemma of retreating ignominiously or unleashing a massive war over tiny islands of little strategic value to anyone. Fortunately, China's leaders, detecting no economic or strategic significance in the offshore islands, ordered no assault.

Washington neglected to analyze Chinese behavior or determine the Sino-Soviet relationship with any precision. U.S. leaders continued to assume that Moscow-Beijing ties remained strong yet vulnerable to American maneuvering. At the Bermuda Conference of

December 1953, Dulles observed that the United States, by exerting "maximum pressure" on China, could weaken Beijing's allegiance to the Soviet Union. An uncooperative approach, Dulles promised, would compel the Chinese to make demands on the U.S.S.R. that the latter could not fulfill, thereby creating strains between them.[86] Dulles defined neither the "massive pressures" he intended to employ nor the Moscow-Beijing ties he intended to break. Lacking precise knowledge of the Sino-Soviet relationship—or any apparent desire to seek it—in August 1954, he feared that the binding Sino-Soviet ties might continue for 25 years. In February 1955, he informed Chinese Ambassador George Yeh that the breakup could come within a year. Then in June 1956, Dulles informed British Foreign Minister Selwyn Lloyd that the natural Sino-Soviet rivalries "might take 100 years to assert themselves." In his noted San Francisco speech of June 1957, Dulles suggested that international Communism's rule in China, as elsewhere, was a passing phenomenon. How the United States might contribute to that passing, and how long it might require, he did not say.[87]

For Washington it was the presumption of strong, perhaps unbreakable, Moscow-Beijing ties that denied the legitimacy of the mainland regime and rationalized continued U.S. nonrecognition. Dulles and his State Department associates argued that recognition of China's Communist government could not weaken its ties to the Kremlin. Meanwhile, nonrecognition assured the containment of Chinese Communist rule in Asia. "Many an Asian has told me," reported Walter P. McConaughy, Director of the Office of Chinese Affairs, in January 1954, "that American non-recognition of the Communist regime in Peiping has had much to do with checking the impetus of the Communist advance in Asia." Conversely, he warned, U.S. recognition would destroy the Asian will to resist the onrush of Communist expansionism. Recognition, Dulles warned an Australian audience in March 1957, would encourage influences hostile to the United States and its allies and further imperil countries whose independence strengthened American peace and security. Shortly thereafter, Ambassador William J. Sebald observed, "A change in the status of Free China would, I believe, have a chain-reaction effect which would seriously weaken the free world." Walter S. Robertson declared even more dramatically in March 1959:

If the United States were to abandon its commitments to the Republic of China in order to appease the threatening Red Chinese, no country in Asia could feel that it could any longer rely upon the protection of the United States against the Communist threat. These comparatively weak nations would have no alternative but to come to terms—the best they could get—with the Peiping colossus.[88]

Beyond containment, nonrecognition sustained the hope of China's eventual liberation. During March 1957, Ambassador Rankin acknowledged that the United States had done much for the Republic of China. But, he noted, the government in Taipei remained "as far as ever from its great objective of bringing about the liberation of mainland China from Red tyranny."[89] What troubled Chiang and his supporters everywhere was the dawning realization that the Eisenhower administration had no policy of liberation.

Long before 1960, the evidence pouring out of Moscow and Beijing dramatized the growing tension between the two countries. The golden age of Sino-Soviet relations had been brief, spanning the years from 1950 to 1955. Symbolically, the break came in 1956 with Khrushchev's tirade against Stalin and his plea for a more realistic and less ideological competition between the Soviet and non-Soviet worlds. The Sino-Soviet alliance was never efficacious. The Quemoy crisis of August 1958, when Beijing coordinated its shelling of the offshore islands with an effort to invoke its treaty arrangements with the U.S.S.R., clarified the growing divergence in Sino-Soviet perceptions of the enemy. Soviet abstinence consisted of clear warnings to Beijing that its troubles with the Republic of China and the United States were, and would remain, its own.[90] By 1960, the Sino-Soviet rift was breaking into the open, soon to render the Communist giants the world's most bitter antagonists. Yet the impact of this split on U.S. Asian policy was scarcely apparent at all.

* * *

Those who condemned the long, costly stalemate in Korea anticipated, under Eisenhower, the peace that Truman had failed to achieve. For some the avenue to peace still lay in victory, not compromise. General Matthew B. Ridgway replied "casualties unacceptable" when the Pentagon sought his views on a general Korean offensive in June 1952. But General James Van Fleet, who returned from Korea in the spring of 1953, declared that the American people could still gain an easy triumph in Korea. "We are ... thoroughly and completely superior to the Chinese Reds in North Korea," he wrote, " ... all we have to do is to start an all-out effort in Korea and the Reds will come begging to us." Eventually most high-ranking U.S. officers accepted

Van Fleet's contention that success still awaited a more determined American effort in Korea.

What had stalled the truce negotiations at Panmunjom during the last months of the Truman presidency was the prisoner of war issue. During 1952, Chinese and North Koreans had crowded the prisoner of war camps—Koje Island alone held 130,000 North Korean and 20,000 Chinese prisoners. Despite the elaborate efforts at indoctrination, thousands of Chinese prisoners signed in blood that they would kill themselves rather than return to China. For Western negotiators, this development proved troublesome, if not embarrassing. UN officials encouraged the prisoners to return to their homelands; they invited Communist spokesmen to interview the prisoners, promising amnesty. Every attempt failed. That tens of thousands refused repatriation was treason *en masse* to Moscow and Beijing. U.S. officials demanded that these prisoners be permitted a choice regarding repatriation; as late as March 1953 Communist negotiators demurred.

Suddenly, for reasons not totally clear, the truce negotiations began to succeed.[91] In part the answer lay in Washington. Both Eisenhower and Dulles created the illusion that they were willing to use greater destructiveness, perhaps even nuclear weapons, to terminate the war. When Eisenhower, following his election, returned from his trip to Korea, he declared publicly in New York that "we face an enemy whom we cannot hope to impress by words, however eloquent, but only by deeds—executed under circumstances of our own choosing." Perhaps Stalin's death in early 1953 was another moderating factor. Late in March, the Chinese and North Koreans agreed to an exchange of sick and wounded prisoners. Shortly thereafter, Communist negotiators accepted the principle of voluntary repatriation, provided that prisoners who rejected repatriation enter a neutral state. When Syngman Rhee discovered that the forthcoming settlement would perpetuate Korea's political division in the vicinity of the 38th parallel, he ordered the release of thousands of prisoners into the South Korean population. The negotiations continued; on July 27, 1953, a formal armistice terminated the war. The worldwide balance of power had become too stable to permit any significant political or territorial changes in areas contested by the major Cold War antagonists.

For Washington the continuing struggle in Indochina remained a simple Communist aggression, emanating from Moscow and Beijing, to be resolved by military power alone. Dulles described the administration's official view of the Asian danger as early as January 1953. "The Soviet Russians," he said, "are making a drive to get Japan, not only through what they are doing in Korea but also through what they are doing in Indochina. If they could get this peninsula of Indochina, Siam, Burma, and Malaya, they would have what is called the rice bowl of Asia. . . . [T]hat would be another weapon which would tend to expand their control into Japan and into India." Vice President Nixon elaborated the danger in December: "If Indochina falls, Thailand is put in an almost impossible position. The same is true of Malaya with its rubber and tin. The same is true for Indonesia. . . . That indicates . . . why it is vitally important that Indochina not go behind the Iron Curtain."[92]

By February 1954, however, Ho Chi Minh's revolutionary forces threatened the entire French position in Southeast Asia. At the besieged Indochinese fortress of Dienbienphu came the crucial test for Washington's Asiatic policies of containment. General Paul Ely, French Chief of Staff, warned U.S. leaders in March that the time for allied intervention had arrived. In his New York address of March 29, Dulles called for the internationalization of the war. "Under the conditions of today," he told the Overseas Press Club, "the imposition on Southeast Asia of the political system of Communist Russia and its Chinese Communist ally, by whatever means, would be a grave threat to the whole free community." Early in April, Dulles and Radford pressed congressional leaders for support of American air strikes against enemy positions at Dienbienphu, but without success. On April 7 Eisenhower informed newsmen that if one more nation of Southeast Asia went down, the others, like a row of dominoes, would follow. Yet he did not support the French at Dienbienphu, for Dulles had failed to secure the necessary British approval for a policy of "united action." The president simply could not obtain the conditions required for a successful U.S. intervention.[93]

Even with the French militarily defeated, Eisenhower was determined to hold the line in Southeast Asia. The 14-nation Geneva Conference, from late April until July 1954, divided Indochina into the independent states of Laos, Cambodia, and Vietnam, the latter separated at the seventeenth parallel until elections, to occur in 1956, determined a single government. As the French withdrew from Indochina, Eisenhower committed the United States not only to the support of Ngo Dinh Diem's new Saigon regime, in control of all Vietnam south of the seventeenth parallel, but also to the eventual elimination of Ho's control of North Vietnam. That single-minded support of Diem overlooked a variety of troubling factors: that Ho had secured the independence of all Indochina from French rule; that

Paris and Washington had placed the mantle of legitimacy on the losers, not the victors; that Ho's cause had been only the cause of Indochinese independence; that he was fiercely independent of all external control; that in achieving victory Ho had defeated good French units, administering 175,000 casualties with 92,000 dead; and that his military power would only increase with the passage of time. How the United States could build, in Saigon, unity and power sufficient to achieve a political and military victory over the forces of Ho Chi Minh remained unclear. From the beginning, the U.S. involvement in Southeast Asia carried the seeds of disaster.

Dulles announced to the press in May that the domino theory no longer applied. The United States, he said, had negotiated a new alliance that would strengthen the other nations of Southeast Asia. The new pact, signed at Manila in September, established the eight-nation Southeast Asia Treaty Organization (SEATO), which included the United States, Britain, France, Australia, New Zealand, Pakistan, Thailand, and the Philippines. These eight signatories promised to act jointly against "any fact or situation which might endanger the peace of the area" south of Formosa. In a special protocol, Dulles managed to include Laos and South Vietnam within the treaty's defense area. As a military arrangement, SEATO was less than promising; the member states, scattered around the globe, scarcely shared any major security interests in Southeast Asia. At Manila, moreover, Dulles warned the allies that the United States, with its global commitments, would fight no more conventional land wars in Asia. It would grant logistical, naval, and air support to Asian forces; beyond that it would resort to weapons of massive destruction.

After 1954, Ngo Dinh Diem shouldered the chief responsibility for defending his country's and America's interests in Southeast Asia. Assured of U.S. support, Diem called off the Vietnam elections in July 1955. Unfortunately, that decision did not terminate Ho's ambitions to unite Vietnam under his regime, but merely shifted his program to infiltration and subversion. Washington found itself powerless to control its Indochinese allies or to desert them. Ignoring official warnings that Diem's fortunes were not promising, the Eisenhower administration surfeited him with advisers, aid, praise, and renewed commitments.[94] During Diem's official visit to Washington in May 1957, President Eisenhower lauded the Vietnamese leader publicly at the airport for bringing to the task of organizing his country "the greatest of courage, the greatest of statesmanship." Diem, in return, thanked the president for the "unselfish American aid which has accomplished a miracle of Viet-Nam." When Diem departed Washington on May 11, the two presidents issued a joint communiqué that "looked forward to an end of the unhappy division of the Vietnamese people and confirmed the determination of the two Governments to work together to seek suitable means to bring about the peaceful unification of Viet-Nam in freedom."[95]

Eisenhower explained his fears, should containment at the seventeenth parallel fail, before a Gettysburg College audience in April 1959, "Strategically, South Viet-Nam's capture by the Communists would bring their power several hundred miles into a hitherto free region. ... The loss of South Viet-Nam would set in motion a crumbling process that could, as it progressed, have grave consequences for us and for freedom."[96] Even as Eisenhower left office he did nothing to reduce the American commitment to Ngo Dinh Diem or prepare an avenue of escape from a war in Saigon's defense.[97] For the moment, the predictable tragedy of American policy in Southeast Asia mattered little. As long as the proclaimed triumphs of the South Vietnamese government and the SEATO alliance guaranteed successful containment at little cost, the Eisenhower administration faced no demands of an explicit explanation of its intentions. Still the intellectual and policy dilemmas of the future were already clear.

* * *

As in Vietnam, the Eisenhower administration rationalized every action or threatened action in the Middle East, Africa, or Latin America in the name of containing Soviet expansionism. In 1953 and 1954 the president authorized the CIA to overthrow the governments of Iran and Guatemala, both devoted to social reform but neither Communist controlled nor tied to the Soviet Union. Premier Muhammad Mossadeq endangered Western interests in Iran when, in May 1951, he seized the British-owned Anglo-Iranian Oil Company and threatened to carry out a nationwide social revolution. When Eisenhower entered office he agreed with the British on the necessity of removing Mossadeq from power, especially when the premier forced the pro-Western shah to flee the country. As in Vietnam, the president did not distinguish between radical nationalism and Soviet Communism. While State Department pronouncements linked Mossadeq to Communist expansionism, the CIA organized a successful coup against the premier and arranged for the return of the shah.[98] In time Iran would compel the United States to pay a heavy price for its easy and triumphant intervention in Iranian political affairs.

Global containment encompassed Latin America, slowly and incompletely, through Guatemala. The Rio Pact of 1947 converted the special hemispheric relationship between the United States and the Latin American states into a permanent collective security system. But the Rio Pact defined no specific danger to hemispheric security; nor did the events of the Truman years require any special financial or defense obligations to the Latin American countries. That changed when Jacobo Arbenz Guzman's democratically elected and reform-minded government of Guatemala granted local Communists a significant role in national affairs. For many U.S. officials, that decision converted his country into a Soviet bridgehead in the Western Hemisphere. Arbenz denied that his government had any connections with the Kremlin. In carrying out his land reform program, Arbenz nationalized only unused lands and left Guatemala's basic power structure intact. When, in 1953, he threatened vast holdings of American-owned United Fruit Company, U.S. officials unleashed an assault on Arbenz's allegedly pro-Soviet government. John M. Cabot, Assistant Secretary of State for Inter-American Affairs, accused Arbenz of maintaining "a regime which is openly playing the Communist game."[99]

At the Tenth Inter-American Conference, held in Caracas, Venezuela, during March 1954, Dulles secured a resolution that declared, "the control of the political institutions of any American State by the international Communist movement . . . would constitute a threat to the sovereignty and political independence of the American States." To terminate Arbenz's Soviet-directed conspiracy in Central America, Eisenhower ordered the CIA to remove him. Shortly after the democratic government's collapse in June 1954, under internal as well as external pressures, Eisenhower accepted the credentials of the ambassador of Guatemala's new military regime under Carlos Castillo Armas, with these words: "The people of Guatemala, in a magnificent effort, have liberated themselves from the shackles of international Communist direction, and reclaimed their right of self-determination."[100] That unfortunate country paid the price of Arbenz's overthrow in decades of mass murders and misrule by successive military regimes. Daniel Graham defined the America's Guatemalan involvement in May 1955: "Deep down everyone in Guatemala knows that Communism was not the issue. Feudalism was the issue, and those who profited from feudalism won."[101]

Following the Guatemalan affair, U.S. economic and military aid went generally to those Latin American governments that had the strongest rhetorical claims to anti-Communism. Former Colombian

President Dr. Eduarto Santos commented bitterly in a speech at Columbia University in October 1954, "The anti-Communist flag in Latin America is being converted into a pirate's flag. The worst enemies of liberty hoist the anti-Communist flag and hide behind it. . . . Unfortunately, this despicable trick finds a sad approval in the United States." Whether military aid added to hemispheric security was doubtful. Washington's close ties with Latin America's military leaders, moreover, incited a deep anti-Americanism among those Latin Americans who believed that progress required revolutionary change sufficient to deprive the ruling elements of their historic social, economic, and political privileges. It required only Vice President Nixon's Latin American tour of April–May 1958 to reveal the depth of the animosity. Except in Buenos Aires and Asuncion, the vice president faced anti-American demonstrations in every capital he visited. For Eisenhower that experience revealed only that the Kremlin was at war with the United States across Latin America.

During Eisenhower's final year in office, Cuba confronted his administration with its toughest and most divisive hemispheric challenge. Fidel Castro's victory over the dictatorial Fulgencio Batista in 1959 provoked general approval in the United States. In April Americans welcomed Castro warmly on his unofficial visit to Washington. But already Castro's relations with Washington had entered a downward spiral. Castro's agrarian reform program, which assaulted large land holdings of American-owned sugar companies, increased the animosity. Castro's social revolution soon threatened American industrial investments as well. In August 1960, the burgeoning inter-American tensions focused on the San Jose meeting of the Organization of American States (OAS), where the United States submitted a 78-page document to support its charges that Cuba had become another bridgehead for Soviet-sponsored revolution in the Americas. For U.S. officials, the Declaration of San Jose, signed reluctantly by most Latin American nations, comprised a firm defense against Communist subversion. Eisenhower responded to the Cuban threat by severing U.S. diplomatic relations with the Castro government and ordering the CIA to prepare a counter-revolutionary assault against the island.

* * *

Eisenhower's Cold War interventionism ultimately encompassed the Middle East, a region that lacked any recognizable Communist-led revolutionary movement. The region's instability was a measure of its intense anti-Western nationalism, aimed largely at the remnants

of British and French colonialism. Unfortunately, Dulles's early determination to extend U.S. global defenses across the Middle East rested
on Britain's status as a regional power. When the secretary toured the
Middle East in May 1953, he discovered that only Turkey, Iran, and
Pakistan—countries near the Soviet border—revealed any concern
for Soviet expansionism. Turkey and Pakistan, members of NATO
and SEATO respectively, readily accepted Dulles's Northern Tier
defense plans. During 1954, Iran and Iraq approached Washington
for assistance. In 1955, Dulles united these four Middle Eastern states
with Britain in the Baghdad Pact. The pact's liabilities were profound.
Not only was it powerless to act, but also its inclusion of Iraq divided
the Arab world, arousing the bitter animosity of Egypt, Syria, and
Saudi Arabia. Pakistan's membership turned India and Afghanistan
into critics as well. Arab nationalists everywhere viewed British
membership as nothing less than an effort to perpetuate European
imperialism in the Middle East. Finally, the U.S. agreement to arm
Iraq defied the 1950 Tripartite Declaration that rationed arms carefully between Israel and the Arabs.

Dulles's Middle Eastern policy quickly brought the United States
into direct conflict, not with the Soviet Union, but with Egypt's
Colonel Gamal Abdel Nasser, dictator since 1952 and a leading pro-
ponent of Arab nationalism and Pan-Arabism. In April 1955, Nasser
attended the Afro-Asian conference at Bandung and there became, with
Nehru, a leading spokesman of Third World neutralism. He negotiated a Soviet-Egyptian arms deal in September 1955, bypassing the
Northern Tier and nullifying the Western Tripartite Declaration on
Arab-Israeli arms. When Britain and the United States refused to
finance his Aswan Dam project, Nasser, in July 1956, nationalized the
Suez Canal Company, owned largely by British and French investors.
Dulles's repeated failures to support British and French interests in
the Suez Canal prompted the two Western powers, in early November,
to occupy Port Said. Led by a strange Soviet-American entente, the
UN General Assembly condemned Britain and France for their military action and compelled their ignominious capitulation. Thereafter
the United States would carry the burden of defending Western and
Israeli interests in the Middle East alone.

Although Israeli, British, and French action against Egypt sparked
the Suez crisis, Eisenhower redefined the subsequent American commitment to Middle Eastern stability. The Eisenhower Doctrine,
adopted by Congress in March 1957, declared, in part, that the United
States was prepared "to use armed force to assist any [Middle Eastern]

nation or group of nations requesting assistance against armed aggression from any country controlled by international communism." Cairo's *Akher Saa*, in response, declared Soviet aggression in the Arab world imaginary. Oregon's Senator Wayne Morse observed bitterly on January 25 that he awaited "the first scintilla of evidence ... that there is any danger of armed attack by the Soviet Union in the Middle East."[102] On February 1, 1958, Syria and Egypt announced their union in the United Arab Republic. Several days later State Department officer William M. Roundtree assured the Senate Foreign Relations Committee that the U.S.S.R. had not converted any Middle Eastern country into a satellite, but had, through deception, "succeeded in exploiting the mistaken belief of some of those countries that they can deal closely with the Soviet Union without risking subversion and ultimate loss of independence."[103] During the summer of 1958, the Pan-Arab movement threatened to overthrow pro-Western governments in Lebanon and Jordan. Washington and London landed troops to save the two governments. Those successes brought at least momentary stability to the Middle East.

In Africa as well, the Eisenhower administration described the political evolution of the 1950s in Cold War terms. Following Ghana's independence celebration Vice President Nixon reported that African development "could well prove to be the decisive factor in the conflict between the forces of freedom and international communism."[104] In its repeated, often ruthless, responses to Third World challenges, the Eisenhower administration managed generally to have its way. This was especially true in Korea, China's offshore islands, Iran, Guatemala, and the Middle East. But the days were numbered when Washington could dispose of every unwanted Third World condition at such limited cost. The challenge of coming to terms with unwanted change in Asia, Africa, and Latin America required less a nuclear strategy than a recognition of the power of nationalism as a force for stability as well as change, and a willingness to coexist with a sometimes troublesome world that otherwise served the nation's interests admirably.

* * *

For Americans overwhelmingly, the country's world role in the 1950s had been satisfactory, even laudable. Despite eight years of perennial tension, the nation had avoided war. Behind the underlying stability had been the outpouring of American dollars to underwrite the country's massive defense establishment as well as the West's unprecedented prosperity. By combining his administration's rhetoric of inflexible anti-Communism, especially in Asia, with his own image of moderation, Eisenhower bridged the nation's foreign policy spectrum with remarkable success. If the proclaimed objectives often defied the creation of policy, they reassured their supporters everywhere that the United States would defend them against any Communist-led aggression. At home, the promises of liberation built a powerful consensus, broad enough to encompass the entire Republican Party as well as most Democrats. The voices of criticism were scarcely audible. Not all congressional Democrats accepted the Eisenhower policies, but even those who objected could never mount an effective assault on official assumptions and objectives.[105] Much of the media refused to question the administration's rhetorical pursuit of the unachievable. This permitted the president to reap untold political advantage from the verbal assurances of liberation even when the promises themselves remained unfulfilled. The government's power to dispose of its critics with such apparent ease was simply a measure of the overwhelming consensus that its purely anti-Communist objectives enjoyed.

Eisenhower seemed to lose his consensus on one issue: the so-called missile gap. In launching Sputnik I in October 1957, the Soviets appeared to be decades ahead of the United States in missile development. The secret November 1957 Gaither Commission Report claimed the Soviets were far ahead of the United States in the development and deployment of strategic nuclear forces, raising the critical question of whether the country would soon become vulnerable to long-range missile attack against which it could not retaliate—and thus not deter. Largely shaped by Paul Nitze, the Report argued that the Soviet Union would likely have a dozen ICBMs operational within a year, while it would take the United States two or three years to catch up—thereby creating a "missile gap." The notion of missile gap was further encouraged by subsequent inflated intelligence estimates and the U.S. Air Force's prediction that the Soviets would have up to 500 operational ICBMs by 1961. As parts of the report leaked to the press, the so-called gap grew. Columnist Joseph Alsop predicted in 1958 that the U.S.S.R. would soon possess one hundred intercontinental ballistic missiles to none for the United States; by 1963, he added, the Soviets would have an advantage of two thousand to 130.[106]

Such assertions of national weakness subjected Eisenhower's apparently moderate defense policies to intense scrutiny in Congress and the press. Democratic advocates of a stronger defense, led by Senators Henry Jackson and Lyndon Johnson, warned the country against the proclaimed missile gap. Eisenhower argued, for good reason, that both the country's defense structure and its military budgets were adequate. The United States already possessed hundreds of bombers and dozens of intercontinental and intermediate-range missiles, positioned in the United States and Europe, and capable of launching nuclear weapons. Between 1958 and 1960 the nuclear weapons stockpile had tripled in size, from apparently 6,000 to 18,000 warheads. Eisenhower was shocked by this level of overkill.[107] Conscious of his failure to control the nation's defense establishment, he devoted key passages of his famed farewell address, of January 1961, to a warning against the power and ambitions of the so-called military-industrial complex.[108] Unfortunately, he penciled out references in his initial draft to a "military-industrial-*legislative*" complex.

Clearly, the Eisenhower consensus on matters of Eastern Europe and China was incompatible with the nation's need to accept forth-rightly what it could not escape. The avoidance of diplomatic accommodation resolved nothing. Eventually the country would consign liberation to the realm of lost causes, but until then it would achieve little in its negotiations with Moscow or Beijing. The administration's verbal devotion to liberation was all that remained of its promise to create a more dynamic, successful foreign policy than that which it inherited from the Truman years. In refusing to deal with either Moscow or Beijing on the bases of interests and power, the administration neglected to exercise the limited options before it. Maurice Duverger reminded Washington in *Le Monde*, April 27, 1954, that it was defying the basic rules of traditional diplomacy:

The entire diplomatic tradition of Europe rests on two unwritten principles: recognition of reality on the one hand, compromise on the other. If the devil himself should be installed at the head of a nation's government, his neighbors could adopt only two attitudes: either try to destroy him by war or negotiate with him a *modus vivendi*. The first attitude is military; the second is diplomatic; there is no third. ... One can almost define the diplomacy of the United States as principles opposed to those which have just been set forth: on the one hand, refusal to recognize disagreeable situations, on the other hand, a desire to obtain capitulation pure and simple.

Eisenhower faced no need to risk his powerful foreign policy consensus by modifying his uncompromising purposes in Europe or China. In both regions the United States confronted conditions that were essentially static. Southeast Asia, however, presented a situation that was dynamic, one whose resolution would require accommodation or war. Washington's posture toward China turned out to be meaningless rather than dangerous, but the conviction that the Chinese antagonist shared in the underwriting of Communist expansionism in Southeast Asia reinforced the American resolve to meet the challenge of Indochina with force. If Eisenhower escaped the necessity of war, his legacies surely assured trouble for those who would follow.

CHAPTER 9

The Kennedy Years

John F. Kennedy inherited Eisenhower's hard-line legacies. But many anticipated, with his election in November 1960, some departure from the established anti-Communist dogmas that would reflect a deeper appreciation of the world's growing complexities and the special requirements that they imposed on national policy. Kennedy's inaugural, delivered before the Capitol on a windy January 20, 1961, carried the promise of a fresh approach to the country's external relations. The new president appealed to the Soviets to join Americans in seeking "to invoke the wonders of science instead of its terrors. ... Together," he continued, "let us explore the stars, conquer the deserts, eradicate disease, tap the ocean depths and encourage the arts and commerce." The instruments of war, he admonished his audience, had far outpaced the instruments of peace. He urged nations to renew their quest for peace "before the dark powers of destruction unleashed by science engulf all humanity in planned or accidental self-destruction."

But on those Capitol steps, Kennedy quickly displayed the ambivalence that would characterize his approach to foreign affairs. He pointed to the scarcely reduced dangers posed by the country's adversaries. "We dare not," he warned, "tempt them with weakness. For only when our arms are sufficient can we be certain beyond doubt that they will never be employed." He instructed the Communist world that the United States would "pay any price, bear any burden, meet any hardship, support any friend, oppose any foe in order to assure the survival and the success of liberty."[1]

Such ambivalence conformed to the continuing divisions in American society, measured by conflicting judgments of coexistence—whether it presaged a successful diminution of the Cold War or the ultimate victory of Soviet Communism. Even the obvious changes wrought by a half generation of European peace offered scant reassurance to those Americans for whom security demanded the uprooting of Communist power and aggression. Until the Kremlin abandoned its rhetoric of world revolution and its support for radical causes, countless citizens, both inside and outside official Washington, would regard coexistence as a continuing struggle for victory by means other than war. Fearing the ultimate destruction of either the Soviet system or Western civilization, RCA Chairman David Sarnoff admonished the nation: "Our message to humankind must be that America has decided, irrevocably, to win the Cold War and thereby cancel out the destructive power of Soviet-based Communism." For Senator Barry Goldwater of Arizona, Washington's previous failure to pursue total victory openly exposed "an official timidity that refuses to recognize the all-embracing determination of communism to capture the world and destroy the United States."[2] *Life* challenged the country "to make irrevocably clear that it is resolved to . . . see the end of Communist efforts to dominate the world." The editorial asked the president to assume leadership "of a full national effort to win the Cold War."[3]

Kennedy required no conversion. Throughout his campaign for the presidency he had pursued a hard-line, uncompromising crusade against the Soviet Union. In Alexandria, Virginia, on August 24, he dwelled on the extreme dangers facing the country. For a decade, he warned, the tide had been running out for the United States and in for the Communist enemy. "These were the times," he said, "when people began not to worry about what they thought in Washington, but only to what they thought in Moscow and Peking." At Salt Lake City, on September 23, he was more specific: "The enemy is the communist system itself—implacable, insatiable, unceasing in its drive for world domination. For this is not a struggle for the supremacy of arms alone—it is also a struggle for supremacy between two conflicting ideologies."[4] Kennedy repeated such fears in his first State of the Union message on January 30. For him the United States had entered a period of national peril. Ten days in office, he averred, had taught him "the harsh enormities of the trials through which we must pass in the next four years. Each day the crises multiply. Each day their solution grows more difficult. Each day we draw nearer the hour of maximum danger, as weapons spread and hostile forces grow stronger." Neither the U.S.S.R. nor Communist China, he declared, "has yielded its ambitions for world domination."[5]

* * *

As president, Kennedy surrounded himself with men who believed, as he did, that only through uncompromising toughness could the United States deal effectively with the Communist world, that the Moscow-Beijing axis, if not monolithic, remained united in essentials and therefore dangerous to the non-Communist world. Only a well-armed United States could carry the burden for peace and stability everywhere. Kennedy selected Dean Rusk as secretary of state over Chester Bowles, Adlai Stevenson, and J. William Fulbright, three intellectuals who had been critical of past decisions, especially those relating to Asia. Contrasted to Dulles, Rusk, a former Rhodes Scholar, appeared urbane and self-effacing. Some predicted that he would introduce a new flexibility in U.S. relations with East Asia. Still, whatever his private views, his public defense of Truman's anti-Communist policies in Asia propounded attitudes and assumptions that varied little from those of Dulles. Nothing in the Kennedy environment would dislodge them. Robert McNamara, the new secretary of defense, entered the administration as an expert on statistical analysis. To McNamara, former president of the Ford Motor Company, everything of importance could be quantified.[6] He built a staff of bright young whiz kids who were convinced that they understood the requirements of the nation's security better than the military professionals.

That spirit of toughness pervaded the Kennedy administration. In external affairs, no less than in football and politics, Kennedy was out to win. Supported by key White House advisers McGeorge Bundy and Walt W. Rostow, he welcomed every confrontation with the conviction that he could not lose. The style and external brilliance of the administration did not conceal its intensity, its propensity for action, its supreme confidence in its capacity to command any crisis. In background, education, outlook, and experience, the Kennedy men represented the nation's anti-Communist Establishment. For journalist David Halberstam, they possessed the Establishment's conviction that they "knew what was right and what was wrong for the country, linked to one another, but not to the country." Later, John Kenneth Galbraith, Harvard economist and Kennedy's choice as U.S. ambassador to India, said of them:

We knew that their expertise was nothing, and that it was mostly a product of social background and a certain kind of education, and that they were men who had not traveled around the world and knew nothing of this country and the world. All they knew was the difference between a Communist and an anti-Communist. But that made no difference; they had this mystique and it still worked and those of us who doubted it . . . were like Indians firing occasional arrows into the campsite from the outside.[7]

For Kennedy and much of the nation's Cold War elite, the Soviet-American competition still dominated international life. In a presumed world of global conflict, military power remained the decisive, essential factor. During the 1960 campaign, Kennedy warned that the "Soviet program for world domination . . . skillfully blends the weapons of military might, political subversion, economic penetration and ideological conquest." The United States was falling behind the Soviet Union; therefore, it was imperative to construct an "invulnerable . . . nuclear retaliatory power second to none" and then develop an ability "to intervene effectively and swiftly in any limited war anywhere in the world."[8] To contain Soviet involvements where U.S. interests were marginal required larger conventional forces than the country possessed.

During his presidential campaign, Kennedy had joined those who charged that the United States suffered from a missile gap. In January 1961 American intelligence began to revise downward its earlier estimates of Soviet missile strength; some experts concluded that the United States had built a 3–1 lead. Still, the president was determined to fulfill his campaign pledge on national defense. His message to Congress on March 28, 1961, asked for a $2.3 billion increase in the defense budget, targeted primarily for new strategic missile systems. "Our defense," he declared, "must be designed to reduce the danger of irrational and unpremeditated general war—the danger of an unnecessary escalation of a small war into a larger one, or of miscalculation or misinterpretation of an incident or enemy initiative."[9]

Yet McNamara was disturbed by the nuclear "overkill" plan he found at the Pentagon. The Single Integrated Operational Plan (SIOP-62), ordered by Eisenhower to combine the military services' nuclear targeting, was completed on December 14, 1960—it was to go into effect in fiscal year 1962, meaning it would begin June 1961. It was initially presented by the Air Force to then Secretary of Defense Tom Gates, various Pentagon officials, and the Joint Chiefs of Staff. The U.S. strategic nuclear alert force consisted of 1,459 nuclear bombs, totaling 2,164 megatons, aimed at 654 military and urban-industrial targets in the Soviet Union and Communist China. Additionally, intermediate forces targeted hundreds of Soviet air and radar bases in Eastern Europe. Should the combined forces be launched in a preemptive strike—in anticipation of a Soviet attack—it would involve 3,423 nuclear weapons, totaling 7,847 megatons, resulting in the deaths of some 285 million Russians and Chinese, severely injuring another 40 million. Moreover, there would be millions of Eastern

European and allied victims as a result of the wind-carried fallout. Only the Marine Corps Commandant, General David Shoup, posed a question. He wondered what would happen if we were not at war with the Chinese. "Do we have any options," he asked, "so that we don't have to hit China?" "Well, yeh, we *could* do that," Air Force Chief of Staff Thomas S. Power replied, "but I hope nobody thinks of it because it would really screw up the plan." Looking at the secretary of defense, Shoup stood and declared: "Sir, any plan that kills millions of Chinese when it isn't even their war is not a good plan. This is not the American way."

On February 3, 1961, McNamara visited the Air Force's Strategic Air Command (SAC) headquarters for a briefing by General Power. Brushing aside the dazzling display of charts and maps, the nimble-minded secretary of defense quickly understood that the plan called for firing four weapons at each single target and that the fallout would be incredible. McNamara was also disturbed by SAC's "Plan 1-A" of SIOP-62 that would launch all of its forces in preemptive first strike against the Soviet Union, China, and Eastern Europe in response to an invasion or impending invasion of Western Europe by conventional Soviet forces. Just contemplating the resulting death and destruction appalled McNamara. The Air Force argued it needed 10,000 intercontinental missiles to carry out its mission; however, the secretary in 1964 set the limit at 1,000.[10]

Even as Kennedy's Washington moved to strengthen its massive military establishment, already beyond discouraging an unlikely Soviet frontal challenge to Western Europe, its emphasis was quite irrelevant to the policy requirements in a world moving toward multipolarity. By the early 1960s Europe's remarkable recovery and the explosive force of nationalism across Asia and Africa created uncertainties that demanded, not larger military budgets, but a reexamination of commitments and attitudes that embodied the perceived insecurities of a bipolar world. The trends were clear and the Kennedy administration, following customary practice, claimed to be offering a new foreign policy, sensitive to changing international conditions. Still its policies reflected no seminal changes, nor did they represent a coherent body of doctrine or even a well-articulated strategic plan. The president sought to keep his options open.[11] Kennedy's initial moves were innovative and promising enough. On March 1, 1961, he announced the formation of a Peace Corps, an ingathering of generally young men and women who, as volunteers, would help to carry American technology, energy, leadership, and goodwill to the underdeveloped world.

The program evoked an astonishingly favorable response, both in Congress and among the country's college students. During September, Congress voted the necessary funds to underwrite the program. The early achievements of specially trained peace corpsmen in education, sanitation, irrigation, agriculture, and town planning quickly created a demand for their presence in many countries of Asia, Africa, and Latin America. The program seemed to reflect the youthfulness and especially the ingenuity that the nation expected of the new administration.[12]

* * *

Kennedy arrived at the White House committed to finding means of employing arms control techniques to curb the burgeoning arms race. The previous administration, despite rhetorical endorsements of the idea, could not field a coordinated arms control policy. Eisenhower's well-publicized "Atoms for Peace" program did little to diminish the prospect of nuclear weapons proliferation, although its companion project, the International Atomic Energy Agency, subsequently established in 1957, would become a cornerstone of the later nonproliferation agreement. In an April 16, 1953, speech following Stalin's death, Eisenhower had challenged Moscow to demonstrate its "sincere intent" for better relations by placing "the Soviet Union's signature upon an Austrian treaty," not withstanding

Figure 9.1
President Kennedy and Peace Corps volunteers (Courtesy: John F. Kennedy Library)

the administration's fear that neutralizing Austria might prove to be a destabilizing power vacuum in the heart of Europe. In early 1955, the Soviets dropped their efforts to tie the Austrian settlement to the reunification of Germany and agreed to Austria's neutralization in a treaty of May 1955.[13]

In March 1955 President Eisenhower created the post of special assistant to the president for disarmament and appointed former Minnesota governor Harold E. Stassen to the position. Following the death of Stalin, the new Soviet leadership offered a comprehensive disarmament plan on May 10, 1955, that marked shift in U.S.S.R.'s policy and indicated a willingness to negotiate. Unfortunately, Washington officials did not respond to the challenge. At the Geneva summit in July, President Eisenhower declared that the U.S. government was prepared to consider a pact for the reduction of arms, but, as he later wrote, the Soviets had "flagrantly violated nearly every agreement they ever made." Therefore, Eisenhower insisted no pact was possible "unless it is completely covered by an inspection and reporting system adequate to support every portion of the agreement." To move toward that objective, he offered the "Open Skies" plan to allow unopposed mutual aerial inspections to minimize "the possibility of great surprise attack, thus lessening danger and relaxing tension." The Soviets viewed the overflight plan as a recycling of Baruch's 1946 inspection proposal and immediately branded it as nothing more than thinly veiled espionage.[14]

While he viewed the prospects of arms control negotiations with the Soviets more optimistically than Secretary of State Dulles and Atomic Energy Commission Chairman Lewis Strauss, Stassen failed to have much impact on policy decisions. Stassen's resignation in early 1958 prompted popular demands to bring the arms race under control. In 1960, the Democratic candidates for president made it a political issue. Hubert H. Humphrey, who headed the Senate Foreign Relations Subcommittee on Disarmament, proposed the creation of a new agency to deal with arms control and disarmament issues. Meanwhile Senator Kennedy introduced a bill to create a separate organization to provide the expertise necessary to provide the president with authoritative advice on these matters.

Once in office, President Kennedy moved more decisively than his predecessors to establish the machinery of arms control. "I have already taken steps to coordinate and expand our disarmament effort," he announced in his January 30, 1961, State of the Union address, "and to make arms control a central goal of our national policy under my direction." He desired to obtain a nuclear test ban, to limit proliferation of nuclear weapons, and to prevent the arms race from spreading to outer space. Kennedy immediately appointed John J. McCloy, who previously had held several high government positions and was a respected Republican banker, to be his adviser on disarmament matters and to prepare recommendations regarding a new arms control agency.[15]

The U.S. Arms Control and Disarmament Agency, based on a bill drafted by McCloy, was established as an independent agency on September 26, 1961. Its mission was to strengthen U.S. national security by "formulating, advocating, negotiating, implementing and verifying effective arms control, nonproliferation, and disarmament policies, strategies, and agreements." It was hoped that the Agency would be able to integrate arms control concepts into the development and conduct of U.S. national security policy.[16]

Amid the tensions of the Berlin crisis, Valerian Zorin and McCloy issued a joint statement on agreed principles for disarmament. Also referred to as the Zorin-McCloy agreement, the September 20, 1961, statement offered goals for negotiation to assure that war would not be used as a way of settling international disputes. In a September 1961 address to the General Assembly, President Kennedy responded to Premier Nikita Khrushchev's 1959 proposal for "general and complete disarmament" by offering one of his own, essentially for "propaganda" value. Both plans primarily sought to influence international and domestic opinion, since neither leader had any reason to expect their plan would gain approval. Extended discussions of the plans by the Eighteen Nation Disarmament Committee (ENDC) would reveal that a major point of contention continued to be that of verification. The United States insisted that verification must not only ensure that agreed limitations and reductions had taken place, but that retained forces and weapons never exceed established limits. The Soviet Union countered that continued verification of retained forces and weapons constituted espionage.

As the informal moratorium on nuclear testing in the atmosphere ended in 1961, the Kennedy administration undertook to develop a sound negotiating strategy aimed at gaining a comprehensive treaty to end all nuclear tests.[17] But partial success would be more than a year away.

* * *

Scarcely two weeks later, on March 13, the president proposed his Alliance for Progress to Latin American ambassadors assembled at the White House. This program implemented the Act of Bogota, signed by 19 nations in September 1960, which established a cooperative program—including a 10-year American pledge of $20 billion—for Latin American economic development. Thus by 1970, "the need for massive outside help will have passed" and each American state would be "the master of its own revolution of hope and progress." The Alliance for Progress, like the Act of Bogota, attached to the promise of aid the requirement for Latin American economic and political reform. In May, Congress voted the appropriations necessary to inaugurate the program.

What troubled the Alliance was the issue of implementation. There was no standard to determine when recipient countries had taken adequate steps toward reform. Moreover, U.S. special interests succeeded in placing a variety of obstacles before Latin American nations' imports. These roadblocks, combined with the doubtful prospect of established Latin American elites being willing to give up their privileged positions, doomed the program from the outset. Despite the American effort to establish task forces on education, land and tax reform, and low cost housing—the essential ingredients in social progress—the Alliance produced little social change and less democracy. Military coups Brazil, Argentina, and Peru during the first year further eroded the impact of the Alliance. On October 6, 1963, Edwin M. Martin, assistant secretary of state for Inter-American Affairs, regretfully reported that the fundamental principle of the Alliance was beyond attainment and acknowledged that military coups were a traditional part of Latin American politics. Latin Americans understood that the Alliance for Progress came in response to the administration's fear of Cuban-based Communism. They soon discovered that such economic and technical assistance programs as the Peace Corps and the Alliance for Progress, despite their humanitarian overtones, embraced Cold War objectives by seeking to render the hemisphere more resistant to revolutionary pressures.[18]

In April 1961 disaster struck in Cuba. In two short years Castro's dictatorial methods, his nationalization program, his clear ties to the Soviet bloc, his support of burgeoning revolutionary movements elsewhere in Latin America, and his constant and intemperate denunciations of U.S. "imperialism" brought Cuban-American relations to the breaking point. Indeed, Eisenhower had broken diplomatic relations with Cuba in 1960. As president, Kennedy inherited a haphazardly planned counterrevolutionary movement, organized and designed by the Central Intelligence Agency, to overthrow the Castro regime in the spring of 1961. At the time of Kennedy's inauguration, some 2,000 to 3,000 rebel Cuban refugees were training in the United States and Guatemala for an invasion of the island.[19]

CIA planners assumed, despite a lack of supporting evidence, that the Castro regime had lost its appeal. With the Cuban people anti-Communist and living under duress, the guerrilla invasion would assuredly ignite a revolution and free the country from Communist domination. Chester Bowles learned of the plan and concluded that it was "a highly risky operation" with little chance of success. He penned a note to Rusk: "If you agree that this operation would be a mistake, I suggest that you personally and privately communicate your views to the President."[20] Rusk indeed shared Bowles's doubts, but preferred to wait for the president to seek his advice. General Edward Lansdale, the government's leading expert on counterinsurgency, took his misgivings to Paul Nitze, then the assistant secretary of defense for International Security Affairs. Lansdale argued that the operation was too poorly managed to succeed. Nitze became uneasy and told his concerns to others involved in the planning. Yet Nitze believed the project necessary and supported it. He explained his decision in his memoirs: "The Soviet Union had inserted itself in our backyard . . . in the form of the Castro regime in Cuba. Like a spreading cancer, it should, if possible, be excised from the Americas."[21] Kennedy himself doubted the wisdom of the invasion, but so insistent were his advisers associated with the planning that he granted a grudging consent after insisting that he would never commit American troops to the assault.[22]

On April 17, 1961, the Cuban refugee assault Brigade struck the Cienaga de Zapata swamps of Las Villas Province (Bay of Pigs) on the south coast of Cuba. There was no popular uprising. Kennedy's refusal to back the invasion with U.S. air power assured Castro's control of the skies. Cuban regulars quickly defeated the vastly outnumbered invading forces—the Brigade's losses were 114 men dead and 1,189 captured. The Castro regime was more solidly in power than ever before.[23]

The president accepted blame for the fiasco, but lamented to his special counsel, Theodore C. Sorensen, "How could I have been so stupid to let them go ahead."[24] Yet so favorable was the public response to such executive candor that Kennedy's popularity soared. Too many in Washington, unfortunately, had failed to accept the reality of the Cuban revolution. The invasion's failure demonstrated both that the Castro regime enjoyed substantial national support and that guerrillas, operating in hostile territory, had little assurance of victory.

Upon reflection, Kennedy and his staff agreed that the decision not to use American forces was the correct one. He asserted before the American Society of Newspaper Editors on April 20 that any unilateral aggression "would have been contrary to our traditions and to our international obligations." However, "should it ever appear that the inter-American doctrine of non-interference merely conceals or excuses a policy of nonaction . . . then I want it clearly understood that this Government will not hesitate in meeting its primary obligations which are to the security of our Nation!"[25]

Washington's growing obsession with Castro received considerable impetus when the Cuban leader, basking in the prestige of victory, began to convert Cuba into a Soviet model with a single governing party, a command economy, and stronger economic ties to the Soviet bloc. The Soviets, in exchange, rewarded Castro with shipments of tanks and artillery, along with the necessary advisers and technicians. Whether the island, comparatively weak despite its ties to the U.S.S.R., merited Washington's official concern was questionable. As a threat to hemispheric stability, Cuba was no match for the 200 million Latin Americans who lived in misery—the real source of revolutionary pressures across the region. Still, for the Kennedy administration, Castro's ties to the Kremlin rendered him the agent of international Communism in the Western Hemisphere.[26] On November 30, the president issued a memorandum committing the United States to help the Cuban people overthrow the Castro regime and institute a government with which the hemisphere could live in peace and security. Thereafter, the administration sent sabotage units of Cuban *émigrés* into Cuba under a covert action plan called Operation Mongoose, with General Lansdale in command. A planning document of February 20, 1962, set the target dates of the operation. After the necessary internal preparations, guerrilla operations would begin in August and September 1962; during October, an open revolt would establish the new government. Another document of March 14, 1962, declared that "the U.S. will make maximum use of indigenous resources, internal and external, but recognizes that final success will require decisive U.S. military intervention." Attorney General Robert Kennedy, determined to get Castro after the Bay of Pigs, was Mongoose's driving force.[27]

During 1962, the Kennedy administration embarked on a variety of maneuvers to weaken the Castro regime. In January, the foreign ministers of the OAS met in Punta del Este, Uruguay, to deal with the issue of Castro's alliance with the Soviet bloc. Secretary Rusk sought diplomatic sanctions against Cuba. Seven Latin American states, including the larger ones, issued a memorandum on January 24, recognizing "the incompatibility between the present regime in Cuba and the inter-American system," but they opposed sanctions. Rusk now limited his objective to the suspension of Cuba from the Council of the OAS. In his plea to the delegates on January 25, he declared that the United States had no quarrel with the Cuban people, or even with the principles of the Cuban revolution, but rather "with the use of Cuba as a 'bridgehead in the Americas' for Communist efforts to destroy free governments in this hemisphere." On January 31, the conference adopted the seven-nation memorandum. On the resolution excluding Cuba, the vote was a bare two-thirds, 14 to 1 (Cuba), with six abstentions.[28] The convention recognized the right of any country to sever trade relations with Cuba. On February 2, the United States instituted a complete embargo. During succeeding weeks the administration undermined Cuban trade negotiations with Israel, Jordan, Iran, Greece, and Japan.

The Kennedy administration never accepted Senator Fulbright's assessment of the Cuban threat. Having learned of the impending ill-fated Bay of Pigs invasion, Fulbright urged the president to "Remember always the Castro regime is a thorn in the flesh, but it is not a dagger in the heart."[29]

* * *

Early in his administration, Kennedy explained his desire to meet Soviet leader Nikita Khrushchev, but warned that the Soviet leader "must not crowd him too much." In his inaugural address, the president acknowledged his readiness to negotiate; soon thereafter he announced his intention "to explore promptly all possible areas of cooperation with the Soviet Union." He assumed that the country's nuclear supremacy would enable him to confront Khrushchev on outstanding issues with some prospect of success. Finally, in June 1961, the young president journeyed to Vienna to exchange views with Khrushchev. The experience was not reassuring. On June 4, Khrushchev warned Kennedy that unless the Western powers accepted the conversion of West Berlin into a free city, the U.S.S.R. would negotiate a treaty with East Germany and assign it control of the access routes into West Berlin. Kennedy reminded the Soviet leader that the West had gained its role in West Berlin by international agreement and intended to remain, even at the risk of war. At the end, Kennedy remarked to Khrushchev, "Mr. Chairman, I see it's going to be a very cold winter."[30] The president's report to the nation, on June 6, reflected a mood of desperation. "I will tell you now," he declared, "that it was a very sober two days. . . .

We have wholly different views of right and wrong, of what is an internal affair and what is aggression. And above all, we have wholly different concepts of where the world is and where it is going."[31] That Kennedy would not challenge established attitudes toward the Soviet hegemony

Figure 9.2
President Kennedy and Premier Nikita Khrushchev at the Vienna Summit
(Courtesy: John F. Kennedy Library)

in Eastern Europe seemed apparent when, in July, he proclaimed "Captive Nations Week" and urged the American people to recommit themselves to the support and just aspirations of all suppressed peoples. Again he affirmed the American goal of German reunification.

Even earlier—in March—Kennedy requested Dean Acheson to recommend an American policy for Berlin. In his report, Acheson advised the administration that any change in the status of Berlin would reshape their alignment of power in Europe. Unless the United States took an uncompromising stand on the Berlin question, Acheson warned, the Soviet Union would dominate Europe and eventually Asia and Africa.[32] Acheson recommended a huge increase in the military budget. On July 25, the president announced that he would submit to Congress a supplemental defense budget request of $3.2 billion for an immediate buildup in conventional forces. This expenditure would increase the Army's manpower from 875,000 to one million. Within weeks the United States dispatched an additional 40,000 troops to Europe. At the same time, the president requested standing authority to call up their Reserves and triple the draft calls.[33] Kennedy's auxiliary defense program pushed the tension over Berlin to a new high. At a NATO meeting on August 4, the allies agreed to support military action in defense of West Berlin's freedom and viability; France's Charles de Gaulle and West Germany's Konrad Adenauer opposed any negotiations with the Kremlin on the future status of Berlin.

East Germany controlled the access routes to West Berlin. Anticipating a crisis, the East German government, in July, began to restrict the exodus of East Germans into West Berlin. The resulting anxiety sent a flood of East Germans across the line, including hundreds of professionals. Forty-seven thousand fled during the first 12 days of August. On the night of August 9, the Communists sealed the border between East and West Berlin. They stopped cars and pedestrians at the Brandenburg Gate as well as all service on the Communist-run elevated rail line. Beginning with a barricade of barbed wire, they eventually sealed off West Berlin completely by erecting the Berlin Wall. Germans watched in despair. Western leaders complained that the barricades broke the four-power agreement on Berlin, but they shrank from the risk of initiating a war.[34] In a gesture of defiance, President Kennedy sent a U.S. battle group from Mannheim down the autobahn through the East German checkpoints into West Berlin. Meanwhile the Soviet bloc had succeeded in impeding the escape of East Germans into the West German Republic.

The Berlin crisis continued until October 1961 when Khrushchev announced that he would withdraw his December 31 deadline if the Western powers revealed some willingness to negotiate. This Berlin crisis died as did those that preceded it with the Soviets reluctant to fight over Berlin and the Western powers reluctant to compromise their principle of self-determination. Khrushchev's actions regarding Berlin, Kennedy later explained to the visiting Finnish President Urho Kekkonen, was part of an effort "to neutralize West Germany as a first step in the neutralization of Western Europe . . . [which] will mean the destruction of NATO and a dangerous situation for the whole world. All Europe is at stake in West Berlin."[35]

* * *

Even as Washington seemed to dispose of the Berlin crisis satisfactorily, its obsession with Castro invited an unwanted Soviet-American confrontation in Cuba. During 1961, Khrushchev warned Kennedy against another armed assault against Cuba, but assured the president that the Kremlin had no intention of establishing bases on the island. The administration readily accepted that assurance, knowing that the Soviets had never placed offensive missiles so far from home.

But in May 1962, Khrushchev addressed the question of stationing nuclear missiles in Cuba. While irritated by the U.S. deployment of Jupiter missiles in Turkey across the Black Sea from his summer villa, his expressed primary motivation was the desire to defend Cuba and secondarily to adjust the strategic nuclear balance. After the Bay of Pigs and Berlin Crisis, Moscow and Havana viewed Kennedy as an aggressive leader and anticipated a forthcoming U.S. military intervention. Consequently, Castro agreed to a missile deployment in Cuba believing that Khrushchev's boasts of a strategic balance was true. In July, Soviet officials negotiated detailed arrangements with the Cuban Defense Minister, Raul Castro, in Moscow. By late July, the CIA reported a large number of Soviet specialists in Cuba, as well as the apparent construction of an air defense system. A U-2 flight on August 29 confirmed the presence of surface to air (SAM) missile sites. For CIA Director John McCone, the expensive SAMs in Cuba could only have the purpose of protecting future Soviet offensive missile bases.[36] On September 4, the president issued a statement that acknowledged the presence of defensive missiles in Cuba and warned the U.S.S.R. against positioning weapons of "significant offensive capability." At a news conference on September 13, the president declared that past Soviet military shipments constituted no threat to the hemisphere, but should Cuba become an offensive military base, he continued, "this country will do whatever must be done to protect its own security and that of its allies."[37] This warning was too late, for Khrushchev had already ordered the transfer of missiles to Cuba.

Kennedy's persistent distinction between defensive and offensive Soviet weapons offered little comfort to the country's anti-Communist elite. In late September, both houses of Congress passed resolutions almost unanimously that sanctioned the use of force to curb any Communist aggression in the hemisphere.[38] As editorial pressure mounted, the president, on October 9, authorized U-2 flights over the western provinces of Cuba to study the SAM sites. On the next day, Republican Senator Kenneth B. Keating of New York, who had not been a particularly visible legislator, informed Congress that he had confirmed refugee reports of construction at six launching sites for intermediate range nuclear missiles.[39] The administration denied the evidence. But on Sunday, October 14, a delayed U-2 flight took photographs that revealed the beginning of a Soviet missile base in the San Cristobel region. Analysts confirmed this discovery on Monday and proceeded to inform Defense and State Department intelligence chiefs, as well as McGeorge Bundy at the White House. On Tuesday morning, when Bundy brought the news to Kennedy, the furious president declared, "He [Khrushchev] can't do this to me!"[40]

Late that morning, President Kennedy convened his top advisers to study the Soviet challenge and recommend a national response. This Executive Committee, later dubbed ExComm, met in absolute secrecy until the president made his decision on October 20. From the beginning, ExComm pondered the meaning of Khrushchev's decision. No member believed that the Soviets meant merely to deter an American invasion of Cuba. Some concluded logically that Khrushchev sought to redress the Soviet Union's exposed strategic inferiority.[41] As CIA Deputy Director Ray S. Cline expressed it, the Soviet leader hoped "to alter the psychological and political perceptions of the balance of power, particularly in Washington." Douglas Dillon, secretary of the Treasury, and the Joint Chiefs accepted that judgment; for them the nearness of Cuba was sufficient to change the strategic balance. Later, Anastas Mikoyan thought that the Soviet missile deployment in Cuba was designed to defend Cuba and secondarily to correct the balance of power. Mikoyan's son later recalled that Khrushchev worried that an American leader "might think" that given "a seventeen-to-one superiority" in intercontinental ballistic missiles a "first strike was possible." To Moscow, this was an "impossible" situation.[42]

Some ExComm members discounted the notion of Khrushchev's strategic challenge completely; they detected little increase in Soviet first-strike or retaliatory capabilities from Cuban-based missiles. McNamara declared that "a missile is a missile. It makes no difference whether you are killed by a missile fired from the Soviet Union or from Cuba." Upon reflection, Kennedy agreed. The United States had thousands of nuclear warheads, the Soviets a few hundred. For Roswell Gilpatric, deputy secretary of defense, the Soviet missiles in Cuba did not alter the military balance. "It was," he recalled, "simply an element of flexibility introduced into the power equation that the Soviets had not heretofore possessed." No one recalled Kennedy's ever mentioning any shift in the balance of power as his reason for demanding the removal of the missiles.[43] The president, however, was painfully aware of the domestic consequences of inaction. The Soviet challenge in Cuba was political, not military. What was at stake, ExComm finally agreed, was the nation's will and credibility. Neither friends nor enemies, at home and abroad, would take Washington's pledges seriously if it permitted the Soviets to place offensive missiles in Cuba. The various dimensions of the challenge compelled the president to draw away from the position that the missiles comprised no threat. He looked to ExComm, in Dean Rusk's opening remarks, to consider options that "will eliminate" them.[44] The *sine qua non* of any U.S. decision was victory.

This seemed to rule out the quest for a diplomatic solution. Adam Yarmolinsky, deputy assistant secretary of defense, asserted later than the group scarcely considered that option. Still, on October 17, Charles Bohlen, en route to his post as ambassador in Paris, advised Kennedy to communicate with Khrushchev privately and base his subsequent policy on the Soviet response. The communication, Bohlen added, "would be very useful for the record in establishing our case for action." Soviet expert Llewellyn Thompson recommended the same course. But when Soviet Foreign Minister Andrei Gromyko visited the president on the following day, Kennedy only repeated his warnings of September 4 and 13. Gromyko discussed Cuba at length without reference to the missiles; the president refused to disclose in conversation what he knew. That revelation would come with an open ultimatum. As author Henry Pachter explained, "Kennedy and the majority of the Executive Committee felt it necessary to have a public showdown with Khrushchev, forcing him to acknowledge the boundaries of his power."[45]

What commanded the ExComm discussions was the need to weigh the alternative applications of force. Dillon, Acheson, Bundy, McCone, Nitze, General Maxwell Taylor, and members of the Joint Chiefs advocated an air strike to eliminate the missile bases, or an actual invasion of the island. Robert Kennedy, in his memoirs, expressed surprise at the extreme hawkishness of ExComm's bankers, lawyers, and diplomats. McNamara introduced the idea of a blockade and attorney general Kennedy strongly seconded the concept. The blockade, or quarantine as it soon was called, was endorsed by Gilpatric, Ball, Llewellyn, Thompson, Sorensen, Stevenson, and Lovett. Finally, on October 18, ExComm agreed to recommend a stop and search quarantine of Cuba. Still the hawks would not concede; several continued to argue for an air strike. That strategy, Robert Kennedy retorted, would be a "Pearl Harbor in reverse." Picking up on the Pearl Harbor comparison, George Ball feared where the air strike would lead: "You go in there with a surprise attack. You put out all the missiles. This isn't the *end*. This is the beginning, I think." How would Khrushchev respond to the deaths of hundreds of Russian soldiers?

On October 20, Gilpatric stated the case for the quarantine. "Essentially, Mr. President, this is a choice between limited action and unlimited action; and most of us here think that it's better to start with limited action." The president concurred. He announced to ExComm his decision to blockade Cuba and was prepared to risk the consequences. He assured the advocates of an air strike or invasion that he did not rule out either option for the future. He now proceeded to prepare his speech for delivery on Monday evening, October 22, to reveal the presence of the missiles in Cuba and inform the world what he intended to do about them.[46]

Kennedy's nationwide telecast embodied the official assumption that the Soviet missiles endangered the hemisphere, that unlike U.S. missiles in Europe, their mission was offensive, not defensive. The president's central warning was clear: "It shall be the policy of this Nation to regard any nuclear missile launched from Cuba against any nation in the Western Hemisphere as an attack by the Soviet Union on the United States, requiring a full retaliatory response upon the Soviet Union." He did not include among his objectives unconditional surrender or Castro's removal. The president delineated the American program: a strict quarantine on all offensive military equipment being shipped to Cuba, continued surveillance of any military buildup in Cuba, an appeal to the OAS and the United Nations for international support and condemnation of the U.S.S.R., and a demand that the

Soviets remove the missiles from Cuba.[47] Adlai Stevenson carried the administration's cause to the United Nations. He urged the Security Council to call for the immediate removal of the missiles to contain the Soviet Union's perennial aggression. Edwin M. Martin briefed the representatives of OAS who voted unanimously to support the Kennedy program. Secretary Rusk assumed the task of explaining the crisis to the ambassadors of the nonaligned and neutral states. He appealed to them to forego their neutrality on an issue that touched the interests of all. In Europe, the alliance held as Britain, France, and West Germany pledged their support.[48] International approval, however, could not resolve the crisis.

Kennedy and Khrushchev, tormented by the potential price of their confrontation, embarked immediately on a correspondence that ultimately led to a peaceful solution. On October 22, Kennedy addressed a letter to the Soviet leader. "I must tell you," he wrote, "that the United States is determined that this threat to the security of this hemisphere be removed." In his response, Khrushchev denounced the quarantine as a violation of the UN Charter and an act of aggression against both Cuba and the U.S.S.R. The weapons in Cuba, he added, were purely defensive. On October 23, Soviet Ambassador Anatoly Dobrynin informed Robert Kennedy that he knew of no new instructions issued to Soviet vessels headed for Cuba. That day, the president dispatched another letter to Khrushchev, asking him to instruct Soviet vessels to observe the American quarantine. On October 24, the quarantine went into effect. Khrushchev again accused the United States of an "aggression which pushes mankind toward the abyss of a world missile-nuclear war." In his letter of October 25, Kennedy urged the Soviet leader to obey the quarantine and make some effort to resolve the crisis. Khrushchev's response of October 26 offered the first break in the stalemate. It implied that the Soviets would remove the missiles along with military specialists if the United States would promise not to invade Cuba or support others who might attempt it.[49] Khrushchev appealed to Kennedy not to push the confrontation beyond the possibility of a peaceful solution.

On the morning of October 27, Washington received another Soviet message that again offered a withdrawal of the missiles from Cuba in return for a no-invasion pledge, but it demanded as well the removal of U.S. Jupiter missiles from Turkey. Kennedy had long regarded the Jupiters so obsolete, provocative, and irrelevant to NATO's defenses that he had ordered them removed. Thus Kennedy appeared ready to consider Khrushchev's second offer. ExComm preferred a showdown without any concessions. The president quickly agreed, not wishing, in Robert Kennedy's words, "to order the withdrawal of missiles from Turkey under threat from the Soviet Union." Then a report from Cuba announced that the country's leading U-2 pilot, Major Rudolph Anderson, Jr., had been shot down by a SAM missile. Pressed by apparent Soviet belligerence, not assured of continued Soviet compliance with the blockade yet determined to avoid any concessions to the Kremlin, the administration had reached a dead end. With good reason, Graham T. Allison called October 27 "the blackest and most frustrating day of the crisis." Facing the necessity of framing a message to Khrushchev, Kennedy adopted the suggestion of Thompson, Sorensen, and Robert Kennedy to accept the first Soviet proposal and ignore the second.[50] After conveying the president's letter to Dobrynin, Robert Kennedy demanded the removal of the missiles in 48 hours or the United States would destroy them. At the same time, he secretly informed the Soviet ambassador that the United States intended to remove the Jupiters from Turkey in four to six months with NATO approval. Whether this hint to Khrushchev, communicated without ExComm knowledge, influenced the Soviet response is not certain, but the president's message of October 27 and Khrushchev's favorable response on the following day, ended the crisis.[51]

Officials, writers, and scholars who advocated an ever-stronger defense quite naturally attributed Khrushchev's decision to remove the missiles to America's superior power and the will to use it. In February 1963, Walt Rostow's Policy Planning Staff, in a postmortem analysis, concluded that the United States had protected its vital interests in Cuba by conveying to the Soviets the knowledge that the administration was prepared to undertake combat operations to achieve its minimum goals. What mattered in the crisis was force and toughness, now enshrined in the instruments of policy. A National Security Council memorandum of October 29, 1962, concluded that weakness had invited the Soviet aggression but firmness would "force the Soviets to back away from rash initiatives."[52] Rostow carried that conviction to its ultimate formulation. In a *New York Times Magazine* essay, he reduced the conflict between the United States and its Communist foes to purely a matter of nerve and skill, backed by a finely orchestrated flexible response. He, like others, made no reference to strategic advantage or the relative importance of the interests in conflict.[53]

For other analysts, the issue was not that simple. James Reston noted as early as October 29 that the Soviets had readily avoided a military conflict over Cuba because the area, no less than history, placed them at a strategic disadvantage; they would not necessarily retreat where the battlefield was advantageous to them.[54] At the same time, no rational Soviet leader would have sacrificed Moscow for the country's minimal interests in Cuba. Whatever the balance of nuclear forces in 1962, Bundy, McNamara, and Cline agreed that no interests in Cuba for either the United States or the U.S.S.R. were worth the price of a nuclear war. Some believed that the chances of war were high. In retrospect, Cline thought them never more than one in a thousand. Khrushchev, recognizing the odds, accepted the settlement as a victory for reason. Fundamentally, the Cuban missile crisis demonstrated the importance of strategic advantage and superior geographic and historical interests in any confrontation, and the possibilities of any policy that reflected such realities.

Still, the final Cuban settlement came hard. Mikoyan, charged with the responsibility of removing all offensive weapons from Cuba, encountered the resistance of a resentful Castro who, for a time, refused to see him. Kennedy's list of offensive weapons included the Ilyushin-28 bombers in Cuba, as well as the missiles. In addition, the

Figure 9.3
October 29, 1962, meeting of the Executive Committee (ExComm) of the National Security Council during the missile crisis (Courtesy: John F. Kennedy Library)

president opposed any Soviet military or submarine bases in Cuba. Castro reluctantly acquiesced on the issue of the Ilyushin-28 removal, but he never accepted the provision for external inspection of the missile sites. Washington did not press the issue.[55] In his retreat, Khrushchev secured Washington's acceptance of a socialist Cuba with a Soviet presence, permitting him to boast in his memoirs that he had secured at least *de facto* recognition of Castro's regime. In November, the Kennedy administration suspended the Mongoose program; in December it redeemed the Bay of Pigs survivors with $54 million in medical supplies and baby food. Thereafter, U.S. policy toward Cuba remained hostile, but accepted the Castro government as a necessity. Khrushchev's limited gains in Cuba could scarcely conceal Soviet humiliation in the missile crisis. Soviet official Vasily V. Kuznetsov commented to John J. McCloy at the United Nations as the missiles were being withdrawn: "You Americans will never be able to do this to us again."[56] Still, the Kremlin's subsequent quest for rough nuclear parity received its incentive, not from the missile crisis, but from the arms buildup of the Kennedy years.

* * *

Kennedy responded to Khrushchev's challenge over Berlin and Cuba with a determination to strengthen Atlantic unity as the foundation of a stronger, more effective, Western alliance. Through his Grand Design for Europe, the president hoped to create greater conformity in the West's economic and political institutions to enable them to meet the requirements imposed by a dangerous world. At Philadelphia, on Independence Day 1962, Kennedy declared that the United States contemplated the European movement toward union, as embodied especially in the Common Market, with hope and admiration. "We do not," he said, "regard a strong and united Europe as a rival, but a partner." Then he continued, "I will say here and now on this Day of Independence that the United States will be ready for a declaration of interdependence, that we will be prepared to discuss with a United Europe the ways and means of forming a concrete Atlantic partnership."[57] At his news conference that followed, the president refused to define what kind of partnership he had in mind, observing that it would be premature to do so before the European nations themselves had made greater progress toward unity.

Kennedy's design for Europe required, above all, a flexible Western defense. To broaden the options required to make limited war more feasible and the nuclear deterrent more credible, he stressed the need for a better choice than surrender or all-out nuclear war. That choice, to be effective, required allied conventional forces strong enough to permit a "pause" in any future fighting sufficient to enable the combatants to negotiate a cease-fire or give the aggressor time to contemplate the consequences of further military escalation. These anticipated conventional forces required a more demanding allied commitment to Europe's defense. The U.S. decision to maintain 300,000 military personnel in the European theater had already undermined the nation's balance of payments structure, whereas Europe, enjoying unprecedented economic growth and prosperity, refused to contribute its share to even the existing conventional forces in Europe. By 1962, Western Europe not only had closed the dollar gap, but also had acquired gold and dollar reserves that exceeded the combined holdings of the United States and Britain.[58]

To maximize Europe's contribution to the continent's conventional defenses, the Kennedy administration opposed expenditures for independent nuclear deterrents. At Ann Arbor, Michigan, on June 16, 1962, Defense Secretary McNamara declared that "limited nuclear capabilities, operating independently, are dangerous, expensive, prone to obsolescence, and lacking in credibility as a deterrent." He asked Europe to avoid conflicting and competing strategies to meet the contingency of nuclear war. "We are convinced," he continued, "that a general nuclear war target system is indivisible, and if, despite all our efforts, nuclear war should occur, our best hope lies in conducting a centrally controlled campaign against all of the enemy's vital nuclear capabilities, while retaining reserve forces, all centrally controlled." McNamara asked that the NATO partners leave full responsibility for nuclear warfare to Washington. In Copenhagen, on September 27, McGeorge Bundy reminded Europeans that the United States could not escape its responsibilities for Europe's defense. Writing in the October 1962 issue of *Foreign Affairs*, Bundy observed that the "present danger does not spare either shore of the Atlantic—or set Hamburg apart from San Francisco.... [W]e may reasonably ask for understanding of the fact that our own place at the center of the nuclear confrontation is inescapable."[59] The administration's preference for a more reassuring flexible strategy did not incorporate any curtailment of the U.S. contribution to Europe's nuclear defenses. Kennedy anticipated that greater military cooperation would eliminate trade barriers and promote a more pervading sense of Atlantic unity.

From the outset, Kennedy's Grand Design for Europe faced the countering views of France's de Gaulle. Long before de Gaulle returned to power in 1958, many French leaders had questioned the wisdom of binding NATO's defenses to the nuclear power of the United States. De Gaulle inaugurated his assault on the U.S. near monopoly of allied leadership in September 1958 when he proposed a tripartite global directorate, including the United States, Britain, and France, to control NATO's decisions. Washington rejected the plan with the argument that the United States could not designate one or two European powers to speak for the others. Secretary Dulles recognized the need for more liberal American atomic secrecy laws to facilitate allied collaboration in the development of NATO's nuclear strategy. In 1958 a modification of the Atomic Energy Act permitted the United States to provide nuclear materials and information to any ally that had "made substantial progress in the development of atomic weapons." Obviously Britain was the only country that qualified.

Washington's rebuff of de Gaulle's tripartite proposal and refusal to share atomic secrets with France reinforced the French leader's determination to build a French nuclear deterrent without American help. This would strengthen France's voice in European affairs and increase the confidence of the French army following France's politically imposed defeat in Algeria. Essentially, however, de Gaulle objected to making French territory a target during Soviet nuclear attack with only Washington having the decision to go to war. In May 1959, he wrote President Dwight Eisenhower, "If there were no alliance between us, I would agree that your monopoly of the possible unleashing of nuclear conflict was justified. But you and we are bound together to a point where the opening of this sort of war, whether by you or against you, would automatically expose France to total and immediate destruction. She obviously cannot leave her life and death entirely in the hands of any other state ... even the most friendly." On September 5, 1960, de Gaulle issued an edict forbidding nuclear weapons on French soil unless France shared in their control. Subsequently, the United States shifted its A-bomb–carrying aircraft from French to British and German bases.[60]

Convinced that de Gaulle would never conform to its wishes, Washington sought an arrangement whereby the European nuclear force, closely linked with that of the United States, would encompass a future French deterrent as well. But that objective required a more effective political and economic union in Europe, and one that included Britain. To that end, the administration placed the full force of its influence and prestige behind Britain's bid for membership in the European Common Market. Earlier Britain had refused to join either the Coal and Steel Community or the European Economic Community (EEC). Traditionally, Britain had avoided ties to the continent, but in 1961 British leaders questioned their country's isolation from Europe. In April, Prime Minister Harold Macmillan informed U.S. officials of Britain's desire to enter the EEC and elicited Washington's support. "We're going into Europe," he informed George Ball. "We'll need your help since we'll have trouble with de Gaulle, but we're going to do it." The British quest for EEC membership faced strong opposition among British conservatives and socialists who feared that EEC's agricultural policies would eliminate Britain's Commonwealth preferences. Macmillan's effort to accommodate Britain's imperial economic interests, especially those of the Commonwealth, cast doubts on British fitness for membership in the EEC or Washington's capacity to help.[61]

Europe's response to U.S. demands for a more equitable distribution of the Western defense burden was hardly enthusiastic. Whatever its lack of flexibility, the Western deterrent had granted Europe a decade of peace without recurrent crises or prosperity-curtailing military expenditures. Many concluded, among them de Gaulle, that it was precisely Europe's inability to fight a successful conventional war that had made the nuclear deterrent effective; apparently the Kremlin understood that any Western decision to resist even a minor Soviet assault could quickly degenerate into a nuclear war. Kennedy's new emphasis on the need of a flexible response seemed to endanger the credibility of the nuclear deterrent and undermine further Europe's confidence in the American commitment to its defense. Some Europeans feared that the United States, in an effort to avoid the extremity of a nuclear exchange, might refuse to act until much of Europe again lay in ruins.[62] Moreover, nowhere in his Grand Design did Kennedy resolve the question of nuclear control. Those who favored stronger trans-Atlantic ties agreed that Atlantic unity required a sharing of responsibility for nuclear decision-making.

Late in 1962, Washington discovered a possible answer to the dilemma of nuclear control in a mixed-manned multilateral defense force. Britain pushed Washington into this proposal when, in November, the Kennedy administration responded to improvements in the Polaris submarine missile by canceling the Skybolt project. Britain had joined the United States earlier in developing this air-to-ground missile; launched from bombers, it could reach targets a thousand miles away. Britain regarded the Skybolt project an American guarantee of its nuclear future.[63] Britain's Defense Minister accused the administration of attempting to deprive his country of a national nuclear deterrent. London's bitter reaction compelled Washington to find a substitute quickly. On December 21, Kennedy and Macmillan conferred in Nassau. There the president agreed to provide Britain with Polaris missiles. To resolve the question of control, the two leaders accepted the principle of a Multilateral Defense Force (MLF) of nuclear-armed naval vessels, initially submarines but later surface ships, manned by mixed NATO crews. The proposal contained no arrangement for an integrated strategy; nor did it diminish U.S. control of its nuclear weapons.[64]

De Gaulle, in a dramatic press conference on January 14, 1963, challenged every facet of the American Grand Design. In rejecting the British application for Common Market membership, the French leader charged the Britain was not sufficiently European-minded to break its ties with the United States and the Commonwealth. He was, he said, simply advancing the emancipation of Europe. British membership in the Common Market would lead to the formation of "a colossal Atlantic Community under American dependence and leadership." France could accomplish little without sacrifice, he informed a French audience in April, "but we do not wish to be protégés or satellites; we are allies among allies, defenders among the defenders." De Gaulle rejected the principle of the multilateral defense force with equal determination. "France has taken note of the Anglo-American Nassau agreement," he declared. "As it was conceived, undoubtedly no one will be surprised that we cannot subscribe to it." De Gaulle dismissed completely the question of the integration of nuclear forces. France, he said, would provide its own nuclear deterrent. The French leader admitted that U.S. defense strategy covered all European targets; what he questioned, he noted, was the American willingness to engage in a nuclear exchange over issues that Washington might regard secondary.[65]

In an apparent effort to protect Europe even further from U.S. influence, de Gaulle, one week after his January press conference, announced the signing of a Franco-German treaty whereby the two governments agreed to "consult before any decision on all important questions of foreign policy ... with a view to reaching as far as possible parallel positions." American officials, wondering about the treaty's implications, soon discovered that many German leaders were embarrassed by Chancellor Adenauer's decision to sign the document in Paris. Actually, in Adenauer's absence members of the German Foreign Office had prepared a preamble that upheld all the Federal Republic's obligations under previous multilateral treaties. The West German government sent its top Foreign Office spokesmen to Washington to assure U.S. officials of West Germany's reliability as a member of NATO. The preamble, in effect, repudiated de Gaulle's objectives. Recognizing his failure to enlist Germany in his anti–Anglo-Saxon crusade, de Gaulle proceeded to ignore the new German treaty and conduct French diplomacy without reference to Bonn.[66] Still, de Gaulle had placed the movement for trans-Atlantic partnership in temporary eclipse.

In Washington, de Gaulle's news conference evoked expressions of muffled rage. Kennedy answered the French leader in a press conference on February 8, noting regretfully that France had denied Britain membership in the Common Market. He challenged de Gaulle's assertion that the United States did not deal with Europe as an equal partner. The president reminded the press that the United States had supported every move toward European unity so that Europe could speak with a stronger voice, accept greater burdens and responsibilities, and take advantage of great opportunities.[67] Only West Germany indicated a willingness to join and defray its share of the cost. Critics noted that the multinational force satisfied no outstanding strategic requirement and offered Europe no significant responsibility for nuclear deterrence. To many international observers, the new defense project was little but an effort to involve West Germany in a system of nuclear defense without upsetting the delicate Cold War balance in Europe. If MLF placed a German in control of nuclear power, it endangered the peace of Europe—as the Kremlin made clear. If, on the other hand, MLF perpetuated U.S. control of allied nuclear defenses, it served no purpose whatever.[68]

To demonstrate his desire to bridge the Atlantic gap with new forms of allied cooperation, Kennedy, in late June 1963, visited West Germany, Ireland, Britain, and Italy. The trip quickly assumed the form of a ceremonial spectacle. In West Germany, the president stressed the concept of partnership. At historic Paulskirche, in Frankfort, he designated the United States and West Germany as "partners for peace." In a clear thrust at de Gaulle, he added: "Those who would separate Europe from America or split one ally from another—could only give aid and comfort to the men who make themselves our adversaries and welcome any Western disarray. The United States cannot withdraw from Europe, unless and until Europe should wish us gone. We cannot distinguish its defenses from our own. We cannot diminish our contributions to Western security or abdicate the responsibility of power." At Bonn, the president issued the same assurance: "Your safety is our safety, your liberty is our liberty, and an attack on your soil is an attack on our own."[69] Kennedy effectively challenged de Gaulle's persistent warnings of America's unreliability; however, he had no measurable effect on French policy. De Gaulle's reading of French economic interests still determined the course of Common Market decisions. When the United States, during the autumn of 1963, pressed the allies for greater defense contributions, de Gaulle replied that the American concept of a "pause" would not prevent nuclear war as effectively as reliance on instant nuclear retaliation. Nothing in the entire spectrum of Soviet behavior could disprove his contention. The MLF issue remained; it would fall to Lyndon Johnson to deal with it.

* * *

For Kennedy and Rusk, the wide-heralded Sino-Soviet rift, demonstrating Chinese independence from Kremlin influence, was not sufficient reason to reexamine the long-established assumptions and intentions of U.S. policy. Conscious of the Nationalist China bloc on Capitol Hill and its power over public and congressional opinion, the president informed Rusk that he had no intention of reopening the China question and wanted to hear no rumors that the State Department was contemplating a change in policy. Shortly thereafter, Rusk informed newsmen that the United States did not anticipate normal relations with the Red Chinese government. In July, the secretary explained why the Sino-Soviet break would not alter Washington's outlook. There was, he acknowledged, solid evidence of tension between Moscow and Beijing, but the width of the gap between them remained unknown. What mattered, Rusk added, was the reality that the "two great systems of power ... are united in general in certain doctrinal framework and ... together have certain common interests *vis-á-vis* the rest of the world."[70] Ambassador Adlai Stevenson argued the American case for nonrecognition before the United Nations in December. To bow to Beijing's demands for the replacement of the Republic of China in the United Nations, he declared, "would be ignoring the warlike character and aggressive behavior of the rulers who dominate 600 million people and who talk of the inevitability of war as an article of faith and refuse to renounce the use of force. ... The notion of expelling the Republic of China is absurd and unthinkable."[71] The Kennedy administration based its rationale for nonrecognition less on China's subservience to Moscow than on its alleged aggressiveness and misbehavior. The mere fact that the mainland regime was independent and permanent did not establish its legitimacy.

By the spring of 1962, it was doubtful that the Kennedy administration could long sustain the country's program of unbroken hostility toward Beijing in the United Nations. British Prime Minister Macmillan, visiting Washington in March 1961, informed the president that the Western bloc could no longer keep the China question off the UN agenda; any effort to prevent it would result in a crushing defeat. Kennedy repeated his assurance to Nationalist China that U.S. policy would not change. Republican leaders in Congress promised to support the president as long as he stood firm. Still, the administration could not ignore Nationalist China's declining acceptance in the United Nations. Rusk suggested a two-China approach, offering Communist and Nationalist China equal representation. Beijing, he knew, would reject the proposal and thereafter carry sole responsibility for its diplomatic isolation.

When the General Assembly convened in September 1961, New Zealand, with Washington's approval, proposed that Chinese representation be placed on the agenda. With a minimum of delay, the Assembly adopted the steering committee's recommendation. To forestall the looming UN decision on China, the administration designed a strategy whereby the General Assembly would establish a panel to spend a year studying the China question. During the November 1962 debates, the chief barrier to mainland China's admission lay in the extreme Communist demands that Beijing represent all Chinese territory, including Formosa. This few countries would accept. On December 15, the General Assembly voted down the proposal to seat Communist China.[72] China's decision, of October 1962, to attack India over the Himalayan barrier not only antagonized its leading supporters in the United Nations, but also embarrassed much of the neutral world that had perennially favored the seating of a Beijing delegation. By its own actions, China ceased to be a live issue in the General Assembly.

Throughout 1963 the Kennedy administration remained firm in its opposition to mainland China as a danger to the entire non-Communist world. Whatever differences separated Beijing and Moscow, those disagreements, ran Washington's official view, were over means, not ends. As one administration spokesman remarked in February, "A dispute over how to bury the West is no grounds for

Western rejoicing." Shortly thereafter, Rusk warned the country in a NBC interview to be "careful about taking premature comfort from arguments within the Communist world as to how best to bury us."[73] Harriman likewise limited the Sino-Soviet quarrel to methods, not objectives. "Both Moscow and Peiping," he warned, "are determined that communism shall sweep the world, but there is a deep difference between them concerning the methods to be employed."[74] Kennedy's Washington carried forward the assumption that China was a special danger to the small nations of Asia. Assistant Secretary Roger W. Hilsman developed that theme in an address of June 1963: "In Asia the greatest danger to independent nations comes from Communist China.... Communist China lies in direct contact with, or very close to, a whole series of free nations.... All these free nations must deal with the facts of Communist China and its ambitions." In his widely heralded address before the Commonwealth Club of California in December, Hilsman repeated the standard formula for nonrecognition: Beijing and Moscow shared the ultimate goal of communizing the world, while China posed an immediate danger to its neighbors.[75]

* * *

In the immediate aftermath of the Cuban missile crisis, Kennedy, in words and actions, sought better relations with the Soviet Union. His willingness to resume negotiations on arms control and other tension-reducing measures reflected a conviction that the Kremlin desired agreements that reinforced the European *status quo* and reduced the dangers of a clash across Central Europe. In his critical letter of October 27, 1962, Khrushchev called for negotiations on a nuclear test-ban treaty. Kennedy, who had earlier sought such a pact, assigned it a top priority. Once again, negotiations quickly snagged on the question of on-site verification, as the Soviets continued to view intrusive inspections as thinly disguised spying. Finally, on May 30, 1963, Kennedy, joined by Macmillan, suggested a conference in Moscow to resolve the conflict. The president addressed the status of Soviet-American relations in his noted American University address on June 10. He attacked those who argued that any discussion of peace and disarmament was useless until the Soviets adopted a more enlightened attitude toward the world. He continued:

I also believe we must re-examine our own attitude—as individuals and as a Nation—for our attitude is as essential as theirs. And ... every thoughtful citizen who despairs of war and wishes to bring peace, should begin by . . . examining his own attitude toward the possibilities of peace, toward the Soviet Union, toward the course of the Cold War. . . . [L]et us not be blind to our differences—but let us also direct attention to our common interests and to the means by which those differences can be resolved. And if we cannot end now our differences, at least we can make the world safe for diversity.[76]

Kennedy selected veteran diplomat W. Averell Harriman to represent the United States at the Moscow test-ban negotiations. The Joint Chiefs had long opposed a comprehensive test ban without guaranteed verification and on-site inspection. Kennedy accepted that formula. On July 2, Khrushchev offered a partial treaty, eliminating the problem of inspection by barring tests in the atmosphere, outer space, and under water. Permitted underground testing provided the U.S. defense department and its nuclear scientists with a guarantee, as they put it, to ensure the safety and reliability of nuclear weapons. (Subsequently, from 1964 to 1992, the United States conducted 683 announced tests compared with 494 for the Soviet Union.) On July 25, 1963, Harriman, Lord Hailsham representing Britain, and Gromyko initialed the partial (or limited) test ban treaty.[77]

In the Senate, the treaty, formally signed in August, faced strong opposition from the right. The father of the H-bomb, physicist Edward Teller, complained to senators that "I think through our policy of arms limitations we already lost our superiority. . . . And I think we might repeat the tragic mistake of the 1930s where war has not been the consequence of an arms race, but the consequence of a race in disarmament." But public opinion mobilized sufficiently behind the president to assure a favorable vote of 81 to 19 in September.[78]

This gain for East-West relations did not stand alone. NATO had confirmed in January the removal of the Jupiter missiles from Turkey, fulfilling the president's secret concession during the missile crisis. In June 1963, Kennedy and Khrushchev established a direct communications "hot line" between Washington and Moscow. This was the first in a series of agreements seeking to avoid the fumbling, indirect diplomatic approaches of the missile crisis that could result in a miscalculation of an adversary's intentions. That year the United States and the U.S.S.R. agreed to support a UN resolution barring weapons of mass destruction from outer space, as well as a nonproliferation nuclear weapons treaty.[79] The possibility of nuclear proliferation greatly worried Kennedy. As he told a March 22, 1962, news conference, "Personally, I am haunted by the feeling that by 1970, unless we are successful, there may be 10 nuclear powers instead of 4, and by 1975, 15 or 20." Lyndon Johnson would see these arms control proposals take form and substance.

* * *

Kennedy's limited agreements with Khrushchev, as well as his words of hope and necessity, suggested recognition of the country's limited power to have its way in a world of diversity. To many analysts, Kennedy was committed to a policy of "peaceful coexistence" with the U.S.S.R., with its implication that U.S. security no longer required the pursuit of victory in the Cold War. J. William Fulbright, chairman of the Senate Foreign Relations Committee, as well as many others, anticipated further evidences of official American restraint, leading to reduced tensions with the Kremlin.[80]

Still, in his final speeches, the president focused on the Soviet danger and the burden that the United States carried for the defense of the non-Soviet world. He warned a University of Maine audience on October 19 against "laboring under any illusions about communist methods or communist goals." A month later, he reminded Americans of the many occasions since 1945 when the United States alone had prevented the domination of the globe by the Communist forces. At Fort Worth, on the morning of November 22, he declared:

Without the United States, South Vietnam would collapse overnight. Without the United States, the SEATO alliance would collapse overnight. . . . Without the United States there would be no NATO, and gradually Europe would drift into neutralism and indifference. Without the effort of the United States and the Alliance for Progress, the Communist advance onto the mainland of South America would long ago have taken place.

After reciting the enormous advances in the nation's defense budget and the increase in its military capabilities, he assured his listeners, "We are still the keystone in the arch of freedom." His final charge to the nation to recognize and resist the ongoing Soviet challenge appeared in the speech he was to deliver in Dallas later that day: "We in this country, in this generation, are—by destiny rather than by choice—the watchmen on the walls of world freedom. We ask, therefore, that we may be worthy of our power and responsibility."[81] What concerned Kennedy at the end was not the country's capacity to exist successfully in a divided world but its willingness to assure that success by meeting the Communist danger resolutely wherever it might appear.